UNIVERSITY OF
GLOUCESTERSHIRE

at Cheltenham and Gloucester

Digital Advertising

Andrew McStay
London College of Communication,
University of the Arts London, UK

palgrave
macmillan

First published 2010 by
PALGRAVE MACMILLAN

Palgrave Macmillan in the UK is an imprint of Macmillan Publishers Limited,
registered in England, company number 785998, of Houndmills, Basingstoke,
Hampshire RG21 6XS.

Palgrave Macmillan in the US is a division of St Martin's Press LLC,
175 Fifth Avenue, New York, NY 10010.

Palgrave Macmillan is the global academic imprint of the above companies
and has companies and representatives throughout the world.

Palgrave® and Macmillan® are registered trademarks in the United States,
the United Kingdom, Europe and other countries

ISBN 978–0–230–22240–3 hardback
ISBN 978–0–230–22241–0 paperback

This book is printed on paper suitable for recycling and made from fully
managed and sustained forest sources. Logging, pulping and manufacturing
processes are expected to conform to the environmental regulations of the
country of origin.

A catalogue record for this book is available from the British Library.
A catalog record for this book is available from the Library of Congress.

Contents

Illustrations

Images

Charts

Tables

Acknowledgements

The author and publisher would like to thank the following for permission to reproduce copyright material.

Sony for permission to use images of the REC YOU campaign; Burger King for permission to use a screen grab of the Subservient Chicken campaign; Projector for their permission to use a screen grab of the Uniqclock online campaign; Journal of Virtual Worlds research for permission to use a conceptual model of advertising and marketing opportunities in virtual worlds

Every effort has been made to trace all the copyright holders, but if any have been inadvertently overlooked the publisher will be pleased to make the necessary arrangement at the first opportunity.

1 Introduction

Advertising as a business, social, cultural and creative practice is undergoing seismic changes. Digital no longer represents fringe advertising media, but rather a set of expanding practices that, as a collective, is progressively becoming a dominant global advertising media form. Unlike other media that have traditionally jostled for position, digital does not compromise. Increasingly other media develop and work with digital as it not only positions itself as the dominant form but also establishes itself as the terrain from where all else spring.

Digital media, the leveraging of vast tracts of data and new creative ways of using media are quickly rewriting the rulebook of advertising. We only need to think about our own media, communication, information and digital purchasing habits to realize this. Although each traditional media form carries its own benefit (for example, newspapers do not require electricity or chargers), digital platforms offer timeliness, relevance and a greater chance for advertisers to understand what happens to their advertising expenditure. They also raise significant ethical questions over privacy.

The advertising community has traditionally spent its time trying to interrupt users and the daily experiences and media content they are engaged with (Kim, 2008). However, people are not entirely happy with this. Whereas people living in advanced economies have in the past been hostage to mass media, these industries seem much less certain now. In many ways control over media flow and methods of consumption now lies with the user. As such, media producers and those in the advertising industry have to pay more attention to the preferences of their audiences. A report produced in early 2009 by the UK's Institute of Practitioners in Advertising (IPA) makes similar observations describing that the future of advertising is predicated on a consumer-led world (IPA, 2009). It suggests that 'if social media does take the lead in the future of brand communications then permission-based advertising could become the norm and understanding this is vital for success, requiring a fundamental shift in mindset. Brands will have to earn the right to be in this space' (ibid).

The era of "interrupt and repeat" is coming to an end as advertising segues with users' new media habits. It is becoming very difficult to gauge differences between marketing and advertising, and if it were not for the fact that clients and marketers still employ agencies to come up with ideas, the title of this book would be different. The current era has more to do with engaging ideas represented through a variety of media. The central word here is *engagement*. Although advertisers and marketers have always sought to capture interest and eyeballs, the contemporary period is more social and interactive. However, despite the apparent relaxing of communication reins, advertisers and market researchers are drilling down ever deeper to find our preferences, dislikes and more importantly other cognate products and services we may be interested in. Digital advertising represents a new paradigm of advertising that perhaps paradoxically, simultaneously gives a degree of control to both the consumer and the advertising community. Cookie data from advertising servers, user data from website analysis tools and attitudinal feedback from survey companies all ensure that, in theory, we see messages deployed for micro-segments including ourselves. Audience targeting is work in process although this development has a long way to go before we find ourselves in the refined targeting scenario envisaged by many science fiction authors, journalists, academics and common folk alike.

I intend to take a critical look at advertising that underpins and generally pays for media services we use, in particular those of a digital nature. This book avoids empty digital rhetoric and instead offers a grounded account of what is occurring and what the techno-social ramifications of digital advertising are. Although the term digital advertising may conjure up images of rage at pop-ups, as we'll see, digital advertising is much more. The big idea of this book is to offer an account of digital advertising in terms of industry practice, media forms, techno-cultural theorization, legal conceptualizations and creative opportunities. Its aims are thus multiple in that it seeks to chart developments in digital advertising and its associated practices, offering analysis and theorization as to what these mean for users and consumers. It also offers critical inquiry into a field more commonly associated with books that delineate the business of digital advertising, rather than offer a techno-cultural exposition of the ramifications of new digital advertising practices and associated audience profiling.

Ubiquity, language and the everyday

In contradiction to a shining modernist conception of the future, our daily-lived reality is now an always-on and on-demand society.

As of 2009, few are without a mobile phone and internet penetration is growing, albeit not as deeply as you may think even in developed economies: for example, internet penetration in the United Kingdom is still only around two-thirds. Notions of the information economy have been in circulation for decades but manifestation at a ubiquitous level is relatively new. Digital now surrounds many of us. Hardware, software and applications have set in motion a whole range of now firmly embedded cultural activities permeating virtually all spheres of life for some people. Try going without digital communications for a few days and it appears that you have dropped off the radar. Such is the normalcy of mediated communication many of my students consider text messaging acceptable in a classroom environment. These changes are characteristic of many electronic media developments historically. Discourses of new media go through the same boom, reflection, introversion and acceptance processes anew as each medium arrives in the public domain and, in part, recreates it in its own image.

Such is the extension of digital technology into everyday life that people regularly use technological jargon to describe how they communicate and get along with one another. Johnson (2008a) argues that digital lexicon mediates everyday life and that we no longer share work but "files"; we do not work on a computer but are "users"; content shared online is "information" rather than ideas; we "send" messages rather than express them. Johnson ascribes this to a shift in how we think about people and their practices and in many ways this is due to the influence of cybernetics in everyday life and communication. Communications scholars such as Norbert Wiener writing in the 1940s about cybernetics and the nature of communication flow have initiated a lingua franca that to some extent underpins how we conceive of mediated, and sometimes interpersonal, communication today. In addition, these language practices seem to have set in motion an argot where it is acceptable to use technological symbols as a means of everyday grammar: for example, emoticons. Notions of systems, information loops and circuits of communication prove a cold metaphor for human relations facilitated by digital technology despite mitigation from the ubiquitous smiley. These technological discourses have permeated all sorts of advertising communications in techno-lite guises. Johnson offers a range of cases where technological tropes and sentiments are used as sales propositions and a vehicle for dressing up new and "advanced" products, or services where people should "connect". A range of other types of tech-punctuation has also made their way into art directors', copywriters' and typographers' toolboxes. These include dots, underscores, square-brackets, command line syntax and other programming jargon, not to mention the gratuitous use of text-message and instant message (IM) language styles. We are, in more ways than one, increasingly becoming a digital society.

Globalization theorists and writers for years have been telling us the world is shrinking, and arguably it feels smaller for greater amounts of people. Mediation of other places not only occurs through the news and traditional televisual media but it also occurs in blogs, virtual environments, geospatial tagging and videos produced by "friends" the world over. Another reason that the world seems somewhat smaller is because it is easier to engage with. Traditional mainstream media, as a rule of thumb, engender passivity whereas digital media facilitate participation and involvement. We are more than consumers; we are producers and as Jenkins (2006a) reminds us, we live in a participatory culture. What I find most interesting and perhaps even revolutionary is the ubiquity and everydayness of tools such as YouTube and other video sharing platforms. Whereas early adoption of new media in the past has been an avant-garde activity, the relative lack of fiscal resources needed to get involved has led to an incredibly democratic platform for content sharing.

The technological changes that digital media and their support structures have wrought are seeing a return to greater individuality and salesmanship. Press, television and radio (with significant qualifications) all represent massification, at least in their inception, and with a single media purchase advertisers have been able to reach the eyes and ears of large audiences. However, as Faber and Stafford (2005) note, this came with a cost additional to the media buy. It meant that communication was homogenous and often appealing to the lowest common denominator. When critics lambast advertising for being banal, they have a point: much of it is by necessity. The targeting of niche audiences made its appearance with the introduction of cable television that began in the United States *circa* 1948 with John Walson's endeavours to sell more TV sets, with cable subsequently representing any system that delivers television content through coaxial cable or fibre optics (Anderson, 2006). This, and developments in satellite capabilities, ensured the distribution of greater amounts of content and aided in refining processes of categorizing and segmenting audiences. Digital now forms a third-age pertaining to personalization and re-invokes personal selling, albeit in a mediated fashion. For advertisers to become intimate with users and consumers advertisers need to know something about us and our preferences, to generate two-way dialogue with brands, or at least create a simulation of reciprocal communication.

Scholars, students and practitioners

Like me, you will probably have an academic or professional interest in advertising and recognize the centrality of advertising to media. You will know that as a general rule both traditional and non-traditional media are largely funded by advertising revenue. You will probably also be savvy and understand that media over which advertising is carried have been changing radically for a good few years now. You will probably also be a bit sick of hearing about the next "Big Thing". This book thus aims to critically delineate the digital advertising sector and offer insight into key features of the current digital environment. Perhaps more importantly, it aims to theorize the cultural contours of digital advertising and media.

My intention is not to hawk or promote recent media developments; this in fact could not be further from its remit. It instead aims to examine contemporary digital advertising media platforms and offer a balanced assessment of its advertising potential; to examine types of advertising that are already carried, nascent forms and their potential; to query the impact of digital advertising on audiences and assess user perspectives; to describe relevant legislation, and explore regulatory and ethical debates; and to investigate and account for creativity in digital advertising, exploring the role of science and the relationship between innovation and creativity. Given that digital advertising is a relatively young business and creative practice, born in 1994, there are few interdisciplinary studies. Material for this book is derived from interviews with practitioners, industry journals, and a range of academic literature derived from advertising, new media studies, sociology, marketing, art history, law, politics, management, audience studies and technology journals.

For scholars and students of digital media, advertising has long been an aspect of digital culture under-theorized and under-explored. As with traditional media, digital advertising is the key revenue generator for most commercial activities online. This is perhaps a fact that is not always articulated as loudly as it should be within the field of Media Studies. It is fair to say that without advertising the web and other internet platforms would not look the way they do. Whatever your feelings about advertising may be, the fact remains that it is a vital area of study for anyone interested in media as many services and tools we take for granted are now advertising-funded, and as such, money generated from advertising has, in a large part, created the digital media environment that we now recognize. This book thus aims to delineate key trends and characteristics of the digital advertising industry. It aims to help academics studying digital cultures develop an appreciation of digital advertising, the nature of the digital advertising industry, the types of advertising that exist (it's not all banners and pop-ups!) and ultimately to recognize the role of digital advertising in terms of the political-economy of the web and related platforms and environments. Students from a variety of disciplines should also find this text useful as it encompasses new media, traditional media studies, advertising, marketing, design, communications, consumption studies and law.

This book also aims to be of use to advertising and digital advertising practitioners. In putting this text together I have interviewed a range of digital advertising practitioners and interested parties. All have commented that this is a timely text and that greater understanding of communication flows, audience reception and digital culture are paramount for the advertising industry. Practitioners will be well aware of the enormous amount of commentary on digital advertising with each year forecasters proclaiming that the year of X is upon us (please insert chosen medium). Amongst other writings, this book thus aims to sift through the commentary from a range of trade publications. These include the Internet Advertising Bureau (IAB), Advertising Age and a plethora of other interested parties such as Adland, ClickZ and iMedia Connection. My intention is to articulate theorization of digital culture and offer the reader a comprehensive understanding of substantive changes and also digital practices that have stayed the course since the inception of digital advertising. Although commentators continue to draw attention to the transformational aspects of digital life and rapid media development, this book hopes to elucidate on social uses of technology less prone to vagaries of application and media fads. Marketers and those in control of advertising spend may also find a relatively unbiased, academic, objective point of view useful. Practitioners will also hopefully find historical and theoretical material interesting and if these analytical perspectives serve to obfuscate rather than illuminate, then this will book will have failed in one of its objectives.

Frame of reference

In working out how this book could be best structured and conceptualized I considered using the term "new media" and that I may be restricting myself with the prefix digital. However, digital does seem to characterize what is new about the latest swathe of new advertising media. This, however, presents its own problems; for example, the term digital means nothing more than 1s and 0s stemming comes from the Latin term *digitus* meaning finger. This means that digital is not necessarily electronic. It could just as easily be smoke signals, mirrors, Morse code or anything else capable of being "on" and "off" and standing for something else. However, whether internet-based or set on some other technological protocols, digital does seem to be the differentiating characteristic between recent media and traditional media used for delivering advertising. As such, it is a technology and does not necessarily refer to the character or content that is carried on it. Digital advertising here therefore refers to advertising through digital channels, particularly the internet and mobile communication and locative devices.

Although the title of this book is Digital Advertising it has a distinct bias towards internet-based platforms. This focus is largely determined by how much agencies and their clients are spending on online advertising compared to other new media, such as mobile phone campaigns. Figures provided by the IAB (2009a) record online advertising as accounting for over 18 per cent of all money spent on advertising in the United Kingdom with this figure growing year-on-year. Similar figures are reported from the United States although growth is slowing due in large part to global financial troubles. In addition, although this book does not comprehensively cover digital marketing, it frequently strays into this territory. As McMillan (2007) notes, distinctions between digital advertising and marketing are unclear. Traditionally marketing had more to do with purchase related activities and the retail environment; in contrast advertising had more to do with the media. In digital environments this distinction is far less clear than in a world of bricks and mortar.

This book has two central aims, the first being of a more practical orientation. Initially this book aims to describe key trends within the arena of agencies, advertisers and clients and carve out definitions of advertising within digital media and types of media platforms used. The second aim is to reflect upon, and explore, arguments surrounding conceptualizations of digital media. These include changing characteristics of digital audiences, concerns over surveillance of personal data and regulation, ramifications of speed and technology, de-mystifying interactivity, discussion of theories of digital consumption and new media advertising and finally a critical exposition of creativity within the new media advertising environment. The USP of this book is thus its interdisciplinary scope and by extension, this book hopes to offer a diverse range of perspectives on digital advertising in relation to a firm grasp of business practice.

Advertising and the technology that mediates so much of it is changing, but then again, it always has and always will. If anything characterizes the current media milieu, it is change. It is probably also a fair bet to say that change and flux are at the heart of digital advertising. In addition, whereas traditional above-the-line advertising media are fixed, digital is characterized by migration. This book does not aim to be a snapshot of the digital advertising market nor is it a coffee table book with beautiful illustrations of ads. Instead it aims to chart the digital advertising environment and lay down some theoretical bones as to what works and why. In addition, it seeks to address some of the concerns over privacy and the political-economy of digital advertising. With the future of advertising being based on information on users and their activities, this book addresses some of the ethical debates these practices raise. It also examines user perceptions of this scenario: does intensely data-driven advertising paint a Big Brother surveillance society or one where advertising might actually be of relevance to us?

Structure of the book

Chapter 2 delineates the history and business environment of digital advertising; it contextualizes the rise of digital media noting the centrality of advertising to media innovation. It explains that online advertising is currently by far the fastest-growing advertising medium, growing at a rate of 21.8 per cent between H1 2007 and H1 2008 (IAB, 2009a) in the United Kingdom. This represents a slowdown in growth due to financial difficulties advertisers found themselves in. This still represents significant growth, particularly when weighed against the traditional advertising media market with only cinema also recording growth. In outlining the variety of new media advertising platforms, new user orientation to digital media, convergence cultures and Web 2.0, this chapter also highlights key new media agencies that are driving the wider new media market forward in reference to specific case studies of note. I conclude stating that an examination of online advertising is long overdue both in terms of industry practice, as a media phenomenon and also as a techno-social enterprise.

A common misperception of online advertising amongst students new to new media is to equate new media with the internet, and online advertising solely with pop-ups and banners. Although these platforms play a significant role within advertisers' media mix they are most certainly not the entire story, especially given the dominance of search advertising – this maintaining over 58 per cent of the entire online advertising media sector (IAB, 2009a). Chapter 3 is an extended in-depth description of the breadth of formats of online advertising at advertisers' and marketers' disposal, and the relevant advertising opportunities that are offered by these. Platforms discussed include pop-ups and banners (static and rich media); email; search and portals; video; viral; social networks; virtual environments (including an extended case study on Second Life); in-game advertising; mobile and locative.

Chapter 4 describes and critically analyses dataveillance arguments and the notion that we live in a "control society". Dataveillance, advertising and tracking of personal data have been a concern for users since the beginning of the marketization of the online environment. Dataveillance refers to the systematic monitoring of users' activities and personal data through electronic means – in this case over the internet. Some of these concerns are justified, some are not and many are a matter of perspective. In this conception of society, citizens and consumers are monitored through their data trails both online and offline. In a Weberian (1994) sense this is referred to as an iron cage, caused by a desire for control by those who seek to manage people. Users and consumers are configured as dependable variables that can be counted upon by the advertising, marketing and data-mining industries to behave in a predictable manner. Decisions are thus made on how best to market and advertise wares to their data-doubles and are decided upon by impersonal data-aggregators. Chapter 5 asks what users' perceptions of digital advertising are: do they like it or hate it, are they aware of it or indifferent, and why? More centrally this chapter examines user perceptions of digital advertising and potential concerns over privacy. This involves an account of risk, trust and perceptions of threat and contagion. It inquires into what extent users trust marketers' and advertisers' motives through what Giddens (1990) portrays as expert systems, and to what extent legislation addresses these concerns. Although there are many reports from both academia and business offering quantitative detail of digital advertising audiences, currently there is very little qualitative discussion of how users consume advertising. As a starting benchmark, this chapter initially inquires into countercultural literature as generated in the late 1990s and early 2000s by cybercultural writers and writers who characterized early digital audiences as being anti-advertising. Developing the inquiry into digital advertising audiences, this chapter notes the quietening of cyberpunk-inspired cybercultural discourse and highlights the role of the 'everyday'. However, although bipolar conceptions of utopia and dystopia have quietened, privacy and the encroachment of business demonstrably play a factor in user conceptions of digital advertising.

Chapter 6 assesses these perspectives on dataveillance in terms of international legislation and regulation on privacy focusing in particular on the United States, European Union and United Kingdom. It also discusses the complications that arise, and how these are dealt with, when data moves across borders and zones of regulation. For example, whilst US-based websites are not required by law to inform users about placing cookies on users' hard drives as long as cookies are not combined with personally identifiable information, EU law requires that users be notified when personally identifiable information is collected about them. This chapter does not discuss collection of digital data alone but instead broadens the remit to information technology and the use of genetic data by data miners as a privacy concern. It also explores regulations and laws in the United Kingdom regarding advertising to children and the shift from traditional advertising to online forms of marketing, advertising and solicitation. Finally, it inquires into the legal status of video viral advertising whose content is deemed inappropriate for traditional televisual viewing.

Drawing on interviews with producers, Chapter 7 explores and assesses changing modalities of creativity in the online advertising environment. It also explores tensions with advertising practices pertaining to scientific methods. It examines polar viewpoints of employees of creative departments worldwide that subscribe to conceptions and discourses of creativity predicated upon romantic notions of the artist as genius (Weisberg, 1993; Negus and Pickering, 2004), and those practitioners who see it as a method to be refined (Hopkins, 1998 [1923]). In doing this it explores the relationship between creativity and innovation. In exploring creativity through innovation this chapter touches on artificial intelligence and advertising creativity in Web 2.0. Using a range of examples, it offers an account of interactivity, telepresence and community involvement. This chapter also explores relevance in regards to the current web and the nascent semantic web that will offer higher degrees of personalization. Whilst one-to-one advertising (Lindstrom, 2001) was part of the failed promise of the dot.com boom/crash years, current models of personalized advertising appears to be having more success with consumers, particularly hard-to-reach youth segments (Nelson, 2007). It also highlights the role of participation and explores in more depth interactive and trans-media storytelling, and media characterized by convergence. These invoke broad strategies conceived in both technical and creative terms where innovation and creativity exist as ideal and happy bedfellows.

The book concludes with reflections on an interview I conducted with Kalle Lasn, both "culture jammer" and editor of Adbusters. Adbusters represents a range of interest groups broadly anti-corporate and I was very interested to hear his perspective on new forms of advertising given his perspectives on traditional sorts. Thus drawing upon key tracts of our discussion I use this as a vehicle to offer conclusions on topics raised throughout the book. These include the role of digital advertising for contemporary consumption practices; fluidity and immaterial labour; the capacity of personalized digital media to aid in artisanship and postmodern trends of self-image construction; risk, digital and genetic segmentation; haptic developments; Adbusters and web 2.0. The book finishes with a consideration of what lies beyond the horizon of what Lasn calls the electronic beach.

Questions for further discussion

- ▸ To what extent should social media form the focus of a brand's advertising activities?
- ▸ How do current conceptions of information society compare to those incarnations described in the 1970s and the 1980s?
- ▸ To what extent do "classic" distinctions between marketing and advertising still apply? Does the notion of an "advertising agency" make sense any more?

2 The History and Business Environment of Digital Advertising

Digital advertising is now a mainstream activity funding a high proportion of platforms and media content online. It is a media option that has been around since 1994, perhaps longer if you include the frowned upon practice of spamming bulletin boards and newsgroups. In putting together this book there have been numerous signs that have confirmed digital advertising's place in the media mix. At the time of writing this was highlighted by the campaign waged by team Obama in the US elections who spent nearly $8 million on digital advertising through October, the month before the election, on Google, Yahoo, Facebook, news websites, advertising networks and in-game advertising firm, Massive (Kaye, 2008). In the September prior, ClickZ (2008) recorded "Obama for President" spending over $12 million, taking up the position of third largest advertiser. As Virzi (2008) asked post-election, was Obama's triumph in the US presidential election determined by "Mad Men" or the "Next Gen?" Text-message campaigns reaching young voters (deemed those under 35) are certainly thought to have contributed to the great numbers of young voters. In true web 2.0 fashion users also got involved contributing innovations including Obama '08 iPhone and iTouch applications. Many donations from grass-root supporters that funded this campaign were also paid through the web. As Thorson and Watson (2007) describe, US political campaigning on the web gathered steam in 1996 with both major party candidates for president having web presence, limited email campaigns, audio and video clips. It is instructive to note that although digital seems to constantly undergo the "Next Big Thing" year-on-year, it is a maturing industry. In addition as financial events in 2008–2009 have demonstrated, although the continued and growing use of digital by private and public bodies alike are testament to the growing mainstream employment of digital, it is during tough economical periods that advertising and media strategies are tested. It is not only the use of digital when times are good that counts but also its use in an economic downturn that perhaps solidifies it as a viable media option. When budgets are tight measurable and accountable digital advertising proves an attractive option.

Setting the scene

The history of media and reproducible content can be dated to *circa* 500 years ago. Recognizable forms of advertising emerged through several key technological developments from the fifteenth century onwards. Most notable is the break from scribal culture and the invention of the printing press between the years of 1436 and 1440 by the inventor Johannes Gutenberg, and for the United Kingdom the printing and translation of books into English by William Caxton. Although printing had existed in other countries prior, Gutenberg's printing press was the first to employ metal movable type that led to a printing press that was reliable and capable of producing copy after copy of books and pamphlets. Interestingly the first book printed for the mass market was the Bible. This was the first time that it was possible to disseminate information widely, quickly and relatively inexpensively. This marked a significant shift from what Innis (1951) describes as time-based media that are durable and heavy yet permanent to forms that are space-based and light and portable. Importantly books can be transported over large distances. Due to innovation in printing, the church was able to strengthen and maintain its role as a cultural unifier in Western Europe.

This has bearing on branding and advertising today and it is also worth reflecting here on the power of media and carriers of content. Even in this early period, media displayed their power to aid in shaping popular consciousness and various sub-strata of power, ethics, governance and daily habitus. Moving ahead to the late eighteenth and early nineteenth century in a period where social and economic life was still primarily agrarian the wheels of the industrial revolution began to turn along with the shift towards even larger cities and hive living, at least within Western societies. Whereas in agrarian lifestyles, culture was fragmented and lack of transportation networks prevented widespread cultural mixing, urbanization promulgated the notion of mass societies. Alongside industrialization and the concurrent exponential growth in manufacturing, production and social centralization, the rise of the mass media provided a powerful new engine of culture and gave manufacturers a means of reaching mass audiences newly versed in the delicacies of consumption and the riches produced by industrially forged muscle. Following Innis (1951) again, each new communication technology serves organized commerce and the market system. They help to draw in producers and sellers from remote places giving access to information and the capacity to advertise. Innis would also argue that in the longer term, use of media also draw small enterprises into larger systems by bringing them under the influence of central institutions such as banks, corporations and commodity exchanges.

Market driven popular culture and its media was improved through a range of technological innovations, not least the advent of wet plate photography, the phonograph, higher quality printing, commercial catalogues, magazines, newspapers, postcards, flyers and radio, the first truly space-based medium. Linking people across time and space, mass media and the consumptive values these innovations promoted and generated what Benedict Anderson (2006 [1983]), in reference to newspapers and nationhood, describes as 'imagined communities' where topics of discussion, frames of reference, values and perceptions are shared across space by individuals who need not know each other. In the United Kingdom the introduction of the Education Act in 1870 also guaranteed education for most of the population that in turn helped foster a more literate population and also a population more interested in newspapers, magazines, advertising and the process of consumption in general. In addition, the growth of the mass media also inculcated a form of sociality through the creation of common knowledge about not only politics and public sphere issues but also of sportspeople, figures of little personal consequence and the emergence of "celebrities".

The early twentieth century saw the professionalization of the advertising business. Up to the latter half of the nineteenth century manufacturers mostly prepared their own advertising copy, with journalists sometimes being drafted in, and publishers being resistant to the idea of illustrations and alterations to the column-based format of newspapers (Leiss et al., 2005). This ascension of the agency world included the rise of outdoor advertising as a means of representing a new modern world characterized by the city, transport, entertainment, shoppers, office workers, managers and labourers. This world looked very different from the agrarian one that preceded it and although advertising existed in a variety of print-based and mercantile forms prior, it never looked as organized as this. In addition to the rise of print-based media the early twentieth century saw the expansion of radio. Radio was perhaps the technology boom most akin to that we have experienced with the internet. The term "new media" is often wrongly assigned to digital media: instead it is instructive to look to radio and the impact it had on society, business, news reporting, warfare and entertainment. As Lessig (2001) notes, in the United States, early and unregulated radio included a wide range of educational, religious and non-commercial services. However, commercial organizations such as National Broadcasting Company (NBC) and Columbia Broadcasting System (CBS) were effective in influencing government as to how the radio spectrum should be organized. This commercialization brought with it the "chatter" of commercials. Polls carried out at the time indicated that listeners hated these, although eventually people got used to them and opposition died down (ibid, p. 74). As Marvin (1988) observes, there is very little beyond technological innovation that is new about new media. She notes that such enthusiasm and fascination is an intrinsically "modern" quality that started with the invention of the telegraph and that all developments since have been elaborations on this innovation. Examples of the recurring discursive construction of "new media" can be found in advertising itself. Jones observes that the figurative copy of AT&T's (American Telephone and Telegraph) advertising campaign for universal telephone service (conducted from about 1910 through the 1920s) is very similar to more recent telecommunications advertising – mixing transportation and communication language to produce such images as "the information superhighway" that was part of AT&T's public relations campaigns for the entire twentieth century (Jones, 1999, p. 277). So although the impact of the internet has been profound, many of these techno-cultural practices have also been experienced in the early twentieth century as radio and telegraphy changed the way people relate to space and place through the facilitation of phenomena like near real-time information transmission, global news organizations and transnational business, more broadly causing shrinkage of the globe.

The twentieth century also saw the legitimization of advertising as it became used for a variety of ends. Governments, for example, first adopted the techniques of advertising during WWI thus establishing shifting and symbiotic relationships with both commercial culture and the media industry. Not-for-profit companies also began to use advertising. In addition to press and the explosion in consumer and business-to-business magazines the 1930s also saw the introduction and adoption of radio. For many countries the period following WWII saw a binge on consumer goods. In terms of media, two major changes occurred after the war in the United Kingdom. First, television replaced radio as the major broadcast medium, and second, an alternative commercial network was born that has continued to expand since. This saw the innovation of a medium that is 'a creature of an economy able to produce and distribute goods on a huge scale, and of a society so complicated that its business is unable to operate with person-to-person communication' (Bogart 1958, cited in Leckenby 2005). The first television station to launch in the United Kingdom in 1932 was the non-commercial carrying BBC and the second was the ITV network in 1955 showing the first television advertisement for Gibbs SR toothpaste.[1] Channel 4 launched in 1982 saw greater account of niche demographics, audiences and the tightening of consumer segmentation. Cable and satellite carriers were also launched in the United Kingdom increasing the amount of channels at audience's fingertips, if not necessarily the quality.[2]

Domesticating digital

Whereas up until the 1970s television was the dominant media technology, computers made their entrance into the domestic sphere of non-specialist users. Arguably home-computing for enthusiasts began with the advent of the Altair 8800. Soon after, engineers from Intel founded their own company and built the Z80, a chip more powerful than those made by their previous employers (Wurster, 2002). This and the Z81 became the processors for a range of microcomputers, including the fondly remembered, for me at least, Sinclair ZX81. Although there were enormous developments in terms of hardware, software and programming languages what is perhaps most important to take away is the affordability and ease of use of microcomputers produced in the 1970s. Using BASIC as a programming language, commands were simple. Users could instruct their computers to LIST, PRINT, LOAD, SAVE or RUN. Although the command line interface looked very different from the operating systems we interact with today, they were easy to use. They were also the first real personal computers in that they were compact, low-cost, privately owned and available to a wider variety of people than hitherto seen. The 1970s also saw the birth of Apple and the pre-eminence of IBM-PCs as domestic computers.[3]

The 1960s saw the invention of the internet and the 1990s the web. I do not wish to dwell on these technological developments that have been thoroughly accounted for elsewhere.[4] Suffice for our purpose is to recognize that the internet is an interconnected set of computers and networks that transmit data, or packets (blocks of data), by 'packet switching'. Data is broken down into blocks or packets that are transmitted individually or, importantly, follow different routes across a network to be reconstituted at its destination. These are sent to and from computers with Internet Protocol (IP) addresses that uniquely identifies the receiver from all other computers on the internet. An IP address looks something like this: 128.34.35.204. It is fair to say that internet protocol is as important as the combustion engine of the industrial age. The web (or World Wide Web) is a set of documents that can be accessed via the internet. These web documents are linked together by hypertext and navigated with a web browser, with the first browser being Mosaic developed by the National Center for Supercomputing Applications (NCSA) and released in 1993. With the advent of browsers, use of the web increased at an exponential rate.

It is worth reflecting on the age of the current infrastructure. Whereas in the early 1990s traffic was largely text-based this soon increased with the influence of MP3 music formats and now video sharing. This is compounded by traditional media providers improving their online offerings, for example BBC's iPlayer. To put this into context, Phil Smith, head of technology and corporate marketing at Cisco Systems, comments 'In one day, YouTube sends data equivalent to 75 billion e-mails; so it's clearly very different' (Kelly, 2008). In addition the cables that carry internet data are susceptible from anything ranging from shark bites to earthquakes to terrorist attacks. Although the ubiquity of the internet lends a perception of solidity, services can very easily be disrupted. There has been significant discussion about redeveloping and overhauling the internet but the scale of the project is enormous. Impetus for such a project stems from concerns such as spam email that accounts for 63 per cent to 95 per cent of all electronic mails (Cheung, 2007), identity fraud, viruses, child pornography and terrorism.

The growth of digital advertising

The early 1990s leading up to 2001 is known as the dot.com boom or bubble period. It involved opportunism and venture capitalism, as opposed to traditional companies employing traditional scalable marketing and business techniques. As Lovink (2002) notes the dot.com era was characterized by the desire 'to get there first'. Between 1997 and 2000, the internet was, for many, the site of the future of global commerce. New dot.com companies entered the market at an exponential rate and confidence in the "New Economy" was at an unprecedented high. The internet rapidly moved out of the realm of technical know-how and computer code into the commercial world of journals, newspaper supplements, magazines and general commentary on the internet and IT flourished. Ultimately as Lovink (ibid) notes 'the dot.com saga tells the story of techno-culture gone pop'. Driven by a lack of experience in the internet marketplace and belief that the internet was the land of plenty, many businesses failed to grasp the fact that this growth was unsustainable and that this industry could be hit by recession. In contrast, the investors in the post-dot.com crash era have become savvy to the proposition that businesses growing at the exponential rate characterized by dot.com companies are not sustainable, although internet-based companies do still tend to scale up much faster than offline ones. Furthermore, post-dot.com boom years have seen traditional 'bricks and mortar' retailers entering the online sector to considerable success (Lindstrom, 2001). The post dot.com era has also slowly seen the evolution of broadband whose availability did not match the dot.com business models where many relied on fast connections for success.

A Wikipedia entry claims that the first clickable banner advertisement was sold by Global Network Navigator (GNN) in 1993 to a law firm. The more commonly accepted beginning of web advertising comes from AT&T and their advertising on the now defunct pages of HotWired in 1994 (DoubleClick, 2005), although the online techno-futurist reflection of the McLuhanite Wired magazine lives on at Wired.com. Since then the online advertising industry has grown exponentially and is now the fastest-growing advertising medium, growing faster than any other marketing/advertising channel. It has proved both a cost-effective medium and attractive due to the potential of clearer metrics on advertisers' returns on media investments.

Traditional advertisers and marketers were initially, and rightly, highly sceptical of the online environment as a place to advertise. The web originally shared characteristics with traditional publishing being text and image based and comprised of "pages". Whereas early web pages were remediated (Bolter and Grusin, 1999) press styled interfaces, media opportunities within the web have expanded and offer advertisers a range of multi-sensorial means of reaching audiences. Early advertising on the web thus carried with it a lineage from other advertising media platforms such as outdoor as well as press. Although web advertising shares characteristics with other media forms, there are also distinct differences. Perhaps most important is that traditional advertising media seek to hold attention within a bounded space. Web pages instead are

full of hyperlinks offering to take the user elsewhere. Despite perceptions of online as the latest incarnation of the New World, advertisers in
their quest to colonize this digital new realm brought with them offline
push-based habits that sat uncomfortably with users. Although the dot.
com era was characterized by a scramble for stakes in the new terrain,
many advertisers and the agencies they employed were quick to pull out
when outcomes were not as desirable as imagined.

The online advertising marketplace has now matured through the
dot.com period into one which traditional advertisers are comfortable
placing their advertising as part of their marketing mix, or even utilizing online solely. For many advertisers it no longer appears a fringe
media, but rather as a platform that 'encompasses all of the media before
it and stirs the pot to the boiling point with a large dose of interactivity'
(Sherman, 2008, p. 166). In 2003, the online sector held 2 per cent of the
total advertising spend across advertising media. The growth of online
advertising now supports the entire UK media market (IAB, 2009a).

In mid-2007, we began to see acceleration in the centralization of the
online advertising sector as Google acquired DoubleClick (a company

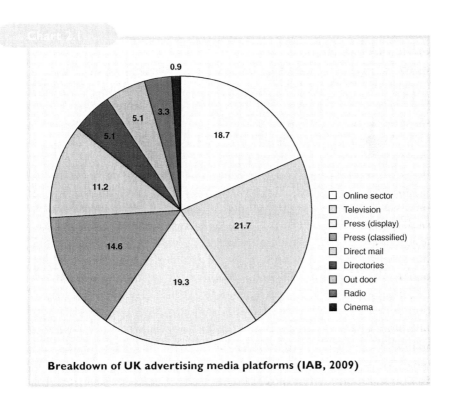

Breakdown of UK advertising media platforms (IAB, 2009)

that specializes in serving advertisements to website visitors), WPP (the UK advertising and communications conglomerate owned by Sir Martin Sorrell) taking over 24/7 Real Media, the purchase of Right Media by Yahoo! and Microsoft buying aQuantive. As Microsoft's Steve Ballmer says 'The advertising industry is evolving and growing at an incredible pace, moving increasingly toward online and IP-served platforms, which dramatically increases the importance of software for this industry' (Clark, 2007). This grab for advertising platforms was driven by a perception that the world of traditional 30-second commercial was over and that the internet is going to be the main advertising environment of the near future. However, not all agencies and advertising conglomerations have fought for technology real estate. Maurice Levy, the chairman of Publicis Groupe, comments that 'We can't compete on a pure technology basis with a Google, Microsoft or Yahoo. What we do know much better is consumers, clients and advertisers' (Sweney, 2008). T In July 2009 the tussle between these groups intensified as Microsoft and Yahoo! formed a search-advertising partnership.

Rodgers (2008) describes a consensus among forecasters that digital advertising will not grow as fast as expected due to the credit collapse in 2008; however, digital is not expected to be as severely affected as other advertising media, primarily due to lower costs and greater accountability. Television in the United Kingdom is expected to be badly affected, although loosening of regulation by the regulator Ofcom may help organizations such as ITV to allow more commercial breaks during their peak-time programmes. In the long term however it is more than likely that digital will grow as a collection of mediums and television as we know it will wane as advertisers increase their digital spend and online carries more televisual opportunities. A report written for Ofcom by Oliver & Ohlbaum Associates (2008) suggests that in a 'stagnation' scenario, by 2020, public service broadcasters may cease to produce revenue due to the growth of user-generated content on the internet, growth in search advertising and growth in web 2.0 TV consumption from on-demand services of traditional broadcasters and YouTube type clip services. However, it is not a matter of newer media displacing "old" media, but rather working out how media forms interact in different ways. It is meaningless to think of a continuum of media or media as a linear set of developments. Media do not arise out of a vacuum but rather inform, develop and interact with other media. As Leckenby (2005) observes, can we think about the internet without the development of television or the radio? No useful medium ever disappears, only the technology and protocols for how content is delivered change. As Jenkins (2006) describes books never replaced the spoken word, cinema did not replace theatre and television did not replace radio. Instead there is a coexistence among media. As such it is more prudent to consider how digital will encompass traditional media.

Online advertising spend, internet usage and consumption patterns

Records taken by Pricewaterhousecooper, IAB and the World Advertising Research Center (WARC) reveal that the entire UK digital market was worth £1,682.5m in the first half of 2008 (January to June). This compares to £1.3m recorded in the first half of 2007 (IAB, 2009a). The share of media revenue breaks down as follows.

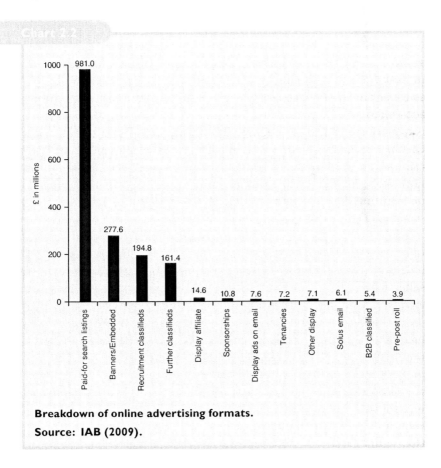

Breakdown of online advertising formats.

Source: IAB (2009).

Compared to 2007 all platforms recorded growth. This is due to the accountability of digital. As McIlroy (2008a) describes, when it comes to making media decisions cost and price as a criterion remained relatively stable (nearly 50 per cent of respondents she sampled rated these as being very important in online, TV, print and mobile), but advertising results are considered very important to an increasing number of media decision-makers. Even in difficult financial times, accountability is becoming more important than pricing.

Money spent on online advertising is biting directly into television's share with online video being a key growth area. However, as we will see in Chapter 3, the two are combining in innovative ways. The online sector is currently characterized in part by contradiction and tension. Whilst it is a growing medium with now solid foundations, many advertisers and media producers are still unsure how to best reach these digital users and audiences. It is clear that online advertising is important, but what is not clear is how best to use it. This is not surprising as it is a moving target, as are online audiences. Compared to traditional media where audiences are relatively easy to discern, online and digital audiences are much more fragmented, mobile and often engaged in tasks and activities as opposed to passive traditional television viewing. In regards to wider digital, mobile phone advertising is still not recognized as a mainstream medium although over 50 per cent of advertising agencies believe that it will be a key medium in the future (IAB, 2008e). The focus, despite the hype surrounding mobile, is with online. The IAB reveals that advertisers in particular (as opposed to media owners or agencies) are cautious about the potential for intrusiveness. One advertiser sampled comments

> I believe that mobile ads will have to be permissioned or requested if they are ever to take off (due to the personal nature of a mobile phone). At present mobile technology doesn't support an ad that is good enough that anyone would want to see. (ibid)

As described in detail in Chapters 3 and 7, although there are opportunities for advertisers the highly personal relationship users maintain with their phones require a careful approach.

Advertising has traditionally functioned as a key revenue generator for media and this shows no signs of abating. In fact the dependence is increasing as people become (arguably) increasingly less inclined to pay for individual or subscription-only media content, particularly in regards to online content. Jarvis (2007) describes that as the media become more dependent on advertising, so advertising becomes less dependent on the media. However, in addition to this scenario are problems with the traditional advertisement/media/audience triad. Advertising is not an individual's first choice as the basis of a relationship with a company. For marketers, it is expensive and inefficient. For customers, it can be invasive and annoying. As Jarvis also observes, targeted advertising is only slightly more efficient and less annoying. Although traditional "presentational" forms of advertising will remain for some time, digital platforms and media do open out the terrain for dialogue and brand engagement. Allen (2007a), in discussion of research from the American research group Forrester, describes that internet advertising in Europe will more than double over the next five years and represent almost a fifth of advertisers' total media budgets by 2012. Although the precision of such forecasting has to be taken with a degree of caution, particularly in light of the unexpected global economic downturn in 2008 and 2009, these are credible figures with the proposed proportion of advertisers' budgets being possibly tame. What makes these figures so remarkable is how relatively recent the dot.com crash was and the lack of confidence in the market that followed. Forrester's analysts expect that spending on online advertising will rise from €7.5b in 2006 to more than €16b (£11b) in 2012. This means 18 per cent of total media budgets will go to email, search, display and other online advertising according to Forrester's surveys of more than 25,000 European consumers and interviews with 24 leading European marketers. Britain should continue to spend the most on internet advertising followed by Germany, France, Netherlands, Italy and Spain.

Aun (2007) in discussion of the same report highlights that Europeans are spending more time browsing the web than watching TV or reading newspapers and magazines and that 36 per cent of those who access the web say they watch less television because they're online instead. Although UK statistics provided by the IAB (2009b) do not correlate, they do represent high internet use. They state that internet users aged 15 and above spend around a quarter of their daily media time online. Around half of users spend time online at least once a day whilst watching television. Furthermore, television is increasingly being watched online with 66 per cent having viewed television or film online, primarily to catch up on programmes missed (58 per cent); on series missed (28 per cent); on programmes sent to me/recommended; to control viewing and watch what I want and when I want (29 per cent); to watch highlights of a programme (21 per cent); watch previews and trailers of programmes not shown on UK broadcast television (25 per cent); and to watch new episodes of programmes not shown on UK broadcast television (22 per cent).

IAB figures from 2008 also show that over three-quarters of UK internet users go online every day with men spending slightly longer online. Top sites visited are those where users can buy a product or service closely followed by map and directions sites. Other key types of sites include price-comparison sites, weather sites, local information services, local government, auction sites, music sites, education sites and news sites (IAB, 2009b). More than 90 per cent of UK teenagers have used a social networking website. The survey of 11 to 20 year olds, conducted by Q Research for MediaGuardian.co.uk, found that one-third of teenagers have at least four social networking profiles on sites such as MySpace, Facebook and Bebo: of those surveyed, 93 per cent said they had registered with a social networking site, and 19 per cent said they 'couldn't live without it' (Kiss, 2007).

So what do online users feel about online advertising? More than two-thirds of online consumers believe that online advertisers do not tell the truth in their advertising (Allen, 2007) although targeted advertising appears to meet with a warmer reception. A third of online consumers said they do not mind adverts if they relate to their interests and are relevant. Allen also reports that 40 per cent of internet consumers trust price-comparison sites and 36 per cent trust online product reviews from other users. In a survey of internet users aged 15 and above, the IAB (2009b) describes attitudes to online advertising. Participants were asked to agree or strongly agree with the following statements: I like to receive emails from companies (18 per cent); banner ads help me find interesting things on the web (23 per cent); I have researched a brand seen advertised online (46 per cent); online sponsorship is an effective way of advertising a product or service (49 per cent); I prefer to see online ads that relate to the content of the sites viewed (55 per cent); and I pay more attention to adverts on sites I trust (56 per cent). As discussed and explored in Chapter 4, trust is a key factor in terms of users, consumers, the online environment and commercial solicitations. According to data provided by TGI.Net, types of advertisements to have prompted an online purchase are in the following order: promotional emails, online advertisements, Sunday papers, direct mail, advertisements on products purchased, fliers or postcards, television, radio, posters, magazines, transport, daily papers and lastly teletext (IAB, 2009b).

Internet usage

The IAB (2009b) describe growth in digital and online advertising being due to continued adoption of broadband and the conception of it being an everyday utility. They observe that the total amount of UK users will reach 31,604m with 30,143m having access at home and the rest only accessing from work. This represents around 60 per cent of UK households with 15.4m now online, taken from a sample in 2007 (ibid); 92 per cent of the 31,143m sampled have broadband access. In addition, 30 per cent of total time spent on the internet is by those above 50 years and online audiences are now more representative of the UK population as a whole than has been seen in the past. Key activities the internet is used for include using email; finding information on a particular subject; visiting the site of a particular product or brand; comparing prices; travel plans; looking at listings; listening to music; researching job opportunities; following sports events/results; instant messaging; and buying at online auction. It is significant how many of these are based on consumerism.

Average daily web use has increased overall with one of the drivers for broadband adoption being social networking sites. Similar figures are being recorded in the United States where in 2008 broadband penetration sits at 55 per cent as of April 2008, up from 47 per cent in March 2007 (Pew Internet, 2008). PewResearchCenter (2007) also report that broadband adoption in the United States has made the halfway point faster than most other information and communication technologies as it took 18 years for the personal computer to reach 50 per cent of Americans, 18 years for colour TV, 15 years for the cell phone, 14 years for the video cassette recorder and 10.5 years for the compact disc player. It has taken about 10 years for broadband to reach 50 per cent of US adults in their homes.

Early in 2009, comScore released statistics detailing the global internet audience and that users over the age of 15 surpassed 1b in December 2008 (comScore, 2009). The Asia-Pacific region holds 41 per cent of the total where China ranks the largest internet population in the world. Europe came in at 28 per cent; North America 18.4 per cent; Latin America 7.4 per cent; and the Middle East and Africa 4.8 per cent. More specifically a report from eMarketer (2009) describes that leisure time spent on the internet continues to rise.

The overall total globally for leisure time spent online is 30 per cent. Although broadband is now part of everyday life for billions, the majority are still excluded from the informational developments. As Haythornthwaite and Wellman (2001) describe, there are large

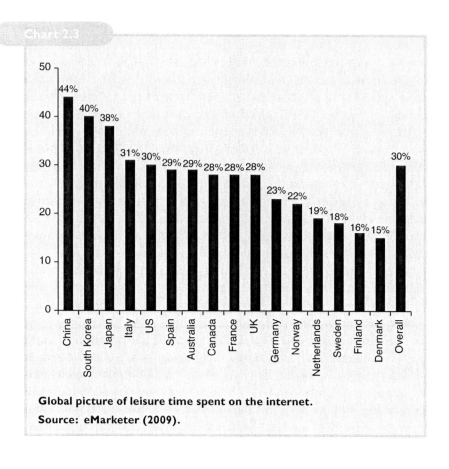

Global picture of leisure time spent on the internet.
Source: eMarketer (2009).

portions of the global population who are not connected to the internet, do not know about it and probably could not access it due to lack of infrastructure even if they are financially able to. In addition, many inhabitants of those in advanced economies also struggle to access; for example, those not able to keep a telephone line connection. Access rates across Europe vary between 40 per cent and 80 per cent with Denmark and the Netherlands maintaining the highest rates. Korea topped the global chart with more than nine out of ten households possessing broadband access at the end of 2006.

Consumption patterns

To be examined alongside advertisers' use of advertising media are ebbs and flows of user consumption patterns. In the United Kingdom, e-shopping represented £46b spent in 2007 with the average shopper spending £661 annually (IAB, 2009b). Although e-commerce continues to grow rapidly and has been heralded as a key contributor to the downfall of many high-street stores in the United Kingdom, these figures should be checked against the wider retail sector. There is confusion here as to the extent it is eroding UK high-street business. For example, in November 2008 UK internet sales only represented 3.8 per cent of all retail sales which, although noteworthy, is not calamitous (The Economist, 2008).

However, in a Nielsen report Paul and Cassar (2008) describe a 40 per cent increase in global electronic purchasing behaviour over two years ending November 2007. This is attributed to convenience and 24/7 shopping convenience for shoppers, who mentioned time-based factors as the motivation for online shopping. Books, clothing/accessories/shoes, videos/DVDs/games, airline tickets and electronic equipment were the most frequently purchased items. Globally the most popular online purchases are still books. This sector benefited from the emergence of new markets including China, Brazil, Vietnam and Egypt. The category with the largest increase proved to be clothing/accessories/shoes, which recorded a rise from 16 per cent to 36 per cent in two years. About one-quarter of online shoppers clicked to buy videos/DVDs/games, make airline reservations or buy tickets and to score electronic equipment such as a digital camera or TV (ibid).

On a regional basis, Europe led the way with 93 per cent experiencing internet shopping, followed by North America at 92 per cent, Asia Pacific at 84 per cent, Latin America at 79 per cent and Eastern Europe, Middle East and Africa at 67 per cent. On a country basis, South Korea topped the charts with the highest levels of online shopping in the world. Ninety nine per cent of South Koreans with internet access use it to shop, followed by the United Kingdom, Germany and Japan at 97 per cent, with the United States lagging in eighth place at 94 per cent (ibid). It is also useful to observe that 60 per cent said they buy from the "same site I buy from regularly". It is thus important for marketers to capture the first sale and maintain and manage the relationship with consumers well. However, around one-third of consumers discover interesting sites when surfing and shopping online and make a purchase. An almost equal number rely on search engines to proffer shopping options, or respond to a special offer (ibid). One area of increasing influence is consumer-generated media and word-of-mouth; for example, consumer produced blogs, internet fora and other types of user/independent reviews. This is particularly relevant with items that are complex, highly priced and highly coveted, such as those in the technology and consumer electronics sectors. It is less likely to influence low-involvement products, and/or those products that consumers want to see, feel or try on (Riegner, 2007).

Keller (2007) cites a range of studies describing that word-of-mouth advocacy is highly important for brands including Proctor & Gamble (P&G), Coca-Cola, Apple, Harley-Davidson and Starbucks. In this environment brands are encouraged to relinquish a degree of strategic control over what their brands stand for, instead listening and reacting to consumer perspectives. The aim is to create brand ambassadors who in a sense will stake their reputation through recommending brands. Such campaigns, more akin to PR, may be tracked through such services such as BuzzMetrics, a service offered by Nielsen. This pertains to examine online conversations about brands, their advertising and how to leverage word-of-mouth as a means of generating credibility.

Digital agencies: trend towards conglomeration

As digital life becomes the norm, agencies have similarly responded by bringing digital strategies closer to the heart of their plans and activities. Moreover, as Cappo (2003) describes, there has been an enormous shift towards conglomerations of advertising agencies in recent years. Heading Advertising Age's Top 50 Marketing List for 2007 are the "Big Five" including Omnicom, WPP, Interpublic, Publicis and Dentsu (Adbrands.net, 2008). It is worth noting that many agencies are starting to think about centralizing their operations around digital, if not actively doing so. Sweney (2007) observes that the advertising giant, the Publicis Groupe, is to launch a 'one-stop' collaborative advertising model to offer media, digital and creative services across its Leo Burnett network (itself a huge agency). This brings together Leo Burnett, the media operation Starcom MediaVest and digital operation Digitas. David W. Kenny, the chairman and chief executive of Digitas, owned by Publicis Groupe goes as far as stating that he intends to reshape the digital advertising strategy for the entire Publicis worldwide conglomerate, which includes agencies like Saatchi & Saatchi, Leo Burnett and the Starcom MediaVest Group (Story, 2007a). The intention is to build a global digital advertising network that uses offshore labour to create thousands of versions of advertisements. Using data about consumers and computer algorithms, the network will decide which advertising message to show at which moment to every person who turns on a computer, mobile phone or eventually a tele-vision. Essentially this is about realizing the practice of personalized advertising that has been long discussed in digital circles. There is also a grab for the smaller agencies that have managed to understand and react to the digital terrain faster than the traditional agencies. Alan Rutherford, vice-president of global media at Unilever, comments

> As a marketer, we have to be playing in the space where the con-sumer is, and we are looking towards our agencies to help us do that. Most of the current agencies have grown up in the old world as has Unilever. Their skills and competencies are in traditional media. And we have to look beyond television because TV is in decline. (Durman, 2007)

Conversely many in advertising believe that these are merely techno-logical developments and that the focus of advertising remains the same: to produce and deliver great creative ideas (see Chapter 7 for more on creativity and the role of the "Big Idea"). This stance eschews techno-determinism and rejects the notion that media possesses the potential to define the scope of ideas for advertising and communicat-ing with audiences. This book argues that techno-determinism and dogmatic reliance on traditional ideas fail to account for successful advertising in the contemporary media milieu. It is not only media that is being reorganized but also people's interactions with them. Ideas and insight do matter, but adopting a Luddite position misses the potential for new digital media. Neil Hughston (Managing Director of Saatchi & Saatchi Interactive) observes

> Well, I think the surefire thing to bear in mind is that a good idea is a good idea so if the idea is good enough it can live in any channel. How you amplify and execute it may well differ and what the kind of user or consumer outtake is will differ depending on the channel you deliver it in. (Interview, 12/11/07)

Initially the digital sector was represented by interactive agencies, which originally meant working with the web. Boundaries now, however, are becoming blurred. As digital becomes more mainstream it is going to be increasingly difficult to say one is digital whereas the other is trad-itional, as are distinctions between non-client side marketing and adver-tising companies. Although there is resistance from traditional creatives and executives, eventually digital and traditional will merge. This is not to suggest some sort of middle ground but rather the normalizing of aspects of digital and the incorporation of traditional into digital. Digital agencies work with a range of platforms but by far the most prevalent are internet-based platforms. In addition to the internet they also use digital outdoor, locative, kiosks, CD-ROMs, DVDs and lifestyle devices (for example, mobile and iPhone styled applications, iPods or PSPs). These agencies may find themselves doing televisual work online both for Internet Protocol TV (IPTV) and viral styled spots so it is growing increasingly difficult to talk in terms of mainstream versus fringe. In addition, digital agencies are also becoming lead agencies in that rather than winning only digital work for being best-in-class specialists, more clients are showing interest in digital agencies to serve as the lead on integrated communications efforts. This is particularly notable in the retail sector and other product categories where there is an opportunity for e-commerce (Parekh and Klaassen, 2008).

Digital and interactive agencies operate in a similar fashion to traditional agencies although they focus on interactive and digital advertising services. Like traditional agencies they offer general services such as strategy, consumer insight, creative, design, management, media and tracking of the consumption of advertising. Additional digital services include video, programming (Flash and otherwise), digital development and deployment. More uniquely digital and interactive agencies may be involved with brand development, developing potential online custom (lead generation), developing digital communications strategies and working out ways of reaching digital audiences and delivering advertising to them, developing rich media advertising campaigns, online video, discussion fora, social networking applications, virtual environments, email communications, search engine marketing and optimization, designing websites, data-mining and assessing advertisers' return on investment.

At present the computing giants are operating in tandem with advertising agencies rather than competing with them, having more to do with media and delivery, as opposed to the remit of creativity belonging to agencies. Although larger groups are buying independent and smaller agencies, some agencies remain independent of the conglomerates. Advertising Age (2008), as listed in Table 2.1, detail the top 10 US interactive agencies and their parent companies. An asterisk (*) indicates estimate and dollars are in millions.

NewMediaAge (2008) provides data detailed in Table 2.2 accounting for UK agencies. As NewMediaAge explains, fee income is money that agencies retain from clients after rechargeable third-party costs such as media, production or hosting have been paid.

Table 2.1 Top 10 US interactive agencies

Rank	Agency [parent]	Headquarters	2007 revenue $	%CHG
1	Digitas* [Publicis]	Boston	345.0	34.2
2	Razorfish [Microsoft Corp.]	Seattle	299.3	27.1
3	Rapp* [Omnicom]	New York	204.0	90.5
4	OgilvyInteractive [WPP]	New York	203.9	16.3
5	IBM Interactive* [IBM Corp.]	Chicago	188.0	NA
6	Sapient [Sapient Corp.]	Cambridge, Mass.	164.0	10.8
7	Wunderman*[WPP]	New York	162.3	11.7
8	AKQA	San Francisco	128.0	30.6
9	Organic* [Omnicom]	San Francisco	125.3	45.0
10	R/GA* [Interpublic]	New York	102.2	33.2

Source: Advertising Age (2008).

Table 2.2 Top 10 UK interactive agencies

Rank	Agency	UK fee income from Digital (£)	Declared UK turnover (£)	Year to Dec. 07	Owner
1	Sapient	50,048,850	58,881,000	Dec. 07	Independent
2	LBi	36,801,819	48,352,379	Dec. 07	LBi International
3	Conchango	30,100,048	34,600,106	Dec. 07	EMC Corporation
4	AKQA	25,518,442	26,618,442	Dec. 07	Independent
5	Digital Marketing Group	23,216,200	40,500,273	Mar. 07	Independent
6	Detica	17,997,992	17,997,992	Mar. 07	Independent
7	Avenue A/Razorfish	17,039,000	22,089,000	Jun. 07	Microsoft
8	MRM Worldwide UK	17,022,000	22,384,000	Dec. 07	Interpublic Group
9	Ioko	16,276,425	20,749,729	Sep. 07	Independent
10	IMG Digital Media	12,211,000	12,436,000	Dec. 07	Independent

Note: Many large agencies chose not to or were unable to disclose their financial information and therefore were not included in this table.[5]

Source: NewMediaAge (2008).

As Sanders (2007) writing for Advertising Age reports, industry executives believe that digital advertising in one form or another is the future of advertising with all the large holding companies spending to ensure they are "futureproof" and relevant to the new media environment. Mark Read, CEO of WPP Digital, on his definition of success observes 'We'll be successful when we won't need to exist anymore. Particularly in five years' time, the boundaries of what's digital and what's not will be irrelevant' (ibid). WPP, Interpublic, Omnicom and Publicis have all been buying interactive agencies, media companies and entertainment platforms. Reflecting the upturn in digital, Campaign magazine, the UK's industry weekly newspaper, reports that 2007 saw profits rise 56 per cent for the top 40 largest digital agencies (Campaign, 2007) with the UK agency Dare winning agency of the year. Significantly Tribal DDB, the digital offshoot of DDB, won Advertising Age's 2008 Global Agency of the Year Award. However, there are significant difficulties in the transition to digital. For example, Greg Smith, chief operating officer of Neo@Ogilvy, a digital media offshoot of WPP Group's Ogilvy Worldwide, sketches out the differences in how traditional media and digital media would tackle buying advertising:

> In traditional media, five people might be responsible for spending $100 million in network and cable television, a task that requires planning and buying the media, ensuring the commercials get to the networks in question and measuring traffic. In digital media, those same five people might be responsible for a budget of only $1 million that involves 1,000 ad placements, the buying of 5,000 keywords on search engines, and tracking and changing the campaign based on the data that come back. Some marketers do this on a daily basis, and many more weekly, making this a continuing, time-consuming task. (Taylor, 2008)

When one considers that traditionally agencies are paid by a percentage of media, the difficulties, and institutional resistance, are easy to appreciate. In addition, shortage of digitally aware staff and the complexity of buying have led to a lag in the adoption of digital and perhaps overuse of traditional formats.

Clients

So who is using digital? As you would expect, there are many advertisers in the telecommunications, technology and media sectors who are using digital and online advertising. It is also not surprising to see financial companies there too. It is interesting to see, however, that the Central Office of Information (COI)[6] made it into the top 10 UK advertisers. Whereas digital advertising once reflected its early adopter user-base, the inclusion of the COI highlights the mainstream nature of digital. Although one of the UK's largest advertisers coming in second in 2007 in terms of advertising expenditure (adbrands.net, 2008), it is instructive to see that the UK government sees online as

Table 2.3 Top 10 UK online advertisers

Rank	Advertiser	Web spend 2007 (£)	% difference 2006	% of all media spend
1	Personal Loan Express	28,518,265	72.42	100.00
2	eBay	19,801,297	397.10	55.89
3	British Sky Broadcasting	15,784,993	−18.79	9.89
4	Capital One	14,736,009	827.86	26.04
5	Microsoft	14,541,370	−3.04	51.40
6	Orange	13,256,323	25.40	14.56
7	Virgin Money	12,721,738	−31.91	67.33
8	O2	10,428,425	−5.93	18.64
9	Amazon	9,886,489	1977.53	98.72
10	COI Communications	8,223,507	117.05	5.12

Source: Nielsen Media Research.

Table 2.4 Top 10 US online advertisers

Rank	Advertiser	2006 ($)	2005 ($)
1	Monster Worldwide	101,637,000	56,588,000
2	Hewlett-Packard Co.	60,906,000	55,021,000
3	Vonage Holdings Corp.	46,415,000	68,938,000
4	Dice	46,243,000	8,645,000
5	Dollar Thrifty Automotive Group	43,855,000	15,902,000
6	AT&T	26,998,000	8,956,000
7	Microsoft Corp.	25,613,000	26,498,000
8	Capital One Financial Corp.	23,811,000	14,598,000
9	CareerBuilder	18,857,000	31,812,000

Source: Market Resource Guide from Crain Communications Inc (2008).

a means of communicating with all its citizens. See Table 2.3 for data compiled by Nielsen Media Research (Brandrepublic, 2008) indicating the top 10 UK advertisers online.

The 2008 Market Resource Guide from Crain Communications Inc reports the 2006 media spend of US' top ten internet advertisers (see Table 2.4). This is derived from analysis of data from TNS Media Intelligence.

Personalized advertising

For clients, agencies and companies such as DoubleClick and Tacoda who deliver behaviourally targeted advertising across an enormous array of websites, a central endeavour is to leverage information they have on their audiences and deliver more personalized advertising, customizable and relevant to them. Personalization involves consumer data generating content tailored to the individual. These involve technological and mathematical applications that are in a constant state of refinement. Like all technological developments, these are heatedly discussed initially, and then appear in the mainstream in a subtler yet more profound guise. As will be discussed in Chapter 4, these are part of wider-scale changes affecting citizens as well as consumers. In many ways we are now an aggregated society. Personalized advertising has been the Holy Grail for advertisers and agencies since the heady days of the dot.com boom period. This is not so much for any creative reason but more to do with return on investment metrics (ROI) and for advertisers to be able to assess which parts of their advertising budget are most effective. The IAB (2008a) note that online advertisements can be shown to specific audiences using demographic information such as age, gender and social class, and that content can be tailored according to an individual's location. In addition, it can be customized to users' online behaviour – thus showing advertisements to large segments of users who have expressed interest in the same thing. Behavioural targeting companies track data about users to show them advertisements for things they are most likely to buy by processing factors such as search terms entered, editorial content viewed, advertisements clicked on and channels or micro-sites visited. They measure browsing and user attention span, and amass information like wish lists, preferences and purchases. We are in the early days of internet-based advertising platforms and later semantic incarnations will involve more knowledge about the make-up of everyday life to deliver personalized advertising. For example, as Story (2007b) describes, Yahoo! has developed a behavioural targeting system where the advertiser (or its agency) provides Yahoo! with the components of its display advertisements that can subsequently be personalized. Personalized elements of the advertising include logos, campaign lines and images. The retailer would share information from its inventory databases that track the items on the shelves in each of its stores. Next, Yahoo! would combine that data with the information it has about its users' demographics and actions online to create a product-specific advertisement. This puts Yahoo! in direct competition with DoubleClick, which was acquired by Google, and aQuantive, which was bought by Microsoft. The difficulty for advertisers is concern over privacy, user autonomy and ethics regarding users' data (as more fully explored in Chapter 6). Grannick (2007) highlights that although advertisers do not collect personally identifiable information about users, they may collect users' IP addresses. These in turn have a fair degree of reliability in revealing post and ZIP/post codes, birth dates and gender.

Story (2008) took the direct approach to finding out how personal advertising can be, asking the four large-scale advertising servers (AOL, Google, Microsoft and Yahoo!) a question: can they show you an advertisement with your name in it? Although none of the companies actually do this, she was interested in whether they could do this. She found that Microsoft could use only a person's first name. AOL and Yahoo! could use a full name but only on their sites, not the other sites on which they place ads. Google wasn't sure; it probably could, but it doesn't know the names of most of its users (ibid). Highly targeted and perhaps personalized advertising presents an interesting scenario for users. By offering up data, they receive advertising they may genuinely be interested in, although this requires the giving-up of degrees of privacy. As suggested in Chapter 6, in coming years this may be a *fait accompli*.

Emblematic of the digital economy is Google. Search advertising has arguably been the most successful digital platform launched. Through use of search algorithms and data aggregation, Google in particular has revolutionized the online and digital advertising industry. Google and Microsoft are also readying themselves to extend their reach into traditional advertising with "Google TV Ads" that operates in a similar fashion to their AdWords programmes (see Chapter 3 for more on this). Whereas many agency figures consider traditional advertising as predicated on creativity, they see the involvement of Google and Microsoft as characterized by sterile algorithms of computer programmers (see Chapters 3 and 7 for more on search and advertising as science). Interest in online-styled targeting techniques for television was highlighted at the 2008 Cannes annual awards where Microsoft announced it had acquired Navic Networks whose software helps direct cable television advertisements to demographically desirably audiences (Pfanner, 2008). At Cannes, Sir Martin Sorrell, CEO of WPP, also remarked that advertising agencies were being priced out of the market in a quest to acquire companies such as Navic Networks, DoubleClick and aQuantive and upgrade their own digital capabilities. 'We coveted them, too', he said during a panel discussion with representatives of Google, Microsoft, Yahoo! and Time Warner's AOL. 'But we didn't have the resources' (ibid). This becomes even more significant when one considers the scale of WPP that is one of the big six advertising holding companies, the others being Omnicom, Interpublic, Publicis, Dentsu and Havas, and the world's largest communications services group employing 100,000 people working in more than 2000 offices in 106 countries.[7] As Johnson (2008) describes, Madison Avenue already is competing with deep-pocketed new rivals. In 2007, the Microsoft Corporation scooped up aQuantive, parent of No. 1 digital agency Avenue A/Razorfish,[8] for $6 b. That is enough to buy one and a half Interpublics. Digital services in 2007 accounted for 12.3 per cent or $4.7 b of worldwide revenue for advertising's Big Four, Omnicom, WPP, Interpublic and Publicis, according to Advertising Age DataCenter estimates (Johnson, 2008). Suffice to say, there are testing times ahead for traditional advertising and communications companies as the technology giants move towards centre-field.

Business, advertising and web 2.0

Much has been written over the last four years or so about web 2.0 and the impact it is having on web-based media. It was not the first tech' ".0"; in 1998, Wired magazine's Chris Anderson and James Daly launched Business 2.0, a monthly magazine that charted the rise of the "New Economy". However, web 2.0's reach has been felt throughout the media environment and is certainly not restricted to advertising. In 2006, *Time Magazine* declared "You" the "Person of the Year," observing that

> We made Facebook profiles and Second Life avatars and reviewed books at Amazon and recorded podcasts. We blogged about

our candidates losing and wrote songs about getting dumped. We camcordered bombing runs and built open-source software. (Grossman, 2006).

Reflecting both on the inane and the genuinely useful, they describe web 2.0 as an enormous social experiment. Advertising has not been slow to embrace web 2.0 although for many web 2.0 discourses are reminiscent of the advent of the web first time around and the investment mistakes made then through over-exuberance. Also, given the centrality of advertising to media, perhaps the relationship between web 2.0 and advertising is more important than most. Web 2.0 is a contentious term that has now entered digital lexicon. Commonly ascribed to Tim O'Reilly (2005), who avowedly protects ownership of the term,[9] it refers to trends in the web predicated on sharing, collaboration and content creation by users. Popular evidence for earlier usage can be found in McCormack (2002) and his book *Web 2.0: The Resurgence of the Internet and E-Commerce*. As Allen (2007a) describes it is a term that arose in the mid-2000s that shifted emphasis away from the web to aspects of the internet such as Voice over Internet Protocol (VoIP) and Video on Demand and similar services and applications that, although reliant on the web, step beyond traditional publishing formats. It is also a rhetorical device in that it expresses a sentiment to move beyond the initial incarnation of the web and its associations with the dot.com crash. It expresses a suggestion that those who survived this period were already using web 2.0 competencies and embracing its potential. Allen states that

> Web 2.0 is, therefore, not a statement of protocols for communication (as the World Wide Web was first for Tim Berners-Lee) but a statement of the business protocols for securing one's investment, from both ends of the investment decision. (2007a, p. 9)

This notion of 1.0, 2.0 and 3.0 (data mining/semantic web) has led to the slightly ridiculous scenario of commentators and technologists claiming rhetorical real estate on the basis of self-branding and consultancy fees. However, in the popular technological imaginary of stories and lore, web 2.0 now represents platforms include web application "mash-ups", content mash-ups, wikis, blogs, social networks and folksonomies.[10] There are a number of technical descriptors of web 2.0, but it is fair to say that the common working division is that web 1.0 is an incarnation based on the web as a source of information, and

2.0 being a participatory web. This is well reflected in a social media campaign launched by Skittles in 2009 that allowed users to take over Skittles.com through a range of social media channels involving Facebook, YouTube, Flickr, Twitter and Wikipedia. Commentary and contributions were not always positive. For example, on Twitter pages a user called xino "tweets": 'Shittles... taste the asshole'; another called tashaa x 3 tweets, 'Skittles sure don't taste like the rainbow when they are coming back up. Fuck i hate being sick'. Although these comments are potentially worrying for brand managers, the fact that consumers are engaging with the brand is deemed by many bloggers and commentators to be a winning outcome for the brand. Rather than the web being something "out there" the web instead is something that we, as users, create and shape ourselves. As a well-circulated YouTube video on web 2.0 produced by Wesch (2007) tells us, 'We are the web'.[11] Tim Berners Lee (the inventor of the web) argues web 2.0 is mere jargon that no one really understands. He argues that the web has always been about people-to-people communication, sharing and consensual building of online spaces. He states that the idea of the web as interaction between people is really what the web is. It was designed to be as a collaborative space where people can interact (developerWorks, 2006).[12] Web 2.0 is thus a term laden with marketing-speak and often adopted and abused by advertisers looking to get ahead of their competitors in search of tech-savvy audiences. Reid (2007) comments 'The original slogan was always to have a web that was easy to write as it was to read,' quoting Robert Cailliau of the World Wide Web Consortium (W3C). Current developments thus reflect technological developments rather than theoretical or philosophical developments.

However, there does seem to have been a distinct cultural shift with the web being used by mainstream audiences as a place to share videos, tag photos and people, create radio playlists, engage in social networking and other activities that involve building networks, communities and data patterns. Although writing as well as reading may have always been the driving idea, there is now a marked shift in popular usage. This, at least in part, is driven by ease of use and average users' understanding that they are capable of using the technology at hand (Gangadharbatla, 2008). Web 2.0 is also intimately tied-up with user-generated content (UGC) where content created by users and consumers rather than media owners or traditional publishers. As the IAB (2008d) note, user-generated content includes written reviews or recommendations online with a large portion of sites now offering their visitors the opportunity to do this, posting comments on news sites, keeping and maintaining a blog or podcast, uploading personal information on a social networking site such as MySpace, Bebo or Facebook, sharing pictures like those available on Flickr, posting video clips on sites such as Google's YouTube, contributing to sites in involving factual information such as Wiki's and finally the referencing or tagging of useful and relevant sites for other internet users, de.lic.io.us. com or Diigo for example. The IAB (2009b) describe that the most popular user-generated activities are communicating or interacting with people they already know; reviewing content submitted by members of the public; watching a video clip submitted by a member of the public; social networking; updating personal profiles; reading personal profiles; submitting an article or comment; online discussion; meeting new people and lastly uploading video clips. It is noteworthy that in contrast to UGC creators who are interested in self-expression, 'UGC users appear more inclined to treat these vehicles like traditional sources and adopt a passive approach' (Daugherty et al., 2008). In addition, motivational factors driving UGC usage include a wish to experience a sense of community, and also to minimize self-doubts through a sense of belonging, and possibly reduce guilty feelings about not contributing (ibid). UGC sites visited by UK users are led by video sharing sites; online community sites/social networking; reunion sites (for example, Friends Reunited); gaming sites (for example, Gamespot or Miniclip); photo sharing sites; virtual worlds (including games such as World of Warcraft and worlds without narrative or gaming function such as Second Life); and online dating sites.

Another phrase to characterize the same phenomenon is social media, with consumer-generated content being applicable to content generated in reference to a brand. For instance, although the general Chinese population have been online for less time than Europeans, or the Americans, online social media and word-of-mouth plays a role in purchase decisions in China whereby 58 percent of purchases are influenced by consumer reviews, ratings sites, forums and discussion boards, blogs and other social media sites. In contrast, about 19 percent of purchase decisions in the United States are influenced by word-of-mouth (Burns, 2007). It appears that in many ways China and other "developing" nations are leapfrogging earlier stages of web history and that the Chinese broadband population has been quicker to adopt a diverse number of web 2.0 technologies for daily use than the US population.

People have and always will place trust in what their peers tell them, probably over what an advertiser will tell them. This word-of-mouth and peer assessed way of making brand and product decisions fits well with notions of 'web 2.0' where users by definition offer creative, intellectual and critical labour for free. This relates to Lazzarato's (1996) concept of immaterial labour. Here consumption is an act of production and 'immaterial labour' (Lazzarato, 1996) where it is unclear whose creative labour advertising (or anything else consumers may make or distribute on producers' behalf) belongs to. Participatory media involves recognizing that media consumers are no longer passive but instead active and are actively involved in meaning construction for brands. The key is that the customer becomes a co-creator of the medium or content carried through or over that medium. Klein (2008) states that established companies should concentrate on using web 2.0 to tap into their client bases and draw upon what has been dubbed the power of the crowd (Howe, 2008). As Spurgeon (2008) describes, the media milieu is now characterized, to some extent, by conversation. New digital media necessitate that advertisers and their agencies think about communication in new ways. This requires a reconsideration of the role of a consuming public and the way they engage with brands. This is an opportunity for brands: whereas many web 1.0 companies did not survive due to initial investment costs, web 2.0 allows companies to harness the content production and interest of users and "crowds".

Web 2.0-styled initiatives can be difficult to manage however. For example, although there are successful advertising ventures into user-generated video content with Pepsi, Jeep, Dove and Sprint staging promotions of this sort, and winners of Doritos' "Crash the Superbowl" competition managing to get airtime during the US Superbowl since 2007, there have been others that have gone awry. As Story (2007c) describes, the Malibu brand, owned by Pernod Ricard, ran a user-generated advertising contest on YouTube in 2007 where disgruntled users believed the outcome of the competition to be rigged. One YouTube user even made a six-minute conspiracy theory video comparing images from a professional Malibu commercial promoting the contest with the winner's video, saying in part: "Wow, the same nose!? The same guy? You be the judge!" In addition, advertisers also run the risk of user-generated work being of poor quality or reflecting their brands badly. Story (2007) also notes that Heinz ran a competition committing itself to picking five of the entries and showing them on television, though not committing itself to a channel or a time slot. One winner received $57,000. In one execution, a teenage boy rubs ketchup over his face like acne cream and then puts pickles on his eyes. Another contestant drinks ketchup straight from the bottle, while another brushes his teeth, washes his hair and shaves his face with it. The net result is that the ketchup looks more like blood.

Convergence

As mentioned above, convergence and web 2.0 are deeply interrelated. Convergence as a term is not unique to web 2.0 platforms nor is it particularly contemporary. For example, Nicholas Negroponte at MIT was working on convergence models in the late 1980s mapping the coming together of industries, objects, apparatus and content in regards to businesses such as telecommunications and entertainment (Bassett, 2008). This was the "teething-ring" theory of digital convergence, in which TV, publishing and computer industries would coalesce to create multimedia hardware.

Web 2.0 notions of convergence have more to do with people and what they do with technology. As will be described in Chapter 3, for example, people use micro-blogging, instant messaging services and mobile telephony as a means of generating constant co-presence across distances. It also involves practices of user content creation, harnessing "the power of crowds" (as with wiki's), digital discussion and content that are now distributed across a range of media platforms far more numerous than has ever existed. Media and content are *visibly* converging. Convergence can be defined as

> ...the flow of content across multiple media platforms, the cooperation between multiple media industries, and the migratory behaviours of media audiences who will go almost anywhere in search of entertainment experiences they want. Convergence is a word that manages to describe technological, industrial, cultural, and social changes depending on who's speaking and what they are talking about. (Jenkins, 2006, p. 3)

The difference, as Bassett (2008) notes, is that web 2.0 versions of convergence are based on 'an understanding of the dynamics of the system (the new media ecology) *in use'*. It contrast to passive media forms and notions of spectatorship where viewers simply watch or listen to advertisements (or wider media content), new forms of media have more to do with participation and interaction. How users and media producers interact is not as yet entirely clear. The problem for content producers is to work out where users are going to be. New media consumers are migratory and show little dedication or loyalty to media platforms. From the point of view of convergence and web 2.0, advertisers need to understand media flow and how to integrate delivery across platforms, in addition to creating greater tools for user-generated content and higher levels of interactivity. As Jenkins (2006a) describes, for some time now fans, audiences and consumers have been dissecting and reorganizing media content online. Advertisers need to create more and varied touch-points with their consumers. Although this potentially sounds expensive, the return on investment and immaterial labour from users interacting with their brands may offset this (also see Chapter 7). Communication thus has more to do with facilitation and engagement than transmission.

Question for further discussion

> How new are new media? What historical, technological, social or theoretical definitions would you say characterize "new"?

> To what extent do you agree with the proposition that 'a good idea is a good idea so if the idea is good enough it can live in any channel'?

> Is any publicity good publicity? To what extent should brands maintain strategic control over their communications in a social media environment?

3   Form and Content: Beyond the Pop-up

A common misperception of online advertising is to equate digital with the online advertising, and online advertising solely with pop-ups and banners. While these formats play a significant role within an advertiser's media mix they are not the entire story, especially given the dominance of search advertising. This extended chapter describes in detail the breadth of formats of online advertising and wider digital advertising media at advertisers' and marketers' disposal.

Platforms discussed include classified, display (static and rich media), search, online digital video and email. Other developments include the leveraging of word-of-mouth, viral advertising and advertising that may be seeded into social networking sites such as *MySpace* and self-broadcasting sites such as *YouTube*. Virtual spaces and advertising are also discussed in light of a case study on *Second Life* and associated environments. Although focused primarily on online media, this chapter also describes advertising opportunities for wireless devices and concludes by summing up the key characteristics of other new media, most notably mobile telephony and advertising opportunities therein. Media here are discussed in isolation rather than how they operate and integrate together. Further, this chapter does not account for how they interact with offline advertising efforts that may be required to drive consumers online in the first place. See Chapter 7 for more on trans-media story telling and how brand values and messages may be relayed through different digital platforms.

Display

Although none of my students claims to have clicked on or interacted with a pop-up, they remain one of the most popular online formats available to advertisers and their agencies. Plummer et al. report a similar perspective noting that the least positive formats are out-of-frame, pop-under and pop-up advertisements (2007, p. 83). The IAB (2009a) break down the display market into banners and embedded that make up the overwhelmingly most popular display format; sponsorships; interruptive formats; display advertisements on email; tenancies;

pre-post roll and other display. As stated in Chapter 2, banners and embedded advertising represent the second most popular digital advertising format with £277.6m worth of media spend and 16.5 per cent of the digital media mix. Online display advertising encompasses all advertising that borders or is included within a webpage in some fashion. As Plummer et al. describe, key types include

▶ *Contextual targeting* that places advertisements on the basis of the content of the page.
▶ *Behavioural targeting* that tracks sites visited offering relevant advertising to a user's history where advertisement displayed need not have to do with the page being viewed.
▶ *Geographic targeting* that refers to customer's registration details involving designated market areas (DMA), area codes, zip or postcodes, time zones or global positioning system (GPS) coordinates. This may also involve internet protocol addresses.
▶ *Daypart targeting* that is more commonly associated with radio and television. For example, use of the internet at work is different to the type of use at home and companies working on behalf of advertisers may tailor their advertising accordingly.
▶ *Affinity targeting* which is the use of sites that maintain kudos with their audience. This has a corollary effect on advertising carried.
▶ *Purchase-based category targeting* that is made viable through tracking of online behaviour. This involves the mapping of a brand's profile customer to users', visitor's profiles and serving relevant advertising.

In the 1990s and early 2000s it seemed that online space was going to follow real life in placing advertising in every conceivable place. Clutter has however now gone down 12 per cent, with fewer display-ad impressions per page view than they were a year ago, according to comScore AdMetrix data (Klaassen, 2008a). The first generally agreed online advertising to exist was hosted by *HotWired* in 1994. Hollis (2005) also comments that online advertising has been in existence since 1994 and properly audited since 1996 when *HotWired* in conjunction with Millward Brown assessed the success rates of *HotWired*'s banner advertising, pronouncing the success of *HotWired*'s campaign and that banner advertising is effective, even on first viewing. Display advertising allows advertisers to know how many users have been exposed to their advertising broadly based on click-through-rates and page-impressions. Whereas page-impressions represent an opportunity for a user to see and click on a banner, for example, a click-through represents the committed action of a user who actually clicks on a banner advertisement in response to its message. Many advertisers see this kind of interactivity as the ultimate measure of effectiveness (Drèze and Zufryden, 1999) although there is confusion over payment, standardization of effectiveness measurements[13] and confusion regarding how effectiveness should be measured in terms of branding and recall (Bhat et al, 2002; Shen, 2002). The Internet Advertising Bureau (IAB) has been instrumental in creating guidelines and formats for advertisers.[14]

Throughout the dot.com boom period (1997–2000), business and academic research focused on whether online advertising was a direct response mechanism or had the power to aid in building brands.[15] Hollis (2005) further asserts that a large proportion of literature emanating from both the business and academic communities doubted online advertising's brand-building capabilities. He cites the following:

> Publishers have to start by admitting that branding, at least in the traditional sense, just doesn't work on the Web. Successful branding happens on TV and radio through a subtle, emotion-inspiring combination of music, images, or voices. Web banner ads that flash catchy tag lines don't do it. (Business Week Online (2000), cited by Hollis, 2005)

Compounding lack of confidence in brand building was the growing awareness that click-through-rates were not converting to sales (Welch and Krishnamoorthy, 2000) and banner advertising being described as the 'black sheep of marketing channels' (Song, 2001). This was also followed by a dip in the online advertising media market share that recovered in 2002/2003 through an improvement in payment and measurement metrics that Lohtia et al. (2003) described as the two top metrics for advertisement reporting and effectiveness measurements. This was further powered by additional effectiveness benchmarks derived from the IAB that focused on examining online in combination with offline media.

Research from CNET Networks in tandem with Starch Research (its founder Daniel Starch pioneered measuring actual advertisement readership in the 1920s) reveal that advertisements which attract the most attention use powerful images employing large and expansive photography: emphasis of contrast between foreground and background lends a 3-D effect and visual spectacle. Red, blue, green-yellow and green are key colours to catch the eye (Plummer et al., 2007, p. 85). In contrast to advertisements that shake and flash to gain attention, simple executions with a clear focal point hold consumer attention. Plummer et al. also highlight that the eye is drawn first to motion and then to copy. In addition, while scanning pages users tend to concentrate on the tops and lefts of pages resulting in an F-shaped pattern mostly regardless of the type of content on the screen.

Furthermore, the growth in rich media also inculcates higher levels of interactivity. Rich media offer more creative potential and capacity for emotional engagement (Sundar and Kalyanaraman, 2004). Rich media differ from conventional banner and pop-up advertisements in that they involve video, high-impact sound and are often interactive in some way. In comparison to static forms of display advertising, rich media have maintained higher click-through rates. These advertisements can be used either singularly or in combination with various technologies, including but not limited to sound, video or Flash, and with programming languages such as Java, Javascript and dynamic HTML (DHTML). These rich media definitions also cover standard web applications including email, static (for example, html) and dynamic web pages where elements of a page may change according to context and conditions; for example, when something happens when a user moves a cursor over an element of a page. These may appear in formats such as banners and buttons as well as transitionals and various over-the-page units such as floating advertisements, page take-overs and tear-backs. Rich media also include in-page and in-text digital video advertisements where the associated content is not streaming in a player environment (IAB, 2008f). Predicated on click-through rates and the desire to understand return on investment (ROI), advertisers have been attracted to this format that gives seemingly straight-talking metrics.

Email

The first email was sent in 1971 by programmer Ray Tomlinson using the ARPAnet, a forerunner to the internet. In 2008, around 210b messages were sent per day: 63 per cent of all traffic was consumer, and 37 per cent corporate email messages. By 2012, this figure is predicted to double to 419 billion messages per day (Radicati, 2008). Email advertising is essentially the same type of advertising as that which drops through your letterbox. It is a form of direct marketing that has its uses but as everyday experience tells us, much of it is junk. Spam is the term widely used for unsolicited email although its remit has been broadened (also see Chapter 6 for discussion of spam and regulation). In 2008, Adland celebrated the thirtieth birthday of Spam noting that the first spam mail[16] was sent to 600 people on 3 May 1978 by Gary Thuerk, an aggressive Digital Equipment Corporation (DEC) marketer (Adland, 2008). The World Wide Web Consortium (W3C) defines spam or Unsolicited Bulk E-mail (UBE) as 'The mass electronic distribution of unsolicited email to individual email accounts, aliases, or mailing lists and archives' (Hernandez, 2007). However, as the Messaging Anti-Abuse Working Group (MAAWG) explains, the precise definition of spam differs slightly from jurisdiction to jurisdiction in local laws. For example, in Europe and Canada spam, or unsolicited commercial email, is based on an "opt-in" approach, whereas the United States has adopted an "opt-out" approach. Nevertheless, it is fair to say that spam may be defined as electronic communications that are likely to be unwanted or unexpected by the recipient (MAAWG, 2007). Either way, figures for unsolicited email range between 80 per cent and 95 per cent.

Although most commonly associated with email, the expression spam also applies to internet forums, mobile, instant messaging, posting within blogs and unwanted advertisements within newsgroups. The term probably derives from a Monty Python comedy sketch[17] where every item in a café comes with spam (a type of tinned meat), but the character, Mrs Bun, does not want spam. Spam was one of the few meats excluded from the UK food rationing policy that began in World War II and continued for a number of years after the war. The British grew heartily tired of it, hence the sketch's humour, where Mrs Bun is confronted by repetitive choruses of spam from Viking Spam singers – everywhere she is surrounded by spam. The Direct Marketing Association (DMA) and similar organizations understandably distance themselves from the activities of spammers and go to great lengths to maintain consumer trust[18] through careful use of consumer email addresses and personal information.

The key advantage of email contact with consumers is the level of intimacy. It is a permission-based format where customers allow businesses to interact with them. As with much digital advertising, relevance is key. Email is now the most popular form of direct response marketing, according to a mid-2008 survey of large US corporations conducted by Direct Partners, New York (Miller, 2008). Email is used primarily by 35 per cent of companies compared to 25 per cent that use traditional direct mail and 21 per cent that use package, statement stuffers or freestanding inserts.

Most email deployment tools allow companies or their agencies to personalize email within the body of the email as well as the subject line. In addition, with email that has been co-opted – where users agree or sign up to receive email (see Chapter 5 for more on co-optation) – companies can discuss previous purchases or buying behaviour. There is a range of email formats that can be received. These are dependent on the type of email client the recipient uses. For example, older plain text clients may only allow black and white text and links will appear as full URLs.[19] More recent clients will receive rich text, colour and accept hypertext. The most up-to-date client at the time of writing provides for HTML and has the same feel and layout as a webpage. These can support animations and images.

Classified

As the IAB (2009a) describe, classified advertising is an enormous contributor to the digital economy. As the third highest digital advertising format, recruitment advertising from companies including Monster and Jobsite represents over £194m of the total digital advertising media spend in the United Kingdom. Other classified advertising from businesses including AutoTrader and the wider automotive industry, directories such as Yell.com, property advertisers including Propertyfinder.com, primelocation.com and the hospitality industry represents over £161m worth of online digital advertising. In total this places classified as the second most popular digital advertising format after search. Like search advertising described below, classified advertising represents an opportunity for smaller-scale advertising to announce their wares and services. Moreover, it allows larger advertisers to target local markets very specifically.

Search and portals

Although Google is today synonymous with search engines, according to Battelle (2005) the first search engine of sorts was a pre-web application designed to access documents held on a range of machines called Archie (archive without the v). Created by Alan Emtage in 1990 at McGill University, his application was based on the internet's file transfer protocol (FTP). It was also similar to today's search engines in that it crawled sources and had a search interface. As a forerunner of today's search engines, it offered an electronic indexing service for locating information that exists on the internet. In 1992, Steven Foster and Fred Barrie, both students at the University of Nevada, created Veronica, an engine that would connect to documents held on a computer. In 1993, Matthew Gray of Massachusetts Institute of Technology (MIT) was responsible for the first web-based search engine titled Wandex. Subsequent important developments in search include WebCrawler developed by Brian Pinkerton of the University of Washington. This engine was the first to index the full text of the document retrieved. AltaVista was perhaps the first recognizable search engine to use multiple crawlers to index the growing number of webpages in the early 1990s. By 1997, AltaVista was the number one search engine handling more than 25 million queries per day (Battelle, 2005); it was not until 7 September 1998 that Google was launched. Other search engines popular in the mid-to-late 1990s include Lycos, Excite, Infoseek, Inktomi, Northern Light and Yahoo!. In the United States, comScore (2009) lists the current five most popular search engines with Google maintaining 65.0 per cent of the share of search enquiries, Yahoo! with 20.1 per cent, Microsoft 8.0 per cent, Ask 3.9 and AOL with 3.1 per cent. At the time of writing it is too early to assess the impact of Microsoft's Bing search engine. Wolfram Alpha is also expected to make a significant impact, with the academic and technology community and those interested in statistics. Shankland and Needleman (2009) describe that whereas 'Google is really good at finding information that has already been put down somewhere, or answering questions that have already been asked and answered...Wolfram Alpha, though, can answer questions that have never been asked before, provided the data to create the answer exists in its corpus of facts and figures'. Although not a Google-killer, it does represent a more semantic approach to search-based technology. According to Plummer et al. (2007) around 44 per cent of searchers use one engine, 48 per cent up to three engines and 7 per cent more than three.

Search advertising now dominates the online media market with around 40 per cent of all money spent on online advertising being spent on search advertising. In 2008, it was expected to generate more than $10 billion business in the United States alone (Klaassen, 2008). This dominance is typified by the now ubiquitous Google Corporation and their Adwords search links on the right hand side and also sometimes just above the search results. The key formats for search advertising include "paid search advertising" and AdWords type services that work by advertising next to search terms. Advertisers only pay when the link is clicked on, as links are "pay-per-click". The advertiser chooses a set of words or phrases that best relate to their business. Advertisers may also bid on words that will positively associate with the advertiser and their brand. When a user has entered a relevant term, the link will appear on the right hand side with the same text or similar appearing in the advertisement itself. The scalability of this stems from the fact that Adwords, and similar programmes from Yahoo! Search Marketing and MSN adCenter, are open to the smallest of advertisers. This means that advertisers only pay if users click on an advertisement. "Contextually targeted search advertising" involves lists of links and advertisements carried on webpages – typically news or blog related – and are relevant to the content of the webpage. Google's version of this is Adsense, whilst Yahoo! offers a service called Search Content Match. Other services involve "paid inclusion" that ensure that specified webpages are included in a search index. This gives the appearance of a natural result. Google does not offer this service. Google is now by far the largest player in the search market with Yahoo! now contentiously allowing them to display Adsense-based advertisements next to their search results. Such expansion has ramifications for antitrust and monopoly laws and regulation. In March 2009, Google controversially announced plans to introduce behavioural advertising, dubbed "interest based" advertising. Whereas advertising prior reflects interests at a specific time, their proposed system collects information from users' cookie enabled web browsers including types of sites visited and pages viewed to offer more highly targeted advertising. As unpacked in full in Chapter 6, this is mired in concerns as to whether advertising should be opt-in or opt-out.

As well as changing the way that wealthier portions of people organize and access knowledge, search has revolutionized the advertising business. Although Google's auctioneering is based on words, there is no technical reason why this should not extend to visuals. MySpace is already rolling out self-serving advertising banners using a search-based system called MyAds that draw deeply on personal data (Morrissey, 2008). In the United Kingdom, search is snapping at the heels of the major commercial broadcasters and will likely surpass them in years to come.

Bizarrely, the inventors of Google originally had very little interest in advertising and were instead deeply suspicious of blending advertising with search results (Battelle, 2005). As Röhle (2008) also observes, the primary function for search is to generate audiences for advertisers via search and to translate users' information needs into consumption needs. Whilst portals (sites such as Yahoo! where search is combined with email, news, stock prices, celebrity gossip and similar features) were cluttered with banner advertisements, Google was keen not to slow the service down with extra load time. Although Google now appears omnipresent, up until 2001 it was struggling to find a business model that would generate any revenue. What is remarkable about the growth of Google-styled advertising is the lack of visual representation involved. Like classified advertising, it is utterly unbranded and based on algorithms (sequences of instructions used for data collection and processing) that only aim to engender relevance to the consumer.

Relevance and usefulness to consumers is generated by the minimal mediation that search advertising involves. The key virtue of search advertising for advertisers is that it targets consumers when they are interested and searching for information about products and services. For consumers, the upside is that they do not receive irrelevant information about products and services they are not interested in. This is a system that is intended to work for consumers and advertisers alike. It also allows smaller-scale advertisers to offer their wares to a public who are interested in their offerings, although as Pan et al. (2007) highlight, it facilitates a rich-get-richer dynamic due to relatively few sites dominating the top ranks.

Interestingly 62 per cent of small businesses in the United Kingdom are not investing in search marketing, even though 76 per cent of those doing so report an increase in sales. The research, commissioned by Microsoft adCenter and conducted by Vanson Bourne, questioned 400 small businesses across the United Kingdom via online questionnaires. Of the respondents not using search marketing, 44 per cent stated they thought it is too time consuming, more than 55 per cent said it is too expensive and 33 per cent said it is too complicated. The results suggest that reluctance to invest in search engine marketing or advertising is not due to a lack of knowledge; in fact, 78 per cent of the businesses not doing search marketing claimed they were aware of the SEM tools available to them (Marshall, 2007).

Search engine optimization

Another key way of driving users and consumers to a particular website is via Search Engine Optimization (SEO). Optimization is the act of altering a website to improve search engine listings. This involves improving or maintaining rankings on search engine listings through the understanding that users are more likely to click on those closer to the top. Because these results are "organic" or "natural" they enjoy a higher trust status and are perhaps considered more authentic than paid-for advertising. Optimizing of search engines requires an understanding of how a search engine's ranking system works. Google uses a system called PageRank as a method of sorting the importance of webpages.[20] PageRank works by ranking the importance of pages by considering more than 500 million variables and 2 billion terms. Pages that they believe important receive a higher PageRank and are more likely to appear at the top of the search results (Google, 2008). Yahoo runs a similar system called Web Rank as does Microsoft with its MSN portal and Page and Domain ranking systems. Other engines of note include AOL and the Ask network.

The original PageRank system works by assessing the amount and quality of in-bound links to webpage with a link working as a form of endorsement. Webpages are important if other important pages point to them. A page with more recommendations from in-links will be more important than a page with fewer. Quality also plays a part. Langville and Mayer (2006, p. 27) use the analogy of receiving a personal endorsement from Donald Trump for a job application. One from him will be more useful than 20 unknown teachers or colleagues. This may be tempered however if one finds Donald Trump is free and generous with his recommendations or links. The importance of these will then drop in significance.

In general terms,[21] to optimize a site, an advertiser must make it relevant by including key terms a searcher will use, particularly in title and headings. Advice on optimization tends to include the following dictums. Key words used overtly and embedded within HTML should be extensively researched. The keywords should also be placed within title tags. These receive a high degree of prominence from search bots as these determine the title of a webpage. In HTML they appear at the top of a page, for example <title>Your title here</title>. Avoid bland and non-descript titles such as 'Andy's Homepage' as search spiders and bots will not notice these. Sites should also be crawler-friendly in terms of how pages link together. They should also contain content that users want to come back for. Lastly, potential advertisers should investigate services that each of the major engines offer via the link at the bottom of their pages. Optimizing is not a dark art and all offer methods, tools and website diagnostics to improve an advertiser's effectiveness.

The future of search

Search engines as described here are still predicated on a largely text-based web not radically different from the original incarnation of the web in 1992.[22] Search engines do not have access to all information on the web with much of it remaining hidden to search spiders. In mid-2008, Adobe provided the Google and Yahoo! search engines with a specialized version of its Flash animation player that reveals information about text and links in Flash files. This is particularly important for advertisers who have traditionally had to decide between building for optimization concerns and aesthetics. Although text-based advertisements are unobtrusive and sit well with text-based search results, they are not the only Google format. Google's insight is that advertisements should be conducive to the format they sit within. As such they are beginning to offer images, videos, news stories and other types of information. Being the owner of YouTube, this is not unexpected as is the fact they have been selling video space on other sites for over two years. More will also be made of locative possibilities. Google again are ahead in these services with their geospatial offerings, Google Earth and Google Maps (competing with Microsoft), delivering the capacity to list and place advertisers' businesses. As mobile phones and other locative media develop, we will see new data layers added to the urban and outdoor environment. As well as the traditional street sign we use to orient ourselves, geospatial media will help us know more about our location through tagged imagery, and allow us to receive and create stories about places, as well as being a format that offers advertising opportunities.

There are many other trajectories that search will follow and innovate. Peter Norvig, Google's director of research, suggests that these include closer links between search and advertising results and more sources that search engines can index; for example, video and audio in terms of speech recognition (Greene, 2007). In general, a focus is on how people interact with the web and how people operate within networks and communities online. Twitter, the micro-blogging service that allows its users to send and read other users' updates, is in the process of examining ways of extracting revenue from its service. This may have the potential to provide a searchable database of what is being said at a particular time. Omniture (an online marketing and web analytics company), for example, employs a program called SiteCatalyst that counts the number of times a brand is mentioned and presents it in a bar graph that can be sorted by day. This classifies Twitter users into segments, such as customers, vendors, employees and other categories. As Learmonth (2009) describes, whereas Google represents an archive of the world's recorded knowledge, Twitter represents what was said on a recorded topic, albeit in brief form. This has been particularly interesting when news has been reported by "twitterers" who may be at the scene of an event before larger agencies can get to the scene. Similarly this is important for news agenda setting. Brands are also keen to get involved with Twitter as a means of generating buzz about their produce and perceptions of closer relationships between brands and consumers. Twitter also represents a potential to leverage a 'group mind' (ibid) where searchers will be able to not only access documents or previous "tweets" but also potentially millions of users. This would allow answers to a query from people rather than documents.

There is also a significant interest in the mobile phone market (more on which below), for example services that lets users search for small businesses by voice. Overall the direction of search and digital advertising is to engender relevance, usability, personalization and advertising that provide users a service of some sort. In addition, Google is also venturing into the terrain of media planning and buying with their Google TV Ads service that is similar to AdWords. The first TV advertisements brokered by Google appeared in January 2009 on two digital-cable outlets owned by NBC Universal. It remains to be seen whether this will set a precedent. Buying space is a remarkably simple system where an advertiser selects keywords and sets a spending limit for each day on the basis of per thousands of people who see the advertisement. Google's system works out where and when the advertisement should be placed on the basis of demographics and other audience data Google are privy to. Given their proficiency in web advertising this is an interesting development to monitor. It is perhaps their involvement that is interesting at this stage rather than their current mechanisms.

Digital Video

As commented on above, digital advertising is far from restricted to text-based search advertising and pop-ups and banners. Driven by the vast growth in video portals such as Metacafe, Veoh, blip.tv, YouTube (owned by Google) and Google Video, there has been a vast explosion in visual content carried across the internet. Whereas the late 1990s and early 2000s represented the audio era for the web, since around

2005 video has been the dominant form of information hogging the network. Although doomsayers foretell the death of traditional television advertising the reality is that much of it is undergoing a process of convergence and remediation (Bolter and Grusin, 1999) and being reabsorbed into digital formats. This, however, is not to suggest that online users will suffer the same fate that television viewers have undergone since the advent of commercial funded television. Viewers, consumers and users hold too much sway and fiscal capital in the online sector to be held hostage to extensive unwanted advertising.

The IAB (2008a) observe that digital video advertising arrived when Mark Cuban's and Todd Wagner's Broadcast.com was sold to Yahoo! in 1998 for a sum of $5.7b. BMW have probably produced the first and most renowned video campaign with "The Hire". This is a campaign beginning on the internet between 2001 and 2002 involving eight short branded films that spanned two seasons with content directed by film directors and producers including, Ang Lee, John Woo and Guy Ritchie. Later comic books produced by Dark Horse Comics carry on from where the films left off. As the advertising industry rebuilt itself from the carnage of the dot.com crash, providers such as Microsoft's Windows Media Player, Yahoo's Launch, The FeedRoom and MSNBC's video content inched the industry forward by selling "test" programs to blue-chip advertisers who wanted to learn about the medium and gain insight. In 2005, augmented by high-speed broadband, Starcom and Mediavest took control of the digital video market claiming Procter & Gamble, McDonalds, Kellogg and Coca-Cola as clients who were to allocate millions of dollars for digital video. This combined with the sale of YouTube to Google made digital video an interesting prospect in the media mix.

Video presents interesting opportunities to advertisers in that it will allow for greater interactivity as advertisers harness web technology to enable users to click-through from their video advertisement to their own website, or roll their mouse pointer over a product to trigger a whole new video presentation or possibly buy the product.[23] Perhaps expectedly, users have negative feelings about online video although users appear to be more receptive to advertising with professionally made video rather than amateur/user-generated video (Mindlin, 2008). In a survey conducted by Burst Media (an interactive marketer services company), about 53.6 per cent of online video viewers recall seeing in-stream – either pre-, mid- or post-roll – ads attached to some form of web programming. However, more than three-quarters (78.4 per cent) of respondents said in-stream advertisements are intrusive and one-half (50.4 per cent) say these ads disrupt their use of the internet (Kaplan, 2008). Shorter commercials appear to meet with more success than longer ones. Honda, for example, have aired shortened commercials to fit with mini-episodes screened on MySpace of series including "Charlie's Angels", "The Facts of Life," "Fantasy Island" and "Who's the Boss", edited from their original lengths of 30 or 60 minutes each to an internet-friendly 4 to 6 minutes.[24]

Viral

Viral in an advertising and marketing context refers to commercial publicity passed on by users through pre-existing social networks. The UK's Advertising Standards Authority (ASA) defines viral as an

> e-mail, text or other non-broadcast marketing messages that are designed to stimulate significant circulation by recipients to generate commercial or reputational benefit to the advertiser from the consequential publicity. They are usually put into circulation ('seeded') by the advertiser with a request, either explicit or implicit, for the message to be forwarded to others. Sometimes they include a video clip or a link to website material or are part of a sales promotion campaign. (ASA, 2006)

As Porter and Golan (2006) note, Steve Jurvetson and Tim Draper from the venture capital firm Draper Fisher Jurvetson (DFJ) coined the term "viral marketing" in 1996 recounting the DFJ marketing strategy of the free email service Hotmail (although Rushkoff (1994) alludes to viral marketing earlier in his discussion of instantaneity and wider media). DFJ's marketing strategy involved the tactic of appending messages originating from Hotmail accounts with the tag line "Get your private, free e-mail from Hotmail at http://www.hotmail.com".[25] As Porter and Golan (2000) also observe, Helm (2000) used the Hotmail case to interpret viral marketing as a method of both marketing and distribution, describing viral marketing as

> A communication and distribution concept that relies on customers to transmit digital products via electronic mail to other potential customers in their social sphere and to animate these contacts to also transmit the products. (2000, p. 159)

Viral advertising is thus advertising that is passed from user to user in a word-of-mouth fashion. Although viral advertising may be composed of pass-along messages, coupons, static animation, photography, Flash imagery or 'advergames', the most notorious advertisements have been short commercials (Kirby and Marsden, 2005). These circulate in an environment of viral video content that is often bizarre, boring, perplexing, political, juvenile, self-aggrandizing, disgusting, voyeuristic, irresistible, ridiculous, parodic and incredibly mundane. Viral at times manages to create or reflect zeitgeists and cultural memes unlike any other distribution channel. Through a content analysis of 360 viral advertisements Golan and Zaidner (2008) find that 91 per cent of appeals are characterized by humour; 28.1 per cent by sexuality; 17.8 per cent by animals; 14.4 per cent by violence; and 12.8 per cent by children. The primary function of 70 per cent of these was branding. Product categories included fashion (84.6 per cent), alcohol and tobacco (82 per cent), food and beverage (66.6 per cent), entertainment and media (65.3 per cent) and automotive (64.1 per cent).

As noted by McStay (2007a), both the advertising industry and targeted audiences of viral advertising have recognized this media platform as one that lends credibility to brands via its anarchic nature and the fact that these materials are readily forwarded between peers who are mostly young opinion formers and city workers, both audiences that are hard to reach (Phelps et al., 2004). See, for example, a viral commercial for Marc Ecko clothing at www.stillfree.com where Air Force One, the US President's plane is tagged with graffiti. Viral is also characterized by humour, originality and, moreover, timeliness due to ease of production and media release. For example, although made without the Obama campaign's participation, "Yes, We Can" – a pop video, put together as unofficial viral marketing by hip-hop producer Will.i.am (of the Black Eyed Peas) and the video shot by Jesse Dylan, son of rock's original protest superstar, Bob Dylan – is a piece of political propaganda, aimed at exactly the young voters who might be inclined to support a socially liberal black candidate but are often apathetic when it comes to actually voting. Will.i.am and Dylan claim that it took just a few days from conception to completion: Will.i.am had the idea while watching a televised political debate on 29 January 2008, and by 2 February it was online, in time for the Super Tuesday polls.

On occasion, viral commercials have also translated into traditional television commercials. For example, Mazda commissioned a web advertisement that was made on a shoestring budget; the car company is said to have preferred the clip to its more expensive TV commercials. Subsequently, it was quickly transferred to television in five European countries (Simmons, 2006). For advertisers, the virtue of viral advertising and marketing lies in its cost-effectiveness, ease of implementation and capacity to target niche audiences including hard-to-reach audiences such as those in AB demographic categories and channel zapping, young opinion formers (Morrissey, 2003). In addition, television fragmentation and concurrent audience fragmentation has led advertisers' thinning media spend to be spread across a wider range of channels. As such, advertisers welcome methods of soliciting consumers within a media platform that carries caché amongst its target audiences, are relatively inexpensive and offer a clearer picture of return on investment. Given that the largest aspect of most advertising campaigns is the media costs that account for around 80 to 85 per cent of the budget (Kelley and Jugenheimer, 2004, p. 4), the benefits to advertisers of using viral advertising are obvious.

Viral advertising is currently the wayward child not only getting into all sorts of trouble but is also being blamed for all sorts of things it did not do. It is a victim of its own success in that it is a genre of advertising that seeks to distance itself from traditional advertising and instead emulate low-budget, user-generated content. As described in greater depth in Chapter 7, it is a format that goes to lengths to not appear as advertising. As Mathieson (2005) describes, the mobile phone sector is also set to undergo a transformation in terms viral and pass-along content. Alstiel and Grow (2006) describe viral as being similar to word-of-mouth advertising in that it is hoped by advertisers that users and consumers will carry advertisers' messages through their own networks of friends and colleagues online.

Rather viral seeks credibility from web users who will refer and forward amusing snippets and detritus from around the web, and viral executions. Most users will not do this with traditional advertising. As such advertisers and their agencies have had to distance themselves from their work. In addition, viral advertising is often more risqué, perhaps edgy and often contains a *visceral sales proposition* (McStay, 2007a).[26] The Encarta World English Dictionary (1999) defines visceral as

vis·cer·al adj

1. proceeding from instinct rather than from reasoned thinking;
2. characterized by, or showing, basic emotions;
3. relating to, or affecting, one or more internal organs of the body.

A visceral sales proposition thus refers to advertising that is physical by nature and does not concentrate on the cerebral as with a unique sales proposition, or the emotional as with emotional sales propositions. Furthermore, this genre of viral advertising also tends to focus on violence or sex in some fashion. Viral advertising, as an expectedly unorthodox format, accordingly reflects young advertising agency creatives' maverick self-styled sensibilities. This is in accordance with traditional notions of advertising creativity that seek to break boundaries, accepted conventions and structures of discipline (White, 2000). In many ways it can be associated with shock advertising. Despite shock advertising often being held as synonymous with Luciano Benetton and the photographer Oliviero Toscani, shock as a creative strategy has a much longer history, for example, Bovril and their 1891 campaign depicting muscular bulls strapped to an electric chair with the headline stating "Bovril by Electrocution" produced by the Victorians depicting two bulls being electrocuted to produce meat essence.

Many viral executions flirt with pornography and other highly graphical forms of representation. The website Kontraband, for example, hosts much other content including fora, spoofs, pictures and other detritus collected from around the web as well as viral. This lends a framing function to hosted viral advertising displayed in that it is an amusing and slightly edgy place to be and gives the brand a degree of invisibility. This is, in fact, the core strategy of viral, to make it indistinguishable from other web content and often to make it appear as user-generated content.

Shifman (2007) asserts that in television, humour is an optional component and that in viral commercials it is almost obligatory,[27] often dependent on adult jokes or observations. The relationship between sexuality and advertising is not a new one. As Cortese (2004) observes, much traditional advertising portrays sexuality as nonchalant, unplanned and perhaps even promoting promiscuity. Whereas shock advertising consciously offends and strategically understands the consumer buttons it aims to press, viral instead assumes a discourse of humour inappropriate for offline television but one that abounds on the web and more specifically within brand opinion-forming target networks. Diesel's recent viral offering, "Safe for Work XXX",[28] produced by Viral Factory, celebrates 30 years in business and makes clear that they still have the capacity to shock. Going straight for the viral jugular they offer a parody of a 1980s porn film through the use of cartoon characters to change adult scenes into ones more innocent, though leaving little to the imagination. A now famous case is Volkswagen's (2005) "Suicide Bomber" whose creators claim was never intended for public release (McStay, 2007a). Suicide

Bomber, an allegedly hoax advertisement,[29] opens with a depiction of a Palestinian suicide bomber dressed in a combat jacket and red and white chequered scarf leaving what appears to be his London-based flat and getting into his Volkswagen Polo car. He drives and then parks outside of a café where diners eat their meals and chat on their mobile phones. This commercial then cuts to the bomber sitting in his car as he pushes the button to detonate his bomb. The blast is contained within the car, saving the diners. The advertisement ends: 'Polo. Small but Tough.'[30] Viral advertising is thus a repository of advertising clutter made manifest through a celebration, or jouissance, of consumer society, trash media and advertising as its key method of articulation. Concurrently, viral advertising extends shock's potential for repeat viewing. Sharing characteristics with the wider viral economy in terms of dispersal, playfulness, copying and abuse of authenticity, content is inherently voyeuristic and facilitates immersion into the advertisement's creative content due to its manipulability and interactivity, and the ease and readiness with which it is passed on within a social network (ibid).

It is not only corporations and large-scale advertisers that have been using viral. The non-governmental organization (NGO), Greenpeace have also used it as way of attempting to get lads to go eco-friendly with a risqué viral advertisement featuring men and women who literally have light shining out of their rear ends. Many advertisements also have lo-fi characteristics and seek to emulate user-generated self-broadcast clips that have, in turn, been influenced by advertising and the form of commercials. Sherman (2007) observes that

> the people's video is influenced by advertising, shorter and shorter attention spans, the excessive use of digital effects, the seductiveness of slo-mo and accelerated image streams, a fascination with crude animation and crude behaviour, quick-and-dirty voice-overs and bold graphics that highlight a declining appreciation of written language.

As brands disassociate themselves from their advertising it is at times difficult to see what is advertising-generated and what is not. This has backfired on advertising at times. A relatively recent example again involves Volkswagen who filed a subpoena seeking the identity of a YouTube user who posted a Nazi-themed parody of a recent VW Golf commercial (Kravets, 2007). Although spoof (both user and agency generated) advertisements will not disappear any time soon, viral has shown signs of maturity with the UK's Home Office using it as a means to address knife crime noting that those carry knives are more likely to be stabbed themselves.[31] Unilever's Dove brand won the top prize at 2007's Cannes Lions International Advertising Festival with the "Evolution" film/advertisement[32] that addresses beauty and media distortion. Created by Ogilvy and Mather in Canada it was heralded as a milestone and an underscoring of mainstream marketers' embrace of the web, where the film was widely distributed. The year 2008 also saw London's Fallon (an advertising agency) win a Cannes Grand Prix award for its work for Cadbury entitled "Gorilla" with the advertisement proving highly successful with television audiences, web users and advertising commentators and critics alike.[33] Cadbury's "Gorilla" highlights well the nature of success in viral advertising and YouTube. As Richard (2008, p. 147) describes, there are clear markers for popularity and success, as demonstrated through prized video responses that offer an interpretation of the original. In the case of Gorilla, this involved a range of grafted-on soundtracks including the UK soap opera Eastenders, Deep Purple and Bonnie Tylor's Eclipse of the Heart that was subsequently released as an official Cadbury advert. Other testimonials include parody, remixes, re-enactment, rearrangement, fragmentation, character spoofs (the guerrilla was also exchanged for Death Vader) and "ego clips" that have to do with branding the self and the seeking of three minutes of fame. More recently Cadbury's "Eyebrows" scored four million views, more than double the number racked up at the same stage by Gorilla.

Social networks

Social networking platforms were probably the most hyped online advertising and marketing vehicle in 2007, although their existence extends back to SixDegrees.com that came into being in 1997 and closed in 2000. Like social networking services we are familiar with today, SixDegrees.com allowed users to create profiles, list their "friends" and, beginning in 1998, surf their "friends" lists. Though still extremely popular and providing characteristics and services that will ensure their survival, advertisers have found it difficult to extract profits from these networks. Some industry commentators have likened it to search engines in the mid-to-late 1990s where there was no clear revenue model until Google unleashed their search-based advertising model. boyd and Ellison (2007) offer characteristics of social networks describing that users

(1) construct a public or semi-public profile within a bounded system, (2) articulate a list of other users with whom they share a connection, and (3) view and traverse their list of connections and those
made by others within the system. The nature and nomenclature of
these connections may vary from site to site.

These forms of social media provided by platforms such as Facebook,
QQ, MySpace, Orkut, Cyworld, Hi5, Friendster, Bebo, Tagged and
variety of others are a means of building online communities. Users
share information about themselves on their profiles including photos,
images, preferences, tastes and join groups with people who have similar interests. Social networking sites facilitate informal communications
and information-sharing across the internet. comScore (2007) reports
that the European social networking community stood at 127.3 million
unique visitors in August – reaching 56 per cent of the European online
population. UK participation in social networking usage proved to be
the highest in Europe, with 24.9 million unique visitors, 78 per cent of
the total UK online population, now belonging to the country's social
networking community. Rupert Murdoch's MySpace is by far the most
successful social network in North America with around 76 per cent. As
boyd and Ellison (2007) describe, this is due in large part to MySpace
allowing a greater degree of personalization by not restricting users from
adding HTML into the forms that framed their profiles and working with
bands and promoters to contact fans. MySpace is followed in popularity
by Facebook, Bebo and BlackPlanet with 12.57 per cent, 1.24 per cent
and 0.87 per cent respectively (Moskalyuk, 2008). In Latin America, Hi5
is the largest social network in the Spanish-speaking countries (except
for Google's Orkut, which dominates Brazil). Facebook is also experiencing significant growth as is Batanga, a local social network. Asia is
the largest and fastest-growing region for social networking. Notably in
China, South Korea and Japan, Facebook has almost no presence. Instead
QQ, Cyworld and Mixi are market leaders in China, South Korea and
Japan respectively. To put this into context, QQ had $523m in revenues
in 2007 and $224m operating profit with 60 per cent of the revenue
coming from services like games, an additional 21 per cent from mobile
services like ringtones with only 13 per cent coming from advertising.
Facebook posted revenues of around $150m. This is generated through
QQ's user-base with QQ reporting more than 300 million users, roughly
the same as population of the United States (Leberecht, 2008).

Social networks are sometimes an extension of real-life networks
of friends but often are characterized by what boyd (2006) describes

as 'imagined egocentric communities'. Friends have as much to do with self-expression, digital cultural orientation and the establishing of online personas and selves. They may be siblings, lovers, school-mates and strangers, though some services such as MySpace facilitate "top friends" (ibid). They thus reflect ongoing relationships between friends and associates of varying degrees of intimacy and antagonism. They reflect a basic human need to belong and to form significant relationships and that there is a greater chance that people will join and participate in social network sites if they rate highly on the need-to-belong scale (Gangadharbatla, 2008). Gangadharbatla also suggests three basic needs that underlie people's group-seeking behaviour, these include "inclusion" that involves the need to belong to a circle of acquaintances; "affection" and the need to be loved by others; and "control" that involves exerting power over others, or giving power over the self to others (Schutz, 1966). In addition, the need for collect-ive self-esteem and the part of the self that derives a sense of identity through knowledge of group membership also plays a significant role. Online networks are interesting phenomena, particularly in light of early cybercultural exploration into discourses of online identity cre-ation, self-presentation, management, maintenance and early com-munity fora (Turkle, 1995; Stone, 1996). In these earlier accounts, the internet and web allowed for identity experimentation and to try out roles, genders and characteristics that do not apply to us in everyday life. Although we may explore identities through the use of avatars in forums and virtual spaces, more social networks sites are closely inte-grated with our offline lives. The earliest incarnation of what we today call social networks and computer mediated communication was 'The Well'. This was a forum that was launched in 1985 as a dial-up bulletin board system (BBS), a precursor to web-based systems. Interestingly, it required that users link their online personae to a real world identity whereas later services did not.[34]

Many users of social networking services spend a considerable amount of effort in presenting their ideal egos and images of them-selves. They are useful for advertisers in a number of ways both overt and covert. Virtually all of these sites sell advertising space and utilize highly targeted advertising programmes. For example, Facebook's tar-geting elements include age, gender, location and interests. They also offer content integration where advertising cannot be skipped. Hi5 also offer targeted display banners, rich media placements and custom spon-sorship services to reach their young audiences. Other services such as AOL's Bebo are less obvious in their advertising and refer to advertisers as "media partners". Their Open Media Platform allows "professional content creators" to sell and serve their own advertising and use content in a word-of-mouth fashion to reach Bebo's forty million plus audience. Similar to other networks, Bebo use behavioural and contextual targeting based on insights from users' interactions. Interestingly Google's Orkut does not offer Adwords and Adsense due to numerous complaints in 2007 from Orkut users, non-profit groups and advertisers regarding advertising appearing with questionable and pornographic content.

Although Facebook utilized display advertising prior, in late 2007 Facebook announced new advertising programmes with founder Mark Zuckerberg stating that advertisers can target advertising to the exact audiences they want. Describing a transition from macro to micro advertising, Zuckerberg told an audience of more than 250 marketing and advertising executives in New York:

> Facebook Ads represent a completely new way of advertising online... For the last hundred years media has been pushed out to people, but now marketers are going to be a part of the conversation. And they're going to do this by using the social graph in the same way our users do. (Facebook, 2007)

Businesses were encouraged to design a page to craft the exact experience they want people to see, in much the same way that users add photos, videos, music and Facebook Platform applications. In this sense both users and businesses are branding the self. This interest in self-presentation derives from a view of Western societies where traditional social structures that aid in forming and nurturing identity are downplayed if not eroded. Fowles (1996) makes a similar point observing

> The signal repercussion of this transition is that self-identity, which used to be handed to the individual through the imposition of societal schema, now must be formulated in lieu of those eroding schema..., and must be maintained without the sureties and precepts they provided, but via self-stabalization. (1996, p. 198)

Within the Facebook site the involvement of the self takes another twist as companies such as Socialmedia use pictures of users' real faces in advertising delivered to their "friends", without users knowing. This format is opt-out rather than opt-in (see more on this in Chapter 6). Both users and businesses are engaging in publicity and Facebook is thus to some extent a popularity contest. Facebook users can interact directly with the business through its Facebook Page by adding reviews, writing on that business' Wall, uploading photos and in any other ways that a business may want to enable. It allows advertisers to create branded pages, run targeted advertisements and have access to intelligence and analytics pertaining to the site's more than 50 million users. Partners can participate in all three components of Facebook Ads, or a combination of them. Although targeting by demographics, psychographics and other profiling methods is nothing new – advertisers, agencies and media planners have been doing this for years – being able to target by relationship status or as finely tuned as TV show preferences is quite unique. Anything that is contained with a user's profile is material for targeting advertising. In addition, Facebook (along with many other social network providers) also offers detailed analytics information in that they can tell advertisers who they are reaching and what kind of trends are appearing throughout the site. MySpace are also engaging in "hyper-targeting" whose programmes analyse information revealed by users on their profile that MySpace in turn utilizes to put people into different "enthusiast" groups, such as music or sports. As will be discussed further in Chapter 6, to the consternation of privacy advocates, who say internet users are unaware of such activity, the social networks regard these detail-stocked profile pages as a kind of 'digital gold', as one Fox executive put it (Stone, 2007). The bane of office managers throughout the world, social networks have become entrenched into a wide range of demographics. Although usage varies globally and from network to network, it appears users are not as young as one may imagine. For example, more than half of US MySpace visitors are 35 years or older (comScore, 2006). However, advertisers have been quick to capitalize on social networks as a means of targeting children. As will be discussed in Chapter 6, this is particularly pronounced in the United Kingdom where regulations have recently been tightened in the offline television sector.[35]

Social networks – as well as blog accounts, favourite websites, desktops and mobile phones – also facilitate the use of widgets. These are embeddable chunks of code and usually third party. Although in digital advertising circles these were very fashionable in 2008, they have been around for some time, for example in the embedding of games in personal websites. In social networking sites they are much easier to configure where widgets can be fun little applications used with a person's profile page. They can also be branded and offer a variety of mini-services and information. Nike's 3-D widget, "Nike Plus Miles",[36] (created by Tribal DDB GmbH, member of DDB Germany), for example, encourages users to run and is bundled with weather forecasts, running news and an integrated RSS Reader. As web-connected television becomes more popular, we can expect to see use of ad-supported widgets on television to deliver social network services. For example, in 2009, Yahoo and Intel introduced its TV application platform called the "Widget Channel" allowing users to interact with their profile and "friends", although not as yet upload video or photos. Key players such as MySpace have shown interest. Branded widgets include refrigerator magnets, lighters, pens, sponsored note pads and other marketing paraphernalia, albeit in digital form. In chunks of code and software they are represented by video players, countdown clocks, make-up simulators, and importantly are inexpensive to distribute, free to the user and often useful. In addition they are extremely cheap to produce and have a high pass-on value (Garfield, 2008).

Virtual environments (case example "Second Life")

The first thing to say about virtual communities is there is nothing new about them. Computer mediated communities have been around longer than the web and its associated protocols. Computer Mediated Communication (CMC) refers to human communication through two or more computers. The WELL is the most commonly cited of the first CMC driven virtual communities.[37] Like Second Life or first/ real life people had weddings, funerals, barbeques and engaged in a myriad of mundane, perverse, outlandish and all sorts of behaviour in-between.[38]

In many ways, virtual environments are the realization of a promise long made by those who see cyberspace as something "out there". The degrees to which users can manipulate environments fluctuate, but they are all simulations in that they vary in their relationship to the real world. Current incarnations bear some resemblance to the real world and this may be indicative of their early stage of development. As Kalay and Marx (2006) describe, in the same way that cars were first thought of as horseless carriages and movies as celluloid records of stage plays, many virtual spaces are modelled on the real world although members and builders are tentatively exploring virtual architectural design principles and lexicon. Kalay and Marx posit four categories of environmental 'shells' in cyberspace:

1. *Hyper-reality cyberspaces*: These attempt to mimic the physical world in every detail.

2. *Abstracted reality cyberspaces*: These obey enough laws of nature to engender believability but do not attempt to create a 'perfect' reality. For example, although one cannot walk through walls, there is more artistic freedom and the environment may take on a more cartoon-like or image processed character.

3. *Hybrid cyberspaces*: These freely mix "real" and "virtual" experiences and facilitate the breaking of laws of nature. For example, users can fly and engage in a range of artistic expression, perhaps reminiscent of Lewis Carroll's (2000) nineteenth century novel, Alice's Adventures in Wonderland. This is often aesthetically rich and disorienting, although fun!

4. *Virtual spaces*: These drop all relationship to the physical world and the Laws of Nature, generally avoiding familiar objects such as walls, doors, windows or floors. Kalay and Marx (2006) cite the space travel sequence towards the end of the movie *2001: A Space Odyssey*, or Char Davies's *Éphémère* as textual examples. Derived from the scuba diving practice of buoyancy control, these latter "experiences" involve the use of breathing as means of navigation as well as full head mounted displays.[39]

These follow a somewhat Baudrillardian (1994) tone in regards to his precession of simulacra where the conclusion of self-referential environments are no longer trying to imitate, duplicate or parody the real. Of the four examples that Kalay and Marx (2006) offer, digital environments most of us are aware of tend towards the second and the third kind. Such creativity and abstraction generate new conventions and codes that must be learned. This has had particular impart for businesses trying to invest in virtual environments. This section makes a case study of the virtual environment that seems to be making the headlines over recent years, Second Life, characterized by being a Lewis Caroll-styled hybrid space. It also refers to all virtual environments as "virtual spaces" despite potential confusion with the four kinds set out above.

As Spence (2008) points out, there are a range of other worlds and the academic community has tended to focus on Second Life. Second Life is merely a fraction of these and has certainly received more than its fair share of press and academic coverage. This book is also guilty of perpetuating this, but mitigation is hopefully granted through the offering of primary interview data from John Lester who leads Linden Lab's customer market development in Education and Healthcare. Other commonly used environments include Gaia

Online, Habbo, Eve Online, Wee World, World of Warcraft, Zwinky, There and Entropia Universe. Google also built Lively that was intended to challenge the pre-eminence of Second Life, although this closed at the end of 2008. More specific spaces are coming online, for example Muxlim Pal, aimed at Muslims yet whose creators hope will also foster understanding among non-Muslims. In the same way that social network sites cater for a range of audiences and others attract people based on common language or shared racial, sexual, religious or nationality-based identities, virtual environments offer similar places and the possibility of user-generated spaces to congregate and communicate in.

From an advertiser's point of view, these can be split into two forms: those that utilize existing environments and those built bespoke for advertisers and marketers. Much of the discussion below is transferable to other environments and given that for many marketers and advertisers Second Life has past its zenith, it is perhaps best to see Second Life as emblematic of emergent metaverses and truly social media rather an end in itself. Although the speed of digital transformation quickly dates case studies, the underlying principles, mistakes and successes in Second Life make the case study worth recounting.

What is Second Life?

A common misconception of Second Life is that it is a game. It is not; it is a 3-D virtual environment or metaverse (derived from Neal Stephenson's 1992 cyberpunk novel titled Snow Crash). Spence offers the following definition of a virtual world:

> Virtual worlds are persistent, synthetic, three dimensional, non-game centric space. Virtual worlds are primarily social spaces that allow for other uses depending on the theme of the particular virtual world. Virtual worlds are either commercial or open source in design and implementation. (2008, p. 5)

As described on Second Life's website,[40] it is entirely created by its residents and came online in 2003. Inhabitants have traditionally communicated via type and text and as with traditional chat rooms, the better the typing skills the more socially successful an inhabitant is likely to be. Voice-based chat was launched in 2007 although with much in-world acrimony. In contrast to gaming it supports its own currency, the Linden Dollar, which can be translated to and from native currency. As such, much business is conducted there, both internally and that which translates to offline life. Examples not only include early adopter mainstream media companies such as Reuters and marketing firms who want to show clients 3-D copies of their work but also include less obvious examples such as underground gas tank firms who want to show pipelines under fuel station asphalt (BusinessWeek, 2006). Inhabitants engage in a range of social, leisure, academic and business activities as with offline life, but importantly this is generated from the ground up from residents. Linden Lab provides the C/Java-style scripting code to allow this to happen, but after this, virtually anything goes. They state in their terms of service that they

> do not generally regulate the content of communications between users or users' interactions with the Service. As a result, Linden Lab has very limited control, if any, over the quality, safety, morality, legality, truthfulness or accuracy of various aspects of the Service. (Second Life, 2008)

The key stipulation is that events or acts do not contravene Community Standards and local law, although this is unclear given the global access of Second Life. It has come to the attention of regulators, however, concerned with sexual "age play" where consenting adults adopt child-like personas. Lynn (2007) comments that proponents are quick to distinguish from paedophilia by saying everyone involved in is a consenting adult and no children are present or harmed. Opponents believe that depicting children in sexual situations with adults is never, ever acceptable – whether in public or private – and that age play should not be tolerated as 'just another sexual fantasy'. Lynn argues the fear is that by stepping in to ban age play specifically and "broadly offensive" sex and violence in general, Linden Lab is starting down a slippery slope of censorship and censure, destroying everything the virtual universe stands for. Many of those worried about protecting freedom of expression are not supporters of age play, yet they aren't willing to ban it outright. In many ways it is reminiscent of the early days of the internet and how to regulate it. Should it be regulated by public sector control of the new environment; can it be left to private entities to self-regulation via the existence of a social contract between stakeholders; should regulation can be hard-wired into the system; or does the new technology warrants a "hands-off" approach from regulators (Guadamuz, 2007)?

What do advertisers think of Second Life?

Advertising Age dubbed Second Life as the most over-hyped media of 2007 (McIlroy, 2008). This is according to 57 per cent of the audience members polled at the Advertising Age Digital Conference session, "What's Worth Your Attention in 2008?" The Advertising Age article notes that 'Second Life has become a quagmire for marketers', according to Steve Rubel, senior VP-director of Insights, Edelman Digital. Neil Hughston, from Saatchi and Saatchi Interactive, similarly comments 'Second Life is kinda interesting and obviously it is established and depends on whether you believe the hype or not, err, and I have an ambivalent view about it right now' (Interview, 12/11/07). Joshua Stylman, managing partner of Reprise Media, advises that marketers should ask themselves three questions before jumping into an emerging media trend: Does it seem compelling? Does it have an audience? Can you engage with that audience? (McIlroy, 2008).

Treatment of Second Life as a pre-existing medium

In addressing these concerns there are a number of issues that need to be considered, most notably that Second Life shares characteristics with the birth of the wider web. When online advertising was launched in 1994 through AT&T and their banner on HotWired's pages, the web was a novelty. The web was too slow, dial-up access was problematic, there were few connected users, content was poor and importantly there was little industry behind it and few clear revenue streams (Jackson, 2006). This perhaps equally applies to Second Life. Although this book does not argue that Second Life will have a similar contribution to media it does argue that many of the same criticisms are being levelled by businesses that have not got to grips with the potential of Second Life. In regards to whether it is compelling, possibly one of the problems in addressing this question is trying to ascertain what Second Life is for. Unlike online gaming platforms it possesses little in the way of narrative or direction, and it is not an information retrieval system. Amongst other things it is instead a set of communities and fora where identities are explored and "lifers" can meet online. It is thus an extension of the virtual communities that characterized the early web and internet. The educational element that in part augmented the development of the web is also highly prominent in Second Life with many universities and colleges getting involved. Its audience and user-base is small and at the time of writing Second Life have 16,785,531 residents. However, numbers of those who regularly access are much fewer with around 522,526 having accessed in the past seven days, 673,827 in the past fourteen, 940,855 in the past month and 1,444,530 in the past sixty days since 27 January 2009. This makes Second Life a very niche medium but one that is well placed for gaining column inches and PR for brands, if not mass direct brand or advertisement engagement.

Advertising in Second Life: Pontiac

As the Second Life (2008a) wiki on advertising describes, Linden Lab views Second Life as a platform and focuses its efforts on development and improvement of the platform. They do not create content or services within Second Life, other than search advertising and paid-for classifieds, although they do offer suggestions to advertisers. These include using Second Life to drive coverage to blogs. As many residents are active bloggers, web users companies have found that by getting involved in Second Life they have generated mentions in web and blog postings through a two-step flow type effect (Katz and Lazarsfeld, 1955). Other companies have an ongoing presence in Second Life and gain attention and visitors by providing technical talks (for example, Intel) or concerts. This is a form of pull advertising in that it gives audiences and users a reason to visit and interact with an advertiser/marketer. It also blurs the distinction between PR, marketing, advertising, retailing and customer services. Second Life also recommends active advertising and direct engagement with users and visitors. Although perhaps the most difficult, they comment it may be the most rewarding, advertisers can create a presence that drives the message or experience advertisers want users to have with their brand or product. For example, if the product was a soft drink, advertisers could provide a script (a small programme) that had people laugh and dance whenever they took a virtual drink. Objects could be given away and distributed virally. These could include a notecard with more information, a coupon or a direct link to a website. As with offline environments, there are many social and popular places that display posters or kiosks that can distribute information, links, objects, or provide teleports to sponsored locations. Virtual world environments present new opportunities and approaches to building and maintaining brand equity through engagement in the flow experience (Park et al., 2008). There are also advertising networks in Second Life where advertisers can pay to have their advertising displayed. Some are limited to images whilst others host some degree of interaction with the content. Person-to-person advertising is also an option. Imax has had success, for example promoting

Harry Potter: *Order of the Pheonix* giving away free in-world tickets. Also, as with TV and radio in real life, Second Life can carry streaming advertising through in-world channels. Audio and video can also be streamed from parcels (small pieces of land) although land parcels are used as method of spoiling others' land through deliberately ugly advertising. Park et al. (see Figure 3.1) offer a useful conceptual model of advertising and marketing opportunities in virtual worlds:

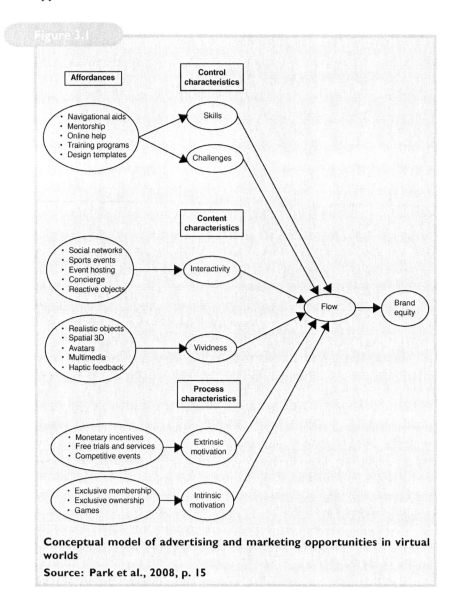

Figure 3.1

Conceptual model of advertising and marketing opportunities in virtual worlds

Source: Park et al., 2008, p. 15

Here affordances, or factors made available through a medium, represent opportunities for advertisers and their agencies. Control characteristics involve skills necessary, or capacity for action, in nego-tiating such high-involvement media; challenges refer to difficulties experienced in navigating spaces, building or interacting with objects (see Novak et al., 2000). Process characteristics involve motivations for people to begin navigating spaces. These may be extrinsic (goal oriented) or intrinsic (involving personal motivations). These elem-ents help engender a sense of flow that Park et al. (2008) consider as absorption through activity. They define this as intrinsically enjoy-able. They also state that through flow, there are a number of benefits for advertisers and marketers:

> In the context of virtual worlds and marketing, relevant outcomes from these categories that are of particular interest include persua-sion, attitude belief, product belief, product awareness, attitude towards brand, attitude change, purchase consideration, customer confidence, purchase intention, user satisfaction, and behavior change. (ibid, 2008, p. 13)

Although there is much advertising agency interest in web 2.0, par-ticularly advertising through social networks, in-game advertising and locative media, interest in Second Life has lately been much more circumspect. As Sudhaman (2006) notes, this is a positive develop-ment as agencies will not simply aim to 'be there' as with some of their clients in web 1.0, but rather their entrance into Second Life has been, or will be, much more strategically focused. Bartle Bogle Hegarty (BBH) soon followed by Leo Burnett was the first agency to enter Second Life whilst digital players have emerged on the scene to help brands and larger agencies navigate the Second Life. The Electric Sheep Company offers creative, technical and strategic services that originated in Second Life itself. It includes Reuters, AOL, CBS, Yahoo, Sony BMG and NBC amongst its roster of clients. Others include the branding and PR agency Rivers Red Run that is working with BBH and Millions of Us that is handling assignments from Toyota and Leo Burnett.

In an interview I conducted in 2007 in Vancouver with John Lester of Second Life, in relation to advertising and strategy he repeatedly noted the carmaker Pontiac and the manner in which they entered Second Life and engaged with the community itself, although Pontiac subsequently left Second Life. As Morissey (2006) from Adweek described, Pontiac aimed to generate a car culture that was hitherto not to be seen in Second Life. Tor Myhren, executive creative director at Leo Burnett in Detroit, Pontiac's advertising agency (along with Millions of Us and Campfire for the Second Life project) notes 'Right now there isn't a car culture in Second Life, but we know there's a huge car culture with human beings...Certainly there's going to be one there and we want to be part of it' (Morissey, 2006). Pontiac bought a 96-acre section of Second Life and created an island titled Motorati Island.[41] In attempting to foster a culture of cars they solicited the Second Life population to submit proposals for how they would create a car culture on the island. In engendering this they held events whereby inhabitants and visitors could talk to the Pontiac engineers. Describing this as a combination of advertising and marketing, John Lester enthusiastically comments

> Well I think things like what Pontiac did is brilliant; where they created this community; they wanted to raise awareness of their brand, they wanted to advertise essentially. They actually did it in a way that was just so respectful of the community and engaged the community. And it's also above and beyond just letting people know about Pontiac like showing a picture or something right. They have the whole professional amateur concept. They have residents in Second Life who are professional amateurs in terms of car design and engineering actually talking with Pontiac engineers giving them feedback about new designs and so it's a combination of advertising and learning more about customers, getting insights from them, you know. I think the most innovative advertising in Second Life is things that are much more multi-faceted than purely just sticking up a poster somewhere. (Interview, 18/10/07)

In wider discussion of successful advertising in Second Life, I asked him about brandscaping[42] and techniques developers are using to transmit their brands' values. Although he pointed to this as a growth area, he focused his comments on the more traditional practice of forms of sponsorship:

> I think that seems to be the trend from my perspective of companies that are...that are really thinking this through a lot. Again the other thing that I think is really innovative but at the same time pretty prosaic is the sponsorship thing. Right now there is an organisation called the Second Life Ballet that started up about almost a

year ago. A number of them were .... dancers in real life; they had a musician and a choreographer and they actually designed these ballets that were performed live in Second Life. Really beautiful, live music, dancers, set design everything and people loved it. And they didn't have enough space to hold all the people who wanted to come watch it. And so they were looking around for something, what to do? They were trying to figure out should we charge money, we're not really business people; we need to get a business manager. And they got in touch with IBM and IBM said we'll give you space on our island because we think this is really great and actually IBM as a company is a very, very strong supporter of the arts, right. So I thought that was just brilliant because it was like, here's a company that is supporting in Second Life things that are ... you know core values of a company. In the physical world it's the same; IBM sponsors all kinds of arts things, art shows and arts festivals, they sponsored the Boston cyber arts festival, last fall. And...I think they're doing the same thing in Second Life. (ibid)

As Burns (2008a) highlights, users of Second Life (and similar environments) tend to market their events predominately within Second Life itself, using billboards and other resources the realm provides to its users. Corporate residents tend to use "out-of-world" marketing channels such as blogs, corporate websites, social networking groups and advertisements. Greg Verdino, chief strategy officer at social media consulting agency Crayon, argues that rather than simply creating branded spaces corporate brands should integrate social media and community capabilities. Community, as with all aspects of social media, is the important element as social support or friendships are popular reasons (in addition to search for information and aid in goal achievement) for joining a virtual community (Riding and Gefen, 2004). More recent environments have placed a greater emphasis on realism and emulating real world places as opposed to the Alice in Wonderland potential of Second Life. These falls under Kalay and Marx's (2006) descriptor of hyper-reality cyberspaces that attempt to mimic the physical world in every detail. Metaversum's Twinity, describing itself as powered by "real life", have scanned 50,000 buildings in Berlin, the German capital, using 3-D mapping data currently used for things like satellite navigation and Google Earth. There are significant advertising opportunities here as tourists orient themselves before arriving, for example. Other companies are planning similar recreations of other cities, including London and Moscow (Simmons, 2008).

Beyond Second Life

As York (2007) notes, although Second Life has undergone a dip in popularity with advertisers, other more youth-oriented environments are attracting significant interest from marketers and advertisers. Through Webkinz and a myriad of other commercial and proprietary online virtual communities, children (particularly girls) are feeding pets, buying shoes and making salon appointments. To enter Webkinz a toy pet must be bought and with it comes the secret code that lets you access the virtual world where children can care for their virtual pet, answer trivia, earn "KinzCash" and play games online. Be-Bratz is another virtual world where children create their own characters, play with pets and make new friends. Similar to Webkinz children must purchase the offline tool to access the community (in this case a USB key that comes with the doll). Steiger (2008), a writer for Advertising Age, also an ex-employee of Linden Lab, comments that Second Life and similar environments are merely the beginning of a category. He observes that for brands, the key factors to recognize are as follows:

▸ Virtual worlds are a significant and fast-growing market.
▸ Virtual worlds are a subset of social media, which accounts for 30 per cent of consumer internet activity in the United States according to comScore.
▸ Virtual worlds turn the web into a "place", allowing users to connect face-to-face in real time.
▸ Early data suggest that levels of brand engagement in virtual worlds are extremely high. Millions of Us, an agency specializing in virtual worlds, has conducted some 60 engagements in virtual worlds for clients with engagement per user ranging from 2 to 24 hours.

Key changes to take place are for clients to recognize that virtual environments have a very large and active user-base. Media and technology heavyweights including MTV and Sony will be scaling up their offerings in the area. Another development to take place is for virtual worlds to plug into existing social networks with add-on features such as rooms and places where people and their avatars can meet. Whilst we adults write academic papers, hold conferences and lengthy debates on topics such as web 2.0 and implications of virtual realities, kids (and folk marketing to them) are quietly pushing the boundaries. Rather than hanging out in shopping centres or malls, many kids are congregating online buying virtual goods for their avatars and online pets.

As Wu (2007) observes, people (adults too) spend over $1.5b on virtual items every year. Pets, coins, avatars and bling: these virtual objects are nothing more than a series of digital 1s and 0s stored on a remote database somewhere in the ether. This is not strange at all. Humans living in wealthy economies spend an inordinate amount of time grooming, purchasing clothing, applying make-up, buying status and positioning goods and spend most of their social lives posturing and articulating desirable identities depending on social setting. Goods that facilitate this are then services. Digital goods are no different. They are services and objects that create real value for people. This is perhaps the proposition or mantra to be adopted for advertising and marketing in virtual environments and perhaps the wider web: rather than pushing advertising at people, it makes much more sense to create items and services of value and let people do with them what they will. This is especially the case with non-branded environments (as opposed to those similar to the aforementioned Webkinz) where anti-establishment discourses abound.

In-game advertising

Agencies and networks involved with in-game advertising include Neue Digitale, JOGO Media, Double Fusion, IGA Worldwide, Engage, NeoEdge Networks, EnterMedia, MetaAdverse, Game Creative and Microsoft's Massive Incorporated, as used in Barack Obama's presidential campaign. Although there exists non-paid-for advertising that is incidental and there to heighten gaming realism, this section deals with paid-for advertising and placement. For example, sports games set in stadiums and race circuits will normally carry billboards and advertising. Other examples of incidental advertising stem from the mentioning of brands or their use within games as way of forwarding the narrative, for example the use of branded cars such as Lamborghinis. These situations normally require permission from the owner of the brand involved.

As with other media, the games industry is broadly keen to involve advertisers to offset development costs. As the Economist (2007) describes, today's games can cost as much as $20m to develop whilst selling prices appear to have reached a ceiling at $60 in America and £45 ($90) in Britain. Extra revenue from advertising could help to pay for development as games become more elaborate and expensive. Although games developers' focus is on the game and the storyline, they are now thinking, in addition, about ways that advertising may fit into the narrative. The Economist further observes that as a rule of thumb, game publishers earn about $5 profit per copy sold. Static advertising typically provides $1 of profit, but by the end of this year dynamic advertising could double that figure. According to a report carried out by Double Vision and Interpret, across a variety of game types, 81 per cent of gamers are exposed to at least one advertisement every other minute, and 75 per cent see advertisements at an even greater frequency – at least one a minute. While the industry standard counts a cumulative 10-second exposure as an impression, the study finds exposure of half-a-second is enough for a gamer to notice an in-game advertisement (Burns, 2008a).

Advertisers see games as a useful route to target the "Lost Boys" or the male 18–34 demographic, who are increasingly neglecting television in favour of computer and video games. The make-up of the gaming audience is not as uniform as it was once considered; instead, it is fragmented along many demographics. Games are not a realm of teenage boys any longer; in fact, the under-18s (boys *and* girls) account for only a third of the audience (Vedrashko, 2006). Citing a report from eMarketer, IGA Worldwide suggests that video-game advertising is destined to grow to a $2b global industry by 2012 making games the fastest-growing major advertising medium. Most games now carry advertising either in-game or around the game although there are exceptions. For example, The Sims does not carry advertising as, according to Julie Shumaker, EA's director of video-game ad sales, they 'realized breaking the Sims fantasy in this case would detract from the player's experience, so we declined' (Jena, 2006). As a result, advertisers are making significant investments in the in-game environment as an effective strategy to reach target audiences. In 2006, Nielsen Media Research launched GamePlay Metrics, a rating service for video games. The ratings service pertained to establish new metrics for the buying and selling of advertising in video games, while also tracking the activities of gamers across other media platforms, such as TV and the internet (Nielsen, 2006). Nielsen also claim they can offer data on how video game play affects or complements the use of other electronic media, showing, for example, what television programmes gamers watch when they're not playing games.

Despite perceptions that users of electronic media are anti-advertising, a recent survey carried out by Neilson BASES and Nielson Games on behalf of IGA Worldwide finds that 82 per cent of consumers either had no problem with advertisements placed in games, or 'were not particularly fussed if ads were included or not'. Sixty-two per cent found games more pleasurable if they contained advertising, as it heightens the gaming experience, on the proviso that it is not interruptive to game play and promotes relevant products to them at the same time (IGA Worldwide, 2008). Given that the gaming demographic is notoriously difficult for advertisers to target, this study has some importance. Over 70 per cent of consumers who were most opinionated about in-game advertisements, felt the advertisements make them feel better about the brand, feel more favourable towards the brand, make them more interested in the brand and believe the ads are for innovative/cutting-edge brands. The participating brand advertisers included Taco Bell, Jeep and Wrigley and Electronic Arts and Activision provided game titles. However, anecdotal evidence from gaming fora suggest gamers find both advertising content and the manner in which it is delivered invasive. Edge, a multi-format computer and video-game magazine, has a number of threads on their forum dedicated to the encroachment of advertising. Many users are anti-advertising, particularly regarding television advertising that is considered banal. They are also suspicious of what they perceive as the onslaught of marketing and advertising content. One poster sums up the majority view posting that 'Do I like advertising? No. And do I want it in games? By and large no, but if it's used to add to the illusion and not distract from it, then I can let it slide.' Another comments that 'If games get to the same level as the gratuitous advertising in iRobot, then I would really have a problem with it. Having someone drink a bottle of Coca Cola in clear view is fine, but having Will Smith say "WOW I LOVE MY CONVERSE SHOES CONVERSE IS AMAZING" actually in the movie, then it becomes a problem' (Edge, 2008). The task for advertisers is thus to embed advertising without it interrupting gameplay. Again, as with virtual environments, it is a question of ensuring flow. Both gaming companies and brand managers have to recognize to what extent users are willing to engage with branded content, for example additional levels or characters. Gamers demand realism: if advertisers offer this without affecting gameplay or attempting to highlight brands and logos too significantly, users appear not to mind.

Static and dynamic in-game advertising

In-game advertising has of course been around for years. The first in-game advertising arrived in 1978 in the guise of Adventureland by

Scott Adams, who inserted an advertisement for his then forthcoming game, Pirate Adventure (Edge, 2006). As a report for eMarketer (2007) describes, early Sega racing games for the Atari 2600 console featured Marlboro display advertisements on the raceway, and high-profile early 1990s' titles such as Zool (a rival to Sonic the Hedgehog) and the FIFA International series contained advertisements for Chupa Chups (a lollipop manufacturer) and Adidas, respectively. More recent developments in the in-game advertising sector involve the business of pushing out dynamic in-game advertising. The value of this sector is expected to leap from $56m (£30m) in 2005 to $732m (£398m) by 2010 (Hardy, 2006). Forecasts vary: Verna (2007) estimates that by 2011 video-game advertising will grow at a compound annual growth rate of nearly 23 per cent, reaching nearly $2 billion.

As the IAB (2008b) describes, historically advertising within games presented advertisers and marketers with several hindrances. For brands wanting to obtain a placement within a game they had to do so during the production process of the title, which meant the negotiation of lengthy lead times. Once the advertisement was in the game it could not be changed, updated or easily measured. However, the introduction of dynamic in-game advertising has resulted in a flexible, updateable and creative alternative for advertisers looking to access multiple niche audiences. Similar to how a website rotates different display advertisements through the same fixed space dynamic in-game advertising can change the messaging on the same billboard in a game. This requires billboard space insertion into the game, as well as a broadband-connected gaming system to work. Marketers can now serve their advertisements into a game in real time and select the type of game and placement they require, for example President Obama's campaign used in-game advertising, including online modifiable games such as Guitar Hero, Burnout Paradise and Madden 09. These were employed in "swing states" such as Ohio and Florida. Advertisers can specify the number of impressions that should be served. Units of advertising can be tracked close to real time so advertising placement companies can determine how many times a character walks past or interacts with an advertisement. They can also ascertain the quality of viewing and whether users position themselves so they can see the advertisement more clearly, the distance at which it is viewed and whether a viewer pauses to look at it. However, dynamic in-game advertising requires an internet connection so advertising units can be simply turned off if a connection is not vital to the gameplay.

Gaming in virtual environments and massively multiplayer online role-playing games (MMORPGs) are another key aspect of in-game advertising.[43] The worlds themselves are held on servers owned by games manufacturers and accessed via software paid for by the client/game player. By definition they are always online. Perhaps the most famous of these is World of Warcraft, as immortalized in the South Park episode 'Make Love, Not Warcraft'. World of Warcraft records eleven million people worldwide registered as players, paying around $15 a month to explore the fantasy role-playing universe of Azeroth. They are broadly based on traditional fantasy game universes such as Dungeons and Dragons and involve the character or protagonists improving themselves, gaining extra powers, experience points, weapons and wealth as they make their way through various levels and environments. Although there are forays into genres such as Science Fiction, by far the most popular is Fantasy. As Chen et al. (2005) notes, of all the genres of online games, MMORPGs (Massive Multiplayer Online Role Playing Games) have become the most popular among network gamers, now attracting millions of users who play in evolving virtual worlds simultaneously over the internet. Although stereotypically players are isolated individuals, MMORPGs engender a great deal of social interaction albeit mostly computer mediated. There have also been significant concerns about addiction given their absorbing nature and the amount of time often dedicated to them. This was highlighted in 2007 when a Chinese man dropped dead after a three-day internet gaming session. User perspectives about advertising in MMORPGs are again mixed. If a game is free to play then many are acquiescent. If a game is subscription based then many are not. Whilst some accept advertising that fits with the context, environment and genre, many wonder how this plays out in a fantasy setting. To some extent users feel this depends on how clever and relevant to game play the advertising is, although also there seems to be a degree of suspicion about whose interests are being served when advertisers become involved in MMORPGs. In-game advertising has no clear established formats so success is difficult to gauge. As Samuels (2008) notes, even sellers of in-game space do not have the same impression of what constitutes an impression. This is due in part to the rapid change occurring within the games industry itself and the lack of dependable research conducted.

Advergames form the last advertising opportunity discussed here within games. Mäyrä (2008) defines advergames as games that operate at some level as an advertisement for a company, product or political view. Advertising agencies and marketers tend to view advergames as complete games dedicated to a brand. They are different from in-game advertising in that they require a whole game surrounding a specific product or brand. Advergames tend to be played online or downloaded to a PC. Hernandez et al. (2005) describe advergaming as allowing brands to build awareness by prolonging exposure of a brand to a target audience. Whereas traditional advertising offers at best two or three minutes of brand engagement, games may deliver significantly more depending how sticky the game is. Although many advergames use formats derived from classic games of the 1970s and 1980s, established companies have created or augmented their own so to reflect their brand values. The vacuum cleaner company Dyson, for example, a company that markets itself on principles of innovation and quality, uses mentally challenging games involving telescopes and potting balls.[44] Similar to reasons for playing regular video games, reasons cited for playing advergames include fun, entertainment, enjoyment of playing games, "to relieve boredom" and "to waste time". That they are free was also cited as a reason in addition to the chance to win prizes, catchy graphics, browsing the internet (presumably games were found in passing) and curiosity (Youn and Lee, 2005, p. 325). The main reason cited for not playing games is a general lack of interest in games overall, little use of the internet and that when online, users are focused on the search task they are engaged in. Due to the blurring of entertainment and advertising they stand in an ethical crossfire given their obvious appeal to children (see Chapter 6 for more on children and ethics).

Mobile telephony, locative and outdoor

The first mobile call was made in 1973 with commercial mobile telephony launching in 1983. Today in the United Kingdom there are more mobile phones than people. Globally more people have mobiles than landlines with some countries leapfrogging ailing landline infrastructures to get to wireless. Japan in many ways represents the future for mobile telephony and people's relations with their phones or *keitai*. As Ito (2005) comments, whereas the internet can be thought of as a colonizing of the virtual, mobile is about the colonizing of the settings of everyday life. In discussion of Fujimoto (2005), Ito (2005) observes that whereas the PC internet is something that demands our attention, the mobile represents a refreshment 'analogous to sipping a cup of coffee or taking a cigarette break. It is a street-level device packaged and mobilized in the ongoing status displays of everyday life' (p. 9).

Mobile represents a range of opportunities for advertisers, sponsors and marketers. Current estimates for mobile advertising are cautious, with consultancy Forrester predicting revenues of under $1b by 2012, although Google's Eric Schmidt claims this figure is too low and fails to take into account that the mobile web is reaching a 'tipping point' (Reuters, 2008). In the United Kingdom the internet advertising trade association, the IAB, is now representing the big five UK mobile companies – 3, O2, Orange, Vodafone and T-Mobile – to help drive the growth of mobile advertising. These five companies are also working with other bodies including the UK's Institute of Practitioners in Advertising (IPA) to establish common formats for advertising. This is in part to ready them for Google's entry into the marketplace that is yet to be felt fully. Stafford (2005) describes that mobile commerce will be used to facilitate, deliver, support and sell goods and services. However, more centrally, it is expected to facilitate business events and act as a promotional medium. This requires significant trust on behalf of the user and evidenced credibility on behalf of the business. Its usefulness to businesses lies in the ability to target of-the-moment, or close to real-time, sales messages. The IAB (2008c) divide mobile phone advertising into categories of mobile internet advertising and mobile marketing. Forms of mobile internet promotions include websites designed for mobile phones, search engine marketing, traditional banner advertisements, video advertising and ringtone downloads. Mobile marketing and promotional strategies that do not use the internet may include text-message campaigns, mobile commerce and Bluetooth marketing. Increasingly phones are becoming 3G (and higher) enabled that allows much higher data access and transfer speeds.[45] As with PCs, applications are proving popular with users and marketers alike. Kraft, for example, had success with branded mobile applications in early 2009 with a recipe and shopping list application for iPhones. Designed as a food-planning and time saving tool, it not only charted high on the most popular 100 paid-for download lists, but consumers also paid 99 US cents for it. Other companies to have early success include Uniqlo, Adidas, Chanel, Audi A4, Levis and Burger King. iPhones and Apple's App Store have driven the expansion of this market with 1 billion applications served, 35,000 applications available and more than 30 million devices in the market (Schmitt, 2009). As with many other technology sectors, it is the male 16-34-year-old market that have taken the lead in adoption of "smartphones". Concern in Europe has been expressed however in relation to the targeting of children, particularly in regards to health risks and over-usage.

Mobile internet

Mobile internet usage in the United Kingdom is rising steadily with 7.3m people accessing the internet via their mobile phones, during the second and third quarters of 2008 (BBC, 2008b). BBC news, Sky sports and the BBC weather are the most commonly visited sites. The mobile market has seen an increase of 25 per cent more people getting online via mobile, compared to PC access of 3 per cent. Although the PC market may be reaching a saturation point, it also reflects a changing relationship to the internet. As seen in Japan, growth in access to the internet via mobile devices far outstrips stationary PC access. In the West, Wireless Application Protocol (WAP) is a type of browser used by small devices to render pages. Despite being pronounced dead by the technology press on a number of occasions it has instead developed into the mobile web or WAP 2.0. It is written in a mark-up language called Wireless Markup Language (WML) although the more recent version WAP 2.0 is written in Extensible Hypertext Markup Language (XHTML). Essentially the mobile web offers a version of webpages that carry limited features compared to PC-accessed websites. They take into account that there will be an incomplete keyboard, a small screen, limited connectivity (less upload/download capability) and less processing power in the handset itself or that too much battery power is used up. In Japan – also generally considered ahead in mobile network infrastructure – the company most commonly associated with mobiles (or cell phones) is DoCoMo. In 1996, they launched "i-mode" that offered wireless internet, web and email access. By 2001, third-generation phones were introduced (McVeigh, 2003).

Unsurprisingly social networks are some of the most used services. In the US market researchers found that 46 per cent of those who use social networks have visited their favourite services on a mobile phone. From that group, nearly 70 per cent visited MySpace on their mobile phone and 67 per cent visited Facebook (Reisinger, 2008). Free to users, MySpace are looking to a mobile offering that provides advertisers with sponsorship opportunities and the promise of targeted ads based on profile information.

Mobile advertising still some years away

Until recently network speeds have placed physical restrictions as to content that can be carried over networks. Mobile has been slower to catch on due to wariness over alienating users through invasive strategies. To highlight how prized phones are, a study called Mobile Life carried out across the United Kingdom by Carphone Warehouse (2008) and the London School of Economics questioned 1256 people aged 16 to 64 on a variety of topics, including whether they would sacrifice being able to own or use a mobile phone ever again for £1m (one in three people claimed they would not). In addition, the study claims that mobile replaces the television as the most essential technology.

Maurice Levy, chairman and chief executive of advertising group Publicis, told a summit in Paris: 'It will be slow, it will take time but it will be there' and that in the long run it is in the interest of consumers, advertisers and phone companies (Reuters, 2008a). Many believe this is the most lucrative of markets due to the ubiquity of mobile phones and that users mostly have them with them at all times. Hamid Akhavan, head of Germany's T-Mobile observes 'There are people on this earth who in their life will never have a TV or a laptop but they will have a mobile phone. [So] thinking logically, there is no reason why mobile phones should not be the most powerful tool for advertisers' (ibid). As with traditional media, advertisers find access to markets through lowering tariffs for consumers. As carriers launch data plans that allow users to do more on their phones with fewer fees, there are huge opportunities for companies to add content and advertise to those devices. Blyk, a carrier start-up run by the former president of the Finnish mobile firm, Nokia, is targeting UK's 16–24 year olds and is one of the first to capitalize on this. They have signed deals with advertisers including Coca-Cola, L'Oréal and Buena Vista (part of the Disney media empire), recruitment company Stepstone, Yell.com and the mobile gaming group I-play (Wray, 2007). Many involved in digital advertising are seeing it as a potential to get further involved with cross-media promotions. Norris (2008) reports that there are two main foreseeable advertising opportunities: search advertising and all that it entails, and display advertising both indiscriminate and behavioural. Microsoft is to run display advertising across its MSN UK portal with clients including Yell.com, SanDisk and Nivea Visage. A survey commissioned by Ingenio also finds that sponsored text links that appear as a result of web searches would be users' preferred form of mobile phone advertising. Text messages from an advertiser were the least-supported form, presumably due to feelings of intrusion (Aun, 2008). Studies of text messaging and advertising tend to support the view that perceived utility and the utilization of contextual information are the strongest positive drivers of consumer acceptance of mobile advertising (Merisavo et al., 2007). Nasco and Bruner II

(2007) present similar findings describing that 'it would be a mistake to merely replicate the form of advertisements presented on TV and the computer monitor' (see Chapter 7 for more creative examples). User awareness also presents problems for those who would like to see increased take-up of advertising and marketing. Norris (2008) notes that a recent survey by Ofcom stated that only 44 per cent of mobile users were actually aware that they could access the internet on their mobile phone. Vodafone also recently estimated that 27 per cent of its customer base regularly used their mobile for browsing, collecting emails or instant messaging, predicting this figure to reach at least 50 per cent by 2010. Improvements in the interface, as with seen haptic developments such as Apple's iPhone, have seen web searches via mobiles and smartphones rise dramatically.

Looking forward: Locative media

Some of the most exciting developments occurring in new media revolve around locative media and the grafting of electronic information onto the real world that can be navigated by wireless enabled laptops, smart phones, GPS-enabled devices and a range of other hand-held devices. Whereas many accounts of cyberspace render geography obsolete, navigating the real through the virtual has gained importance in recent years. This invokes a geospatial web that involves 'integrating cartographic data with geotagged knowledge repositories and environmental indicators' (Schari, 2008). Locative media is thus about layers of digital information shaping our experiences of the urban environment. Mobile media until very recently has been one of the least discussed forms although most of us do not leave home without a phone, digital music/video player, laptop or some such form of wireless media. As Huhtamo[46] (2004) points out, even McLuhan had little to say about the potential for mobile media. McCullough (2006) describes how inscriptions and sign making have characterized almost all cities throughout history. What we are seeing through the advent of locative media, and the data cloud through which it navigates, is an extension of that. Much as electrification did for power infrastructure a century before it, pervasive or ubiquitous computing brings mobility, precision, personalization and embedding to urban annotation or what Murthy (2006) more accurately describes as spatial annotation. Rather than thinking about computers as something desktop-bound, computers are increasingly everywhere, or pervasive and ubiquitous. Locative media allow us to access information about those places whilst we are actually there. However, the trick for advertisers, as with other forms of digital advertising, is to engage users and consumers into generating this content themselves. McCullogh (2006) further comments

> The goal of 'urban markup' is a way to characterize this complex problem as a bottom-up rather than top-down process – that is, like the World Wide Web, to invite many more people to become authors and producers, and offers many more filters for those who remain consumers. A bottom-up approach addresses how people play, appropriate, and occasionally resist the situations they encounter.

Rather than merely assuming people are tourists or lost, there is the potential for interesting ways of engaging with the environment through electronic means. This means that advertisers do not simply bombard phones in range with coupons, publicity, push advertising, tokens and similar.

Personalization is a significant opportunity for businesses engaging in m-commerce. As Rashid et al. (2006, p. 3) describe, m-commerce can be defined as a set of business activities conducted over wireless and mobile networks through applications on hand-held devices. Given the intimate relationship many users already maintain with their phones, personalized advertising is a logical extension of an existing relationship. Advertisers need to tread carefully as although mobile shares many characteristics with online advertising, a phone is part of an individual's personal identity, more like a favourite item of clothing or accessory than a piece of technology (Perlando and Barwise, 2005). Although advertisers and their agencies have access to high quality data upon which to create consumer segments for pre-cision targeting on socio-demographic characteristics, spend, usage and other behavioural information (IAB, 2008e), the depth of feeling that phones engender requires that advertising should be opt-in as opposed to opt-out. It is instructive to again look to Japan where PC access to the internet is less common and the relationship to phone is perhaps more intense. As McVeigh (2003) posits, mobile usage fosters a deeper sense of individualism that has to do with an understanding of the self, characterized by individualized interiority that is created through consumerism. This 'personal interior space not only requires expression and exploration but is also filled with demands, desires, and cravings that need satisfaction' (ibid, p. 25). As such phones are not merely a communication tool but also a mode of expression and object to be personalized. In Japan this has involved use of "techno-cute" accessories and other means of humanizing cold technological objects (Hjorth, 2003). Use of cute, or *kawaii*, symbols, characters, avatars, ring melodies, games and accessories (and their subversion) have led to a huge economy of customization and personalization. "Hello Kitty" is perhaps the most well known signifier. Notably usage of the cute aesthetic and sensibility is not restricted to females but has also been embraced by men.

Whereas the previous two chapters have focused on laying down a practical exposition of the business environment that digital advertising consists of and operates within, and this one the media opportunities and characteristics available to advertisers, the following chapter lays down some critical frameworks and understanding with which to conceptualize new digital media.

Questions for further discussion

▸ If search is biting into television revenue, what happens to the process of branding? Are traditional advertising media necessary for branding?
▸ To what extent should viral be integrated into a company's marketing communications?
▸ What advertising opportunities do geotagging and locative media offer?

4   The Business Practice and Cultural Contours of Dataveillance

As alluded to in Chapter 3, behavioural targeting relies on a large amount of consumer data to deliver advertising that is timely, relevant and perhaps customized to the individual. Of particular concern for many is the lack of transparency of data gathering processes and what happens to users' data when collected. The extraction of data to translate into capital is a form of corporate surveillance. This chapter examines the wider picture of data surveillance – dataveillance – and charts the cultural contours of a society relied upon to generate data. This is done through understanding market research, the development of segmentation, current attempts at the configuration and surveillance of the user as a data-double and aggregation of information gathered. This presents an interesting paradox as it involves a scenario where surveillance and the delivery of advertising is more abstract yet at the same time more personalized. Whereas audience research has in the past involved panels of people, door-to-door research, TV set-top boxes as well as surveys, information is now mostly remotely collected although on an exponentially larger scale. This chapter further queries the extent to which we live in a 'control society' (Deleuze, 1992; Clarke, 2003; Yar, 2003) by examining the delivery of personalized advertising and the remote construction of users' data-doubles more closely.

A history of surveillance, business and consumers

Lyon identifies surveillance as being 'any collection and processing of personal data, whether identifiable or not, for the purposes of influencing or managing those whose data have been garnered' (2001, p. 2). Surveillance does not necessarily mean people watching each other but rather it seeks out 'factual fragments abstracted from individuals' (ibid). It is the enormous growth in computational power that has led to such a marked increase in surveillance capacity and application. Surveillance is not inherently wrong or bad. Like many practices and technologies, the question hangs over the nature of the application of these processes.

The wider picture of surveillance

The beginnings of surveillance are intimately tied to the notions of modernity and rationality. As Giddens describes, the term modernity refers to 'social life or organisation which emerged in Europe from about the seventeenth century onwards and which became more or less worldwide in their influence' (1990, p. 1). Giddens characterizes modernity as being comprised of a number of developments and political, social and economic changes. These include more broadly the *pace of change*. Although older societies have of course developed, the pace of technological change in modernity was extreme. Change was not restricted geographically either; the *scope of change* involved much deeper and wider interconnections between nations and the spread of businesses where then and now 'waves of transformation crash across virtually the whole of the earth's surface' (p. 2). The third feature of the break, or discontinuity, that modernity engendered was the *nature of modern institutions*. Many of the organizations born then were hitherto unseen, for example the intersection of culture and geography that formed the nation state, the dependence of production of goods and objects upon inanimate power sources (coal to gas to electricity and nuclear energy) or the wide-scale commodification of products and wage-labour where workers sell labour to employers.

Conceptions of modernity and rationality are commonly associated with Max Weber, one of the three founding fathers of sociology (the others being Durkheim and Marx). Weber was interested in the idea and expression of rationalization as found in both technology and the organization of human activities in modernity. He was particularly interested in the role of bureaucracy and administration, or the controlling, managing and coordinating of complex tasks. This according to Weber involves rational action, or the 'methodical attainment of a definitely given and practical end by means of an increasingly precise calculation of means' (Gerth and Mills, 1946, p. 293). Weber saw this form of rationality as the dominant mode of action in modern industrial societies. This for him was not only restricted to business and industrial processes but also found expression in a range of discourses and practices including education, science and Western classical music (he was interested in the standardization and coordination that governs modern symphony orchestras as compared to Asian orchestras and others that he saw as characterized by inventiveness and spontaneity).

Bureaucracy for Weber was something essential to modern societies yet also distasteful. He observes

That the world should know no men but these; it is in such an evolution that we are already caught up, and the great question is therefore, not how we can promote and hasten it, but what we can oppose to this machinery in order to keep a portion of mankind free from this parcelling-out of the soul, from this supreme mastery of the bureaucratic way of life. (cited in Mayer, 1943, pp. 127–128)

Suffice to say, Weber was somewhat pessimistic about bureaucrats and more importantly, the nature of operations it engenders. He described this rationalization as an iron cage that traps individuals (Weber, 1994). Business tools such as the punch card, the assembly line and the automation of the workplace may have helped businesses, but for workers corporations were perceived as dehumanizing machines. Simmel, writing in 1903, offers a bleak depiction of modern cities describing a worker's life in the metropolis thus:

he is reduced to a negligible quantity. He becomes a single cog as over against the vast overwhelming organization of things and forces which gradually take out of his hands everything connected with progress, spirituality and value. The operation of these forces results in the transformation of the latter from a subjective form into one of a purely objective existence. (2002, p. 36)

Techniques of administration involve disciplining procedures. This is perhaps seen most explicitly in Taylorism and the factories of Henry Ford where humanity was stripped to service the logic of machinic management. These were exercises in efficiency and the application of "scientific management" so as for humans to behave more like machines. As Robins notes, this was structural enterprise and a 'megamachine that paced and disciplines the workforce' (1999, p. 112). Nowadays monitoring in the workplace and human resource management routinely employs techniques to monitor workers' presence at work, their whereabouts, their activities, performances, use of time and the like (Hendrickx and Castro, 2002). Examples of such surveillance and developments in discipline include electronic recording, video-surveillance, time registration, black boxes, badges, data-logging and monitoring of email and internet use.

Staples in discussion of Foucault (1977) and discipline states that 'the modern individual is now born into a sea of regulations, petty rules and subrules, and fussy inspections, a world where the supervision of the smallest fragments of life and body takes place in the context of the school, the barracks, the hospital, and the workshop'

(2000, p. 20). Yet, in addition, modern institutions have provided obvious benefits. Modernity then has positive and negative aspects, which Giddens (1990, p. 7) describes as 'double-edged characteristics'. Whereas pre-modern society typically had more to do with kinship and lineage, modern societies were characterized by efficiency. In attaining efficiency administrative tools were created. Amongst these were surveillance and the watching and recording of phenomena, employees, individuals and groups of interest to a particular set of administrators whether these are of a governmental or business nature. There is a long political and cultural history of the relationship between the state, its borders, its citizens and the extent to which surveillance is used in the name of administering borders and the degree to which governments monitor their own citizens (Bigo and Guild, 2005). Although it is difficult to pinpoint an exact date of the germination of surveillance societies we can see inclinations beginning with the advent of the nation state and its strict control of boundaries, and the intensification of capitalist enterprise in the nineteenth century. Today, the United Kingdom, along with China, Russia and the United States has emerged as one the most heavily surveilled nations in the world. Gus Hosein, of Privacy International, explains the UK's ranking, noting that 'the country has the world's largest network of surveillance cameras, plans for national identity cards rich with personal and biometric information, and little government accountability when personal information is lost' (McKenna, 2007). In other words: 'Is closer and closer social control the inevitable price of "progress", a necessary concomitant of the continued development of modern social forms' (Robins and Webster, 1999, p. 108)?

Rather than becoming embroiled in a discussion of geo-politics, nationhood, security and legitimacy this chapter prefers to concentrate on capitalist uses of surveillance and dataveillance techniques,[47] although on occasion government and business interests intersect.[48] For example, as the Economist (2007) describes, two days following the 11 September 2001, attacks on New York and Washington, Frank Asher, a drug dealer turned technology entrepreneur, decided to examine the data amassed on 450 million people by his private marketing data-service company, Seisint (now taken over by the LexisNexis Group), to see if he could identify possible terrorists. After giving each person a risk score based on name, religion, travel history, reading preferences and so on, Asher came up with a list of 1200 "suspicious" individuals, which he handed to the FBI. Unknown to him, five of the terrorist hijackers were on his list. A broader example of the intersection of government and business can be found in concerns over governments' potential to subpoena data from data-rich companies.

Monitoring consumers

From a business point of view dataveillance has its origins in the will to rationality, greater understanding of consumers and the desire to not only know more about them but also to be able to reach them in "real-time". As Castells notes

> the core of the transformation we are experiencing in the current revolution refers to technologies of information processing and communication. Information technology is to this revolution what new sources of energy were to the successive industrial revolutions. (2001, p. 30)

Dataveillance processes are grounded within businesses' fervour for effective administration and quantifiable return on investment. It is a function of bureaucracy, a process that alleges to be impersonal. Whereas Ford's factories utilized the logic of the machine, many work places today use electronic surveillance both overtly and covertly as a means of controlling and bringing employees into line. Productivity now may be measured from afar rather than the window above the factory floor. Bureaucrats and managers seek stability and predictability and one way of ensuring this is to have as much information as possible. As Lyon (2001) observes, during the mid-twentieth century and the growth of computers, this came to include market research and the gleaning of information from other companies. In addition to the streamlining of business processes and employee management – and the dreaded term, human resources – surveillance is also useful for market and audience research.

Digital audiences are now being asked (sometimes) to take up a place within the circuitry of consumer culture as determined by probability aggregates upon which personalized offerings can be made, particularly in regards to behavioural targeting.

The ABCD of segmentation

A key aspect of any business that wishes to sell products or services is to understand as best as possible their consumers. As Arvidsson (2004) describes, audience market research has been in existence since the mainstream use of advertising developed in the nineteenth century. In the twentieth century, when it started to get into its stride post World War I, it developed as an attempt to curtail and limit the irrationality of the consumer and mobility of identity. As Leiss et al. (2005, p. 136) observe, Stanley Resor who purchased the Thompson agency in 1916 was the first to support research into consumer behaviour in addition to media hiring a number of behaviourist scientists to study advertising and audiences in a systematic manner. This again was carried out under the auspice of rationality and a need to construct specific categories of consumer.

In discussion of the difference between segmentation and differentiation between audiences, Smith (1956) describes the need to create consumers favourable to the seller. He describes that 'In its simplest terms, *product differentiation* is concerned with the bending of demand to the will of supply. It is an attempt to shift or to change the slope of the demand curve for the market of an individual supplier' (1956, p. 5). This is done through advertising and promoting differences between a product and its competitors. Segmentation conversely was about the demand side of the market and represents adjusting product and marketing efforts to consumer or user requirements. Smith uses the example of introducing a refrigerator to the market with no freezer compartment. Manufacturers are responding to distinguishable preferences of the refrigerator market whose frozen storage needs have already been met. Smith further observes that one of the reasons for greater focus on segmentation and needs and wants of smaller units of consumers derives from the capacity of manufacturers to decrease their minimum manufacturing unit. This represented a release from earlier constraints imposed by mass production. He also notes that many firms in that period reached saturation in their main markets and needed to attend to smaller or fringe markets that although small individually were of importance in the aggregate. The ability of businesses to operate was thus contingent on market research.

Although there was much academic innovation occurring in the 1970s, Wind (1978) describes that "real-world" segmentation followed *a priori* and clustering approaches. The first is

> a priori segmentation design in which management decides on a basis for segmentation such as product purchase, loyalty, customer type, or other factor. (1978, p. 317)

The other approach involves a

> clustering-based segmentation design in which segments are deter-
> mined on the basis of a clustering of respondents on a basis of 'rele-
> vant' variables. Benefit, need, and attitude segmentation are examples
> of this type of approach. As in *a priori* segmentation studies, the size
> and other characteristics (demographic, socioeconomic, purchase
> and the like) of the segments are estimated. (ibid)

Subsequent developments in the 1970s include flexible clustering that
uses conjoint analysis whereby variables and factors that people make
decisions with can be monitored. This gives the flexibility of building
up segments based on decisions that people make and subsequently
gives insight into their choices as to why they prefer one product over
another, or what it is about a piece of advertising that resonates with
them. Another development to emerge with advances in computing
power is componential segmentation that seeks to predict which type
of consumers will be most responsive to which product feature.

Underlying motivations

The 1950s saw interest in motivational research that sought to understand underlying motivations to consumer behaviour. This was
broadly based on Freudian psychology and came to popular attention
via Vance Packard's *The Hidden Persuaders* published in 1957. It is in
this form of research that advertising for many became synonymous
with psychological manipulation. One of its most famous practitioners
was Ernest Dichter who adapted psychoanalytical concepts to marketplace behaviour, tapping consumers' subconscious to understand
feelings about products. Major agencies such as McCann-Erickson and
Young & Rubicam in New York, and Geller and Weiss (later Edward
Weiss & Co.) in Chicago adopted the technique of in-depth interviews
and hired psychologists to conduct and analyse the data (Stern, 2004).
Dichter also displayed a distinct sensitivity for the process of distil-
ling ideas and presenting them in an easily digestible fashion often
using slogans of his own. For example, whilst conducting interviews
for the Ivory soap account he came up with the slogan, "wash your
troubles away", based on his insight into the reasons why people take
baths, observing that daily bathing has a ritual function and is a process whereby sinners wash themselves with soap and hot water to
cleanse their bodies physically, emotionally and psychologically (ibid).
Although Dichter's work became discredited in academic circles and

decreasingly cited in relation to motivational research, his work still indirectly informs teaching on opinion formation (DePaulo, 1990).

Motivational research borrowed from Freud a belief that people's real motivations were hidden and that they can be elicited through free-association. The next major shift in audience research was the development of psychographics that in some ways borrowed from motivational research, and its insistence on examining the complexities and minutiae of everyday life. Psychographics represents a more organized attempt to understand and classify consumers by their attitudes, opinions and interests. As Ziff (1971) explains, the 1960s witnessed widespread prominence and interest in psychographic segmentation. This developed out of the recognition that demographics has limited application in some product sectors and where it is necessary to know what people think in addition to designators such as age, sex and so on.

The impact of digital

Computational power in the 1960s allowed for exploration of a greater set of variables of consumer make-up, behaviour, wants and interests. As Green observes, 'a major factor contributing to the increased generation of data is, of course, the computer. It is only fitting, then, that the computer share in the task of making some sense out of the morass of output it can so blithely generate' (1970, p. 15). He also comments that computers were highly useful for market segmentation analysis, new product development, attitude measurement more generally, and that to process algorithms necessary to conduct these analyses requires the capabilities of high-speed computers. It is interesting to note the centrality of the algorithm to working out consumer segments and predictive patterns. In conceiving of the future Green envisages that

> large, interactive 'data analyzers' with visual display and hard copy, auxiliary output will be developed and made available on a real-time basis to marketing technicians and managers alike. The analyst will be able to try a number of ways of summarizing his data and looking for significant patterns without the long delays associated with batch processing procedures. (1970, p. 17)

The will to speed and real-time analysis is palpable. Green also states that the 'limitations of current methods are many and serious, but the core ideas embedded in the procedures appear both exciting and, in some cases, profound' (ibid). Another key analytical tool for advertisers and marketers that strongly impacts on today's targeting mechanisms is geodemographics. Phillips and Curry (2003) unpack the history of geodemographics explaining it as a social and geographic categorization tool to emanate from the United States and soon thereafter Canada and Europe. It uses publicly held data and private computing to work out the best sites for businesses and also to pinpoint direct mail drops. It is a system that divides the landspace into discrete spaces occupied by homogenous groups of household and individuals. This started through use of the ZIP (Zone Improvement Plan) code to organize households in the United States under post offices with each of these serving around fifteen thousand households.

By 1970, these files were computerized and by the mid-1970s CACI and Claritas had created the first geodemographic targeting systems by combining mapped ZIP code data and census generated socio-economic information. By the 1990s, their systems had proliferated and they were now using a range of publicly held information sources (Phillips and Curry, 2003). Importantly however, they were also using information provided by consumers from returns such as product registration cards. Becoming highly refined in their profiling they were also beginning to be able to refine geodemographic searches into much smaller units.[49] More recent is the recognition that individuals are fluid and mobile entities and that they can only map consumer behaviour by understanding that consumers have lives outside of the home. Data gatherers are keenly interested in locative mapping, locative devices and geospatiality. It is this desire to map and quantify that Phillips and Curry (2003) describe as the 'phenetic urge'. Rather than categorizing by containers such as the home, demographers and those interested in their data have begun to 'understand regions as constituted by the patterns of activity of individuals' (ibid, p. 144). Demographers are monitoring mobility. What is increasingly becoming more noticeable is how personal data is becoming. Greene (2008), for example, discusses research from Massachusetts Institute of Technology (MIT) that pertains to 'mine reality'. Mobile network providers have been able to roughly locate users for some time now through the phone pinging with the nearest mast. Service providers also record the duration of call and the number dialled. With many handheld devices now having the processing power of low-end desktop computers that can collect and utilize GPS data; this has led to a myriad of possibilities including analysis of the spatial proximity to other Bluetooth-enabled devices and friends, colleagues and family within a social network. Importantly, as will be described further in Chapter 6, legal statutes and regulations are lagging behind technical innovation and social change. However, both technical and practical caveats apply. Although there is a general will to quantification of both user action and intention, it is incorrect to suggest that measurement of online audiences is predicated solely on digital collection techniques. For example, as with research on traditional media forms, companies such as Nielsen and comScore utilize both telephone surveys and consumer panels, that is people who have agreed to give information to researchers over a period of time, usually for some sort of incentive. Other companies such as InsightExpress use pre- and post-testing as a means of generating insight; this is to ascertain factors such as effectiveness, coverage, reach, frequency and audience profiles. Panel members will install software on their computers to obtain a representation of their online media consumption. As Plummer et al. (2007) note, this is not without methodological concern, as it does not measure usage at work. Perhaps more central is that users' recorded search parameters may differ from their normal habits.

The impact of intensive data mining

As discussed in Chapter 2, many advertisers in the 1990s were gleeful in their adoption of online advertising as a means of reaching consumers. The dot.com boom promised advertisers and marketers much higher returns on investment and information about who is clicking on their advertising. However, although knowledge of metrics (in this case how many impressions were being engaged with) was important in the early days of internet advertising, knowledge of who was clicking was not so important. As Rodgers et al. (1999) describe, this is due to the fact that up until around 1997, internet users were largely well-educated, middle-to–upper-income males. Segmentation was not a significant issue.

Data mining and segmentation returned as a modus operandi as the internet began to be used by a wider range of people. It involves a collection of analytic methods for extracting information from large databases. Hand defines data mining as 'the process or secondary analysis of large databases aimed at finding unsuspected relationships that are of interest or value to the database owners' (2002, p. 637). As we have seen above, database analysts and data miners have been around in one form or another since the 1960s and perhaps before. Due to the vast amounts of data in circulation and held by data gatherers, businesses are in a position to offer personalized advertising experiences derived from data collected both digital and non-digital sources. More accurate profiles mean that companies can result in greater success in 'cross-selling related products, upselling, product affinities, one-to-one promotions, larger baskets, and customer retention' (Han and Kamber, 2001, p. 674). Although internet-based data mining is perhaps now more widely reported on, the offline retail sector remains dedicated to extracting meaning from huge databases of data. Wal-Mart allows suppliers to access data on their products and through data mining identify customer–buying patterns, control inventory and product placement, and create new merchandizing and marketing opportunities. Whereas industrial processes brought new precision to the creation of distribution of goods, now retail machinery aims to learn more of our preferences to tailor price and product offers. Yahoo! for example, in a research paper titled "Squeeze Every Drop of Meaning from Data", discuss new clustering techniques aimed at picking up and structuring innocuous human/advertisement interactions. Their Sponsored Search Group programme

> may initially use machine learning techniques and regression models to predict click-through rates for a particular ad on a particular page. It will factor in such contextual data as what time of day an ad was clicked on, which state or country the user was from, and what words were used in the title of the ad. In fact, the machine learning model will try to extract as many features as it can from the interaction between web pages and ads to predict future actions. (Yahoo!, 2008)

Data mining is now ubiquitous and growing in intensity. Baker (2008) in his populist book on data mining and mathematics, *The Numerati*, describes that in the 1990s

> we had to render everything we sent, the very stuff of our lives, into ones and zeros. That's how we came to deliver our riches, the key to communications on earth, to the masters of the symbolic language. Now these mathematicians and computer scientists are in a position to rule the information of our lives. I call them the Numerati. (2008, p. 9)

Despite allusions to conspiracy theories surrounding Illuminati and those accused of controlling global events behind the scenes, Baker is right to acknowledge the translation of human impulses, purchases, secret wishes, likes and dislikes into digital data to tweak commercial offers and maximize eyeball exposure time. Through statistical analysis computers analyse consumer data in terms of commonalities, variances, repetition, patterns, associations, relationships, reactions to price and placement, classification, clustering and the generation of sequential patterns to anticipate behaviour and (in the case of advertisers) optimize advertising and product offers. Although false positives are regularly generated (oddly, I receive Facebook advertisements for Christina Agueliera's perfume), scientists, engineers and mathematicians are constantly refining systems that are also growing in processor power. Data miners are getting to know us very well, perhaps better than we know ourselves?

Dataveillance, docile bodies and reliance on Bentham's panopticon

Theories of dataveillance find initial expression, although not direct reference in Foucault's (1977) work on discipline. Discipline involves surveillance, individuation and behavioural correction. Here new forms of discipline create what he calls docile bodies. Docile bodies are created through discipline, and not of the spiritual, health or self-mastery sorts. As Moss describes, the kinds of discipline in modern societies produce a docile body 'more powerful yet easier to direct and subjugate, and also more calculable and easier to know, a predicable object from the quasi-scientific knowledge of the social or human sciences' (1998, p. 175). The docile body is created through observation. Somewhat famously, Foucault (1977) argues that this was exemplified in Jeremy Bentham's panopticon, a type of prison that allows observers to watch prisoners without the prisoners being aware they are being watched. This in turn was to create a sense of all seeing "power". Bentham's unbuilt model was an exercise in controlling exponentially increasing prison populations. Foucault revived the idea as a metaphor for the constricting nature of the late twentieth century. Foucault's thesis is an exercise in control and power whereby Bentham's architectural model is a perfect model of disciplinary social control. Reversing the idea of placing individuals in dungeons, the panopticon differs in that the prisoner can always be seen but cannot see his or her jailer. Rather than being held in a dark dungeon banished from view the prisoner is always potentially on view but never knowing when he or she is actually being gazed upon. As Foucault (1977, p. 199) describes, '[h]e is seen, but does not see; he is the object of information, never a subject in communication'. Consequently the key effect of the pan-opticon is to induce a programmed functioning of power through the possibility of constant visibility and self-censoring behaviour. This finds expression today in CCTV (Yar, 2003; Koskela, 2003) and, as Lyon (1994) notes, when surveillance is conjoined with computerized tills and video cameras then we have entered a period of the panop-ticon without walls.

Haggerty and Ericson (2000) observe that within surveillance stud-ies there is a protracted over-reliance on Foucault's (1977) thesis of Bentham's eighteenth-century panopticon. Bentham describes that the 'essence of it consists, then, in the centrality of the inspector's situ-ation, combined with the well-known and most effectual contrivances for seeing without being seen' (1843, p. 44). However as Wood (2003) points out, surveillance is not contingent upon 'sinister forces' wishing to do us harm. Wood states that surveillance can be used

> ...in the name of the efficient servicing of consumer demand, soci-ety and sociality that has moved beyond the modernist project so accurately described by Foucault, towards a new situation of 'unin-tended control'. (2003, pp. 237–238)

As Mann et al. (2004) point out, whereas inmates of the panopticon model were aware of being under surveillance, the modern panop-ticon is a reversal of Foucault's original (1977) thesis where the guards not only remain hidden from view but also actively try to make them-selves unconscious in our minds and activities. This is in contrast to the original formulation whereby the guards make as large an impres-sion as possible through absence. Where the panopticon has a central observatory the modern form of electronic surveillance is much more dispersed. Elmer states that

> ...dataveillance entailed decentralizing the panoptic mode of sur-veillance calling into question the production of risk management tools – computer matching or profiling techniques that attempt to attribute general characteristics to individuals. (2003, p. 236)

Thus dataveillance examines the use of personalized information for segmentation, clustering and predictive purposes. The straightfor-ward notion of surveillance is complicated by the issue of users and consumers being willing participants in the dataveillance process receiving both prizes and punishment. For example, when order-ing products online, clicking on an advert or filling personal details online there is often a reward or prize for delivering such information (Elmer, 2003). However, Lanier and Saini (2008) argue that such incentives can only be ethical when consumers fully understand the terms and conditions underlying these social contracts, as well as 'the actual costs and benefits that can accrue from the exchange relationship (p. 18). Those who decline may be punished and forced to pay more for the same artefact or service. Thus the situation is somewhat more complicated than users watched by identifiable organizations. Instead data collection companies are not readily identifiable and take on a more abstract, ethereal form less easily identifiable and certainly more difficult to contact for the unaware user of a personal computer.

Control societies and 'dividualization

Rodowick argues, 'control societies organize power through the invisible or virtual architectures of computer networks and telecommunications' (2001, p. 222). Inspired by Deleuze (1992), such literature on dataveillance argues that users are designated by codes as opposed to any designation that marks out the user as an individual. The term 'dividualization thus refers to the notion that users and consumers are stripped of uniqueness as a social being and instead are reduced to a figure or variable. Deleuze (1992) makes the point that in a "control society" we are no longer designated by a signature or a number but instead a code. These codes find expression in the clusters and groupings data miners classify us into. This system arguably finds its origin in the Hollerith machine, designed in 1890 by Hermann Hollerith that was used to tabulate the 1891 US Census, although this was to some extent based upon Charles Babbage's unbuilt *Analytical Engine*[50] and the *Jacquard Loom*.[51] Hollerith used punched cards to record information and designed a tabulator and sorter to mark the results. Hollerith not only created the company that became IBM, but as Black (2002) notes, Hollerith systems were used by Nazi Germany in the registering and surveillance of Jewish people throughout the holocaust.

Gere similarly observes, 'Hollerith's invention also helped found a connection that continues unabated to this day, between digital technology and methods of surveillance, control and discipline' (2002, p. 38). Internet protocol addresses do not tell us anything about the user in terms of precise geographic location, gender, class, title or any other markers that marketers and advertisers use to target campaigns. This is not a signature as it reveals nothing about the individual, but instead the activities of the IP address (where on the internet does it go, how long does it stay for, etc.). As Deleuze (1992, p. 5) notes we have 'become "dividuals", and masses, samples, data, markets, or *"banks"'*. Users lose markers that form the individual as a social being and instead are reduced to a figure or variable. This is a step beyond administration and power as conceived by Weber or Foucault. As Lyon (2003) in discussion of Deleuze and Virilio observes, today's surveillance goes beyond that of Michel Foucault's disciplinary society, where persons are "normalized" by their categorical locations, to what Deleuze (1992) calls the 'society of control' where similarities and difference are reduced to code. The coding is crucial, because the codes are supposed to contain the means of prediction, of anticipating events (for example, crimes), conditions (for example, AIDS and SARS) and behaviour (for example, consumer choices) that have yet to occur. This scenario is to be regarded as a datascape whereby information is accumulated, stored and aggregated in an increasingly dispersed and abstracted form. Digital media as a collection of platforms and technologies invoke what Virilio (1997) discusses in terms of *dromology*, meaning the science or logic of speed. When we think about the world we often conceive of it in terms of distribution of wealth, finance and military might. Virilio (1986) instead examines speed as it relates to power, for example in the velocity of dispatching information. Whereas forces such as the military sought to speed up the moving of troops (as well as communication to and from these), acceleration has now more to do with information and the attainment of real-time understanding and transmission.

In this conception of society, citizens and consumers are monitored through their data trails both online and to some extent offline. Users and consumers of electronic information are viewed as assemblages (Haggerty and Ericson, 2000) whereby individuals are read by database processors as a concatenation of demographic and previous web usage. Eschewing humanist notions of identity, dataveillance literature describes users as ephemeral nodes within a cybernetic web of input, output and feedback. In this narration of online and locative environments, users are temporarily configured as dependable variables that ideally can be counted upon by the marketing and advertising industries to behave in a predictable manner. This is not to suggest data-doubles in this view are stable entities but rather they exist as data intersects, as required by advertisers for the purposes of establishing an online target audience and working out future interests. Haggerty and Ericson observe that 'to the extent that the surveillant assemblage exists, it does so as a potentiality, one that resides at the intersections of various media that can be connected for diverse purposes' (2000, p. 609). This becomes especially relevant when one considers that data is never held by one source. It is sold, diffused and used over and again, refined and redefined endlessly as programs on users' computers send information back to remote computers and matrices of users are reconfigured and then disassembled. As Baudrillard famously and presciently comments

> The real is produced from miniaturized cells, matrices, and memory banks, models of control – and it can be reproduced an indefinite number of times from these. It no longer needs to be rational, because it no longer measures itself against an ideal or negative instance. It is no longer anything but operational. In fact, it is no longer really the real, because no imaginary envelops it anymore. It is a hyperreal, produced from a radiating synthesis of combinatory models in a hyperspace without atmosphere. (1994 [1981], p. 2)

That is, the user is reduced to a configuration of algorithms that, according to data miners, have no reference outside of themselves. Whereas the problem for advertisers in the past was how to gather information on users and consumers, the question now is what to do with all of this information. Poster (1996) in discussion of databases and the collection of citizen and consumer information argues that databases act as discourses 'constituting subjects outside the immediacy of consciousness' (1996, p. 14). This means that databases containing information about us create data-doubles or doppelgangers of us that remain largely external to ourselves unless we take the trouble to require information from marketers, data miners or government.[52] Discourse on and about us in a sense operates as a language (ibid). In the same way that language is an abstract system used to represent objects, entities and phenomena, our data-doubles are abstractions of ourselves. Our online data-selves are a complex interplay of power, control, regulation and information, with a variety of bodies and organizations both private and governmental possessing differing levels of access to this data, and thus eventually us. Poster argues that databases reconfigure the constitution of the subject. As linguistic objects (for example, demographic symbols and abstract data used by advertisers, marketers and agencies to represent us), users are constituted as objects without authorship. Because information is passed and sold onto a myriad of third parties, including governments, libraries, hospitals, universities, marketers, advertisers and client corporations, databases operate as language in their own terms.

Users are understood in terms of probability garnered from previous activities in offline and online political, social and commercial nodes, such as the use of store cards, magazine subscriptions and types of websites visited. This is then an arena of control whereby marketers and advertisers seek an audience that is comparable to 'objects' (Fuller, 2003). Poster sees these processes as capitulation to marketing departments and advertising agencies. He describes this process as

> ...a submission to the publicity departments of untold corporations of one's preferences as the information flits at electronic speeds from one's credit card through the computers networked around the globe and finally into the omnivorous databases of the insatiable transnational behemoths. (2004, p. 409)

Ang further states that

> The development of the consumer society has implied the hypothetical construction of an ideal consuming subject through a whole range of strategic and ideological practices, resulting in very specific constraints, structural and cultural, within which people can indulge in the pleasures of leisurely consumption. (2000, p. 185)

Poster (2005) argues that targeting has arrived at a situation in which retailers have more knowledge of consumer preferences than consumers themselves. He argues that we have found ourselves in a 'brave new world of consumption prefigured only in the imagination of science fiction writers' (2005, p. 21). Utilizing Philip K. Dick's science fiction tale *Ubik* (1969), he investigates the mediascape of the hyperreal in light of the emergence of digital advertising. Under the rubric of the cyborg, the networked consumer and 'dividualization, Poster remarks

> With the multiplication and dissemination of increasingly advanced information machines, the Earth has entered a post-human era. Our society has done so under the general regime of the commodity, which, at the cultural level, disseminates itself in the discourse of advertising. (2005, p. 22)

He also asserts that a contradiction arises in the online arena when the drive to expand capital and sell more products conflicts with users' need for greater control over personal data. Potentially the more advertisers attempt to target consumers with personalized messages, the greater the sense of alienation users feel from the production of online advertisements. According to Poster this scenario will eventually hit meltdown and 'the future of digital advertising will be ubiquitous at the cost of a kind of blowback effect in which corporate databases are open to hackers/consumers' (2005, p. 36).

Towards an equiveillant society?

Brin (1996) argues that the privacy game is up and that corporations and governments have won or are at least building a society vastly one-sided in its information flows. Accordingly, Brin laments that the proverbial genie is out of the bottle and there is no way to get it back in. In a society characterized by surveillance and dataveillance he suggests that the only reasonable response is sousveillance, or watching the watchers. The difference in Brin's account is that he suggests we, the citizens and the state, share the same watching apparatus. For example, each and every citizen of a city would be able to lift his or her wristwatch/TV and call up images from any camera in town. This is the mutual disclosure argument. A society characterized by equiveillance is one where all members of society are empowered to use tools of accountability. As computing becomes more ubiquitous and embedded in our lived environment, the capacity to deflect and monitor potential watchers grows. Although a scenario of self-responsibility is perhaps an undesirable one, the other option is to rely on companies and governments to be more responsible with our data. Brin (1996) observes, the alternative to self-responsibility and the development of equiveillance is to pass privacy laws that will be enforced by elites, and trust them to refrain from looking at us. Brin argues that an equiveillant approach invokes a more democratic society predicated on balance and sharing of power. In contrast, in a despotic community, respect and power are not shared but are restricted to the few. The thesis here is that 'freedom is best served when all citizens have enough knowledge to hold each other reciprocally accountable' (Brin, 2008).

Mann (2004, p. 620) defines surveillance as the 'eye-in-the-sky' and sousveillance as 'down to earth'. This derives from French where surveillance is literally watching from above and sousveillance is watching from below. Mann (2004) describes an interesting scenario that involves him in two similar situations with very different outcomes. Wearing visually obvious sousveillance equipment, he entered an art gallery with eyeglasses that captured live images. He was subsequently roughly manhandled out of the gallery. Refining camera equipment to fit a pair of spectacles that looked fashionable and not out of place he entered a jewellers and told them the nature of the spectacles. In contrast to the earlier situation, he was instead asked if he would be interested in commercializing this product. Mann evaluates his artistic and ethnographic experiment reflecting thus:

> It is therefore interesting to note that an inclusionary rather than exclusionary element of sousveillance is possible. While surveillance tends to be exclusionary, and tends to present a very strong 'us versus them' directionality, sousveillance can be made to operate much more like Peer-to-Peer, in the sense of creating a level playing field. The sousveillance landscape therefore may include both shoppers and shopkeepers, wearing personal recording devices. (2004, p. 625)

Another possible configuration of the watching scenario is where citizens and consumers have access to the same tools as traditional power holders. This has similarities with Mann's concept of 'reflectionism' whereby sousveillance is used to mirror and confront bureaucratic organizations (Mann et al., 2003, p. 333). This is then a form of 'detournement', the tactic of appropriating tools of social controllers and resituating these tools in a disorienting manner (Rogers 1994). However, while situationist tactics, as in the sense of de Certeau (1988), aim to disrupt cultural, political and economic established norms of practice, equiveillance aims to create a mutual standoff.

Is an equiveillant society possible? Can we envisage a society where techniques of watching are so ubiquitous and commonplace that those with financial and disciplinary power accept counter-watching as an everyday activity? On the surface this seems appropriate although requiring consumers and citizens willing to monitor elites and importantly holding to account those that abuse our data. However, the power relationships involved favour the corporations and the analytical engines they employ. It is in the sifting, sorting, reorganizing and extracting where meaningful knowledge lies. As Solove observes, to solve the problem, 'a transparent society would have to make each individual as competent as bureaucratic organizations in processing information into knowledge' (2004, p. 74). There are of course problems of power: is power so easily shared? Schneier (2008) refutes the mutual disclosure argument observing that although information mutually gathered by individuals may equal a balancing of power, if the balance of power is out of balance to begin with, mutual surveillance will be of little help.

What users will tolerate in terms of dataveillance, and what they will demand in return – be this services, products or rights – are all questions that need further research. As such, the following chapter explores critically users' perspectives, and how users have been conceived within digital advertising practice and research.

Questions for further discussion

▸ Is closer social control the price of progress?
▸ To what extent do you agree that online space is public space?
▸ 'Data miners are getting to know us very well, perhaps better than we know ourselves?' Is this true and should we be concerned?

5 Conceiving User Approaches to Digital Advertising

Chapters 2 and 3 offered an account of the business environment of advertising and advertising media platforms respectively, whilst Chapter 4 delineated the cultural contours of dataveillance. This chapter offers critical approaches to understanding audiences, users and their perceptions of digital advertising and the data mining sub-processes that increasingly drive it.

In addition to the form, content and delivery of advertising, the dynamics of media audiences have changed, and continue to do so. In many ways the first mass media advertising audiences were homogenous. Reacting to greater segmentation, concurrent media diversification and media technologies that facilitate time-shifting, we are now seeing a more fragmented audience. Media and contemporary communications have in many ways reorganized time and space for users and audiences. In a manner similar to the reorganization of communications methods and patterns between people wrought by the telegraph and the telephone, digital media have set in place new developments in mediated social relationships. Many of these technological developments are, of course, everyday and potentially mundane techno-social practices (overflowing email inboxes come to mind!). The changes in how the online environment is perceived in the past ten years or so is remarkable. Web and internet usage is now an integral part of everyday life for many living in affluent economies. Popular characterization was somewhat different only a few years ago. In the 1990s, when the web was new, the online environment was redolent with Rheingoldian (1993) communitarian discourses and the discourses of being on the edge of new, technologically determined realities. It seems as if in 2000 someone flicked a switch on the internet and turned off all things "cyber". Who now considers themselves as part of a cyberculture – I doubt many Facebook users. Britain's Queen now broadcasts her yearly speech on YouTube, the Vatican has a YouTube channel and politicians routinely make use of the web as a means of reaching young audiences. This has been particularly effective for the

Britain's David Cameron and the US's Barack Obama, now offering a weekly address. Indeed the political image-makers now routinely make use of blogs, podcasts and online video. Digital is now mainstream and has been for some time.

Contemporary media tend to be of a more "on-demand" nature and traditional forms are reorganizing themselves around digital principles. Whereas traditional broadcast programming tends towards a time-constrained linear nature, more recent incarnations allow for asynchronous usage and navigation. That is to say, we are no longer confined to schedules and the beat of the drum of the content provider. Instead there is greater choice and control. For many commentators on new and digital media the defining qualitative difference between these and traditional media are the degrees to which they allow and facilitate interaction. Interactivity shifts the control onus to users and engenders high-involvement media engagement as opposed to passive instrumental media consumption, of the Shannon and Weaver (1949) couch-potato sort, involving an information source, a transmitter, a channel, a receiver and a destination where the message is received. In theory, interactive advertising places the consumer or user at the centre of the commercial communication due to effectiveness being derived from the degree to which he or she engages with the interaction (Stewart and Pavlou, 2002). Herein lies the nub of the development: digital advertising in many ways requires *engagement* from users.

Whereas in years gone by online environments were perceived as anonymous, this is certainly no longer the case. Web companies have a vested interest in learning our interests, search habits and patterns of use and consumption. Although advertisers and marketers have always been interested in this kind of information, the benchmark and quality of information being gathered is of a very different order. This has raised privacy concerns from advocate groups. However, users and consumers themselves have not been as vocal. Defenders of targeting – usually those involved in publishing or advertising – claim consumers are mostly happy with the deal. Users share information and in turn receive valuable advertising that alerts them to useful products and services. Critics counterclaim that users are unaware of targeting processes and that greater transparency is required. As such, this chapter offers a brief account of the cultural history of the internet to better understand discourses of anti-advertising so prevalent online. It then proceeds to account for contemporary perspectives on digital advertising, privacy, ramifications for behavioural targeting practices and begins to assess these in light of regulation more fully detailed in the following chapter.

The departure from cyberspace and the Californian ideology

As you might expect, there are plenty of fascinating accounts and overviews of internet history online, for example Hobbes' Internet Timeline[53] that accounts for the formation of the United States' Advanced Research Projects Agency (ARPA) in 1957, through to plotting the full scale of the web in November 2006. It unpacks the first nodes of the internet, consisting of UCLA, Stanford Research Institute (SRI), University of California Santa Barbara (UCSB) and University of Utah. It also explains that the first attempt to send a message from UCLA to Stanford by Charley Kline resulted in the system crashing as the letter G of LOGIN was entered: so now we know, system crashes are nothing new! Although the internet has existed for some time now, it has undergone significant changes in terms of the culture that it informs and is informed by it. The early period was characterized by small numbers of users based in universities. Highly technologically savvy, these were the early pioneers who foresaw usages not only for military and defence purposes but also for civil communication. Nethistory[54] has a wonderful set of accounts from early users and their first forays into digital ethers, the first computer-mediated-communication (CMC), and the birth of communities connected by hardware and shared wonder at the intimacy and possibilities offered by internet technology. As Condon (n.d.) writing for Nethistory describes, it was not so much the hardware and then high-speed links that was celebrated but rather the people behind the screens. Condon recollects that

> we had discovered a new frontier. We found a way to reach beyond the physical limitations that constrained others (though they didn't know it) and share information, viewpoints, and form friendships. We were bound together not just by common interests in computers or certain fields of study, but by the knowledge that we had stumbled upon a new world – a virtual world.

This was a new world without state influence and without regulation. Frontier discourses of the founding fathers were deliberately invoked by organizations such as the Electronic Frontier Foundation (EFF) founded in 1990 to help protect rights online (Busch, 2006, p. 306), though governments took notice when cyberspace interfered with their rules and laws. For the first time people were maintaining daily relationships and interactions with people whose voices they had never heard nor faces they had ever seen, yet feeling as they shared a special communicative secret others would not be privy to for years to come. This sense of wonderment and the growing legions of Netizens[55] eventually culminated in what came to be known as cyberspace. Bruce Sterling (1992) describes cyberspace thus:

> A science fiction writer[56] [William Gibson] coined the useful term 'cyberspace' in 1982, but the territory in question, the electronic frontier, is about a hundred and thirty years old. Cyberspace is the 'place' where a telephone conversation appears to occur. Not inside your actual phone, the plastic device on your desk. Not inside the other person's phone, in some other city. THE PLACE BETWEEN the phones. The indefinite place OUT THERE, where the two of you, two human beings, actually meet and communicate.

The term cyberspace is not only influenced by the growth of telephone networks and CMC but also virtual reality (VR). The early internet appeared to be imbued with a sense that transcendence could be manifested through technology. Although nowadays much CMC is taken for granted, the early period was characterized by the sense of magic granted to all technologies new and perhaps not fully understood. In some regards it invokes Arthur C. Clarke's discussion of the future and his oft-quoted dictum whereby 'Any sufficiently advanced technology is indistinguishable from magic' (1973, p. 39). As Lister et al. (2003) describe, this version of cyberspace is popularly characterized by headset wearing, computer-generated worlds, and suits and gloves that allow tactile and positional feedback whilst the body remains in real space. The majority of us do not wear suits, although some do spend time in virtual environments such as Second Life, but the point is that these environments are immersive. It is not qualities of realism or high-tech graphics that are important but more the involvement of the self within the network in much the same way that one can become engrossed in a telephone call.

Cyberspace thus became redolent of utopian characteristics and, as Robins (1995, p. 135) describes, 'nowhere-somewhere'. These utopian discourses do not exist in isolation; they have a genealogy and history. They are part of a wider meta-narrative of progress inherited from modernity. Transcendence in modernity found expression in art, science and musings over technology. Geometric boundaries were falling away as mathematicians such as Bolyai and Lobachevsky pushed beyond Euclidean geometry; in art, Cubism and Futurism were seeking a-religious realities beyond the mundane of the everyday, not to mention theosophists, philosophers and mystics whose writings permeated a variety of artistic endeavours in this period. Cyberspace also came to be popularly populated with philosophers, mystics, utopianists and idealists, all of which predicated on technological innovation. However, Robins is rightly scathing of cyberspace hyperbole. He comments that

> All this rhetoric of 'age-old' dreams and desires – which is quite common among the cyber-visionaries – is unspeakably vacuous and devoid of inspiration. It is a familiar old appeal to an imaginative space in which we can occupy new identities and create new experiences to transcend the limitations of our mundane lives. It is the aesthetic of fantasy-gaming; the fag-end of a Romantic sensibility. (1995, p. 139)

Although advances in communicative technology generate absorbing and fascinating phenomena and situations, it is wrong to divorce them from the everyday real world. Underpinning many early accounts of cyberspace is a sense there was/is something wrong with the real world and that cyberspace offers some kind of escape. This escapism manifested in the idea that community could be rediscovered and that a utopia may be established unshackled from the inequalities and ills of the world of dirt and substance. Cyberspace was thus a stage of evolution made manifest through the privileging of mind, spirit, art, expression and creativity (see Coyne, 1999 for a full exposition of transcendentalism and the internet). As Robins (1995) again notes, one has to ask, is this account of cyberspace an alternative society or an alternative to society? Although seemingly unrelated to the world of advertising and marketing, it is interesting to see how many of these tropes and discourses were invoked for campaigns for new technology products and services. Even today, although few use the term cyberspace many of the discourses of transcendence permeate conceptual configurations of the internet.

In recognizing and conceptualizing users of digital media it is instructive to examine notions of cyberculture as informed by cyberpunk as a potential means of understanding conceptualizations of digital advertising. Cyberpunk is a science-fiction form that gained mass prominence in the 1980s, presaged by Phillip K. Dick writings from the 1960s, 1970s and early 1980s that also involved monopolistic corporations. Some of the most popular authors include William Gibson (1984), Rudy Rucker (1988) and Bruce Sterling (1988) focusing on high-technology, urban environments and low-life. It stands in opposition to accounts of modernist accounts of technology and tends to be nihilistic in its outlook. A key feature of the bleak landscape depicted in cyberpunk literature is that of the megacorporations as portrayed by William Gibson, one of the famous proponents of cyberpunk. These are organizations that wield huge power in face of governments whose power is largely ineffective.

Given that usage of the internet was growing in the 1980s and the web was just around the corner, it is no surprise that cyberpunk was to play a part in conceptualizing discourses and practices of digital life in the 1980s and 1990s. Cyberculturalist perspectives of the internet can also in part be attributed to the Electronic Frontier Foundation[57] (EFF) described above. The EFF's remit was, and remains, to defend free speech, privacy, innovation and consumer rights. Distinctly anti-corporate and anti-governmental regulation in its original incarnation it imagined the internet as an unfettered cyberspace based on the purpose of furthering human knowledge and reaching out to other Netizens through electronic networks (Calcutt, 1999; McLure, 2000; Silver, 2000). The EFF, at least in its original form, considered advertising a social and economic practice that hinders the progression of knowledge due to propagation of idiocy and banality (Boudourides and Drakou, 2000; Shade, 2002).

In this view advertising is a tool of the megacorporations and was shunned by early users of computer networks. When the web came online there was significant tension and concern about the encroachment of business and the conversion of online space as places for communication and exchange into online malls littered with the detritus of advertising and marketing. As the web came online in the early 1990s, pop-ups, floating screen-based advertising and banners were irritatingly popular with advertisers and there were many of these given the businesses' revenue model. As Lister et al. (2003, p. 183) reflect, in the development of early online advertising we see the interaction of forces of ownership, investment and perhaps most importantly, ideology. Whereas the pre-web internet was advertising free, the web, became in effect, an open market for people to trade and advertise their wares.

This account of the internet invokes the "Californian ideology". As Patelis (1999) highlights, this involves a techno-determinist view of an inevitably free-market future. The early period of web investment reflected this belief being characterized by dynamism in relation to policy, regulation, development and most notably involved a clear break from this past. In sum, it involved a hyper-modernity. Internetphilia – or freedom through internet-based communication – also involves freedom from restrictions and regulations. However, as Patelis points out this depiction also means free from existing relations, above society and beyond the state. It also maintains extremely similar characteristics with the free-market. In this view the internet as a communications medium wanes and we see not the domination of the internet but the transformation of the electronic environment to one infrastructurally predicated on commerce, albeit one driven by hunger for data.

Identity

The internet is in part a creation of virtual spaces whereby aspects of one's identity can be played out in relative safety not found in the real world, although it may in part affect real word identities. Turkle (1995) describes how online identities are evocative objects for thinking about the self, not only in terms of how we present ourselves online but also on how we fulfil and construct identities for the real world. Identity is malleable and reconfigurable for situations anew. In many cases online where responsibility to others is lessened, the online environment thus conceivably offers a Cartesian means of escaping the physical confines of the body or the "meat" that encapsulates the real self as well as the social and cultural nexuses we are all involved in. As communication has largely been textual, perhaps involving an avatar of sorts, this has led to a degree of disembodiment. This means that markers such as age, sex, race as well as wider legal, financial and personal history are removed. Identity online is to some extent about performance in the theatrical sense, fluidity and liberated from concerns over authenticity. Although performativity and the use of "alts" carries on in virtual environments, it is interesting to see that more recently online versions of the self via social networks resemble real physical identities much more closely. Although these online representations are to some extent idealized versions of the self, they are based on real life. As Slater (2002) describes, there appeared to be a definite schism between online selves and offline selves. This line is now much more blurred and we now see that digital media is something to be studied and configured within existing social relations.

Another key figure in cybercultural lexicon is the cyborg. As Featherstone and Burrows (1995) observe, cyborgs need not necessarily refer to online media solely given the rise of cosmetic surgery and similar practices now widely employed to modify the body. Although the term cyborg invokes visions of Robocop, it is best thought of as a melding or augmentation of the body with technology. The cyborg is a figure of both fiction and fact. Latour (1991) uses the language of hybridization whereby humans and non-human objects form entities by dint of the networks and technologies they share. This is because those from wealthy economies now live in a world where we are indissociably networked with other objects for most social acts we engage in, with agents acting on our behalf. We are to an extent one with our mobile phones, laptops and other technologies we conduct our daily lives with. New networks and technologies stimulate new behaviours.

Ubiquitous usage and the "everyday"

Although remnants remain of early internet discourses that rally against the encroachment of commerce into the online environment, the war was won a long time ago. In many ways it makes little sense to talk of a free internet or cyberspace. Lessig comments 'that cyberspace was a place that governments could not control was an idea that I never quite got. The word itself [cyberspace] speaks not of freedom but of control' (1999, p. 5). Cyber-utopianism is at most a fringe belief with the mainstream of users of digital media engaging readily and perhaps uncritically with commercial websites, players, tools, services, games, search engines and platforms. For example, in the United Kingdom: Windows Live Messenger, Facebook, eBay and Google comprise the top four visited sites (Neate, 2008).

It is notable that the key revenue generator for Facebook and Google is advertising. Although advertising is now mainstream, and advertisers are savvy to the idea that users do not want to be swamped by push advertising over which they have no control, how do users actually feel about it? This is difficult to ascertain. As described in Chapter 3, there are a plethora of formats of advertising ranging from innocuous sponsored links to large screen display overlays. Many users used to traditional advertising do not even recognize much digital content as advertising (McStay, 2006). Also, the differentiation between advertising and marketing is blurred to such an extent that it becomes meaningless to differentiate between them. Is a website advertising or is it a virtual shop window? If an advertising agency creates the website does this make it advertising or does it remain within the remit of marketing?

As Haythornthwaite and Wellman (2001) describe in their now canonical text *The Internet in Everyday Life*, as the internet moves from the preserve of the early adopters and avant-garde into a platform that underpins many social, economic and technological practices, a more "everyday" assessment is required. This needs to deal with people's reactions to digital advertising, in addition to macro events such as laws, regulations and governmental and business practices that bear upon users. As Haythornthwaite and Wellman point out, it is easy to get caught up in the transformational aspects of the internet and forget the uses that everyday users put it to and how it integrates a variety of practices and experiences. Similarly, many commentators have also neglected to place internet use within the rest of human daily experience. After all cyberspace is an extension of both physical and temporal existence, offering a 'common stage for everyday economic, cultural, educational, and other activities' (Kalay and Marx, 2006). Although there are notable accounts of people spending too much time in virtual and gaming environments, for most of us online activities are a small portion of how we spend our waking lives. In addition, the focus on cyberspace and cyberculture also neglects to account for how digital life leaks out into the real world in the form of augmented spaces, the use of the internet in navigating real space (as with locative media), not to mention the use of social networks that do not replace real friends but for most users offer an additional texture and communication channel between offline friends. As Thompson (2008) observes, everyday use of the internet tends towards ambient sociality, or co-presence, in that online communication, however banal and Twitter-like, lends a social dimension to everyday life. Many people use mobile text-messaging in a similar ambient fashion. With reference to Japan and mobile phones (or *keitai*), Habuchi (2005) describes this is a telecocoon, or the production of social identities through small, insular social groups (Ito, 2005). In addition, whereas cybercultural discourse highlights identity experimentation, more recent incarnations of online and digital activities are identity experimentation inhibiting due to them being in effect mutual surveillance tools. However, as Albrechtslund argues, mutual surveillance is not something inherently undesirable. He argues that 'to participate in online social networking is also about the act of sharing yourself – or your constructed identity – with others' (Albrechtslund, 2008).

Resistance and negotiation

As with offline advertising, user and audience behaviour is a balance between what is described here as states of co-optation, negotiation and resistance. The term co-optation here refers to the extent to which users are willing to engage with advertising and the sub-processes that generate highly targeted digital advertising. In understanding user behaviour, clinging to cybercultural discourses is not much use in painting the overall picture. These narratives tell the story of a niche audience who are now far from the mainstream of users. Conversely, the academic journals on digital and online advertising tell us little about *qualitative* understandings of digital audiences. Analysis of online audiences and advertising largely generally consists of *quantitative* experimental and survey research to determine key advertising-related features of online audiences, such as internet demographics and psychographics (Rodgers and Harris, 2003; Assael, 2005), perceptions of online advertising's value (Ducoffe, 1996; Brackett and Carr, 2001), online advertising's interactivity (Liu, 2003; Tse and Chan, 2004) and online advertising's effectiveness (Dahlen, 2001; Gallagher et al., 2001; Dahlen et al., 2003; Martin et al., 2003; Havlena and Graham, 2004). There is much less naturalistic, qualitative research focusing on how people perceive and engage with online advertising (although see Phelps et al., 2004), and even less looking at how audiences perceive notions such as creativity in digital advertising.

De Certeau (1988) indirectly offers useful ways of conceptualizing user behaviour. His notion of the "everyday" is born from a belief in privileging 'ways of operating' and foregrounding these as objects of study rather than them as being part of an 'obscure background of social activity' (1988, p. xi). Whereas many theories of use and consumption of cultural objects look towards macro explanations, De Certeau, along with Lefebvre (1971) and Bourdieu (1984), observes that it is fruitful to look towards microelements of what people actually do with objects created for consumption. In discussion of everyday life, de Certeau details how we find ourselves having to negotiate strategies from institutions involved in representation, consumption and production wishing to assimilate us. In face of producers' "strategies", de Certeau contextualizes these procedures in terms of "tactics" that people use in their reaction to strategies employed. De Certeau (1988) configures producer strategies and user tactics in terms of producers having large budgets, being of a dominant order, as having a site of operation and being relatively inflexible in how they roll out their strategies. Users, however, are considered as more fluid and adaptable. They do not seek to 'win or take over' or address a strategy head-on. A tactic is defined by the absence of power (de Certeau, 1988, p. 38). Instead users reorganize meaning and cultural objects with the awareness that many of the things around them have been created to cater to the lowest common denominator; they expect to have to work on things to make them their own. Although it may be enticing to look to web 2.0 platforms as a means of circumventing producerly strategies, it is instructive to examine this in light of media ownership and advertising. De Certeau's description of strategy as a calculated manipulation of power relationships (ibid, pp. 35–36) is extremely appropriate to advertising given that the entire process of advertising has been predicated upon executing a strategy to best target an audience. It also works well with advertising in that the consumption of advertising is far from straightforward. For example, users and consumers may be resistive and co-optive at the same time. For example, we may watch television advertising breaks during a film, but begrudgingly nonetheless! Highlighting these ways of operating, de Certeau notes that these activities no longer form an incomprehensible background to social life. Instead they should be articulated as a central area of study. As Lister et al. comment 'The concept of everyday life is central to the study of culture and media, but is often absent from accounts of new media technologies' (2003, p. 220). The notion of the everyday is also employed to refute the distinction between the virtual and the material as distinct entities. As Murthy (2006) describes, in contrast to pessimistic images of dystopia and corporate hegemony, there is significant space left for movement and human creativity. In this version of power relationships, although many of the resources that support digital life are maintained by power elites with close affiliation to the states, its expansion and development is engineered by a much broader base who can write software, maintain servers, construct websites and actively engage in annotating both online space and offline (or urban) space. Despite the apparent unity and extension of power that corporations may hold and possess, a closer look shows a degree of fragmentation and fraying, laying open threadbare spots for subversion, exploitation and more common to everyday folk such as ourselves, appropriation.

Active and interactive audiences

By the 1970s, it had become widespread in much "leftist criticism" of the media and in media effects research to describe the mass audience as passive, existing simply to soak up the ceaseless flow of popular programming (Neuman, 1991). The active audience thesis was first championed by the uses and gratification model developed by Katz et al. (1974) as a critique of audience passivity. More recently it has been adopted and extended to focus on digital media by Stafford and Stafford (2000) who identified five underlying factors of web use motivations: a search factor, a cognitive factor, a new and unique factor, a social factor and an entertainment factor. Allowing for global differences in reasons for media use, Roberts and Ko (2000) also use uses and gratification to describe global interactive advertising as involving:

> cross-cultural marketing communications that are planned and executed to actively engage persons in advertising processing through interactivity as a part of overall localized, regionalized, or worldwide strategic communication efforts.

The uses and gratification model has drawbacks, most notably its assertion that mass communication is no more than need gratification and that media effects are demonstrated by ability of people to indicate that their needs have been gratified (Ross and Nightingale, 2003). However, it shifted the emphasis from what media do to people, to what people do with media. In contrast to media determinist notions of audience (or user) behaviour, studies of active audiences acknowledge that users of media are not 'cultural dupes' (Grossberg, 1995, p. 75) and are in fact central to meaning and media form negotiation. More specifically, media and the masses were seen as dimensions of the same overarching political process. As Ross and Nightingale further point out

> Whilst the second half of the twentieth century saw a significant growth in audience studies, with the actual concept of 'the audience' moving through the arc of passive sap to interactive player, it was arguably the 1990s which saw the most significant shift in thinking about the audience with the widespread incursion of the internet into everyday lives and culture and the explosion in talk and reality TV shows. (2003, p. 146)

The advent of the World Wide Web and its development into mass medium(s) has arguably forced a re-evaluation of both how audiences behave and traditional media models. Although displaying surface similarities to the uses and gratifications model (Blumler and McQuail, 1969; Katz et al., 1974), interactive models differ in that audiences are also capable of media production (or at least influencing the media) as well as meaning production. Although the term web 2.0 is problematic, it does reflect well the shift towards user-generated content and participatory culture. Jenkins (2003) argued that interactive audiences are active, discriminating and critically aware, though this is debatable given the plethora of "You've Been Framed" entries that make up large portions of bandwidth-hogging video sharing.

Interactive audiences and user-generated content

Ross and Nightingale (2003, p. 147) argue that because internet researchers are dealing with media with new characteristics, new research methods are needed. They assert that change in technology is paralleled by change in genre and this by extension will refocus the methods used in audience analysis. In a somewhat deterministic fashion they state that the growth of the World Wide Web and its journey to becoming a mass medium requires researchers to rethink the notion of both audience and medium. More broadly, they point to audience-based programming that generates interactive responses on the part of the listener, watcher or user. For Ross and Nightingale, it is this participative aspect that differentiates audience analysis from a traditional active audiences approach.

The viral advertising phenomenon, for example, has delivered an interesting scenario for media audience theorists. Within the context of viral advertising we have seen the emulation of user-generated content as a means of reaching consumers. To some extent this can be seen in sub-cultural guises of incorporation whereby agencies appropriate media and cultural trends as a means of reaching target audiences unwilling to be reached through traditional media. Viral in the past has allowed advertisers to circumnavigate many regulations that impact on how they can communicate with audiences and users. Creatives have been to some extent unshackled from frustrating regulatory hindrances (see Chapter 6 for more on regulation) and can tend towards creating edgier work. A situation has evolved whereby advertisements use low budget production as a means of generating authenticity. Also common is the practice of agencies distancing themselves from their advertising, claiming they have been subject to spoofing, perhaps to gain more PR and column inches and brand notoriety with hard-to-reach users and viewers.

Conversely there is also the potential that viral advertising may be spoofed by users, as with the short viral video that creates a montage out of Unilever advertisements including Lynx and Axe as well as Dove, the ethically posturing soap and body cream brand, that asks 'parents to talk to their children before Unilever does'.[58] Viral advertising is symptomatic of a culture of "prosumers", a term that derives from the video camera industry, that reflects a market niche that sits between consumers and professionals (or producers) (Toffler, 1980). In the user-generated content arena this translates as technology and media within the range of domestic use but capable of producing work for large-scale distribution.

Co-optation and targeting

On the flip side of display advertising, viral advertising and other strongly representational advertising there is search advertising. It is low in mediation and relies on engendering relevance to the user both in time and space. That is, it appears when and where required. If advertising in the future is not relevant, useful or wanted, it will be in trouble. Audiences have long engaged in conscious and unconscious practices of cognitive filtering. Hood and Schumann (2007) observe this involves a coping mechanism of filtering content, cognitive capacity limits and restriction of how much individuals can absorb when stimuli are over-abundant. Moderating factors here include an individual's desire for information; technical ability; inclination to trust and amount of time available to spend online. Contextual cuing also is also part of cognitive filtering. As Hood and Schumann describe, if users are exposed to irrelevant advertising in the corner of a screen, over time this space may be filtered out. Tolerance to repeated information also increases wear-out and the promotion of negative attitudes to digital advertising.

In addition to cognitive filtering users can sift out much digital advertising, particularly online advertising, with applications such as Adblock Plus, a Firefox plugin that erases advertising from webpages. Firefox users can also utilize another plugin called CustomizeGoogle, which strips advertisements from Google search results. Carr (2007) observes that the number of users of Adblock Plus and similar plugins is not yet high enough to spur a counterattack from online advertisers and that most large internet companies are content to ignore advertisement blocking for the time being, perhaps fearing that criticizing the plugins would only raise people's awareness of them. For digital advertising to be successful they have to engender co-optation through relevance. Given that so many web-based businesses are based on advertising, it pays not to upset customers. Another aspect to this is that advertising-based models of revenue have lowered the barriers of entry so people with a viable business idea can quickly get online with an advertisement-based business model. Applications such as Adblock Plus hurt these companies. As Naughton (2007) observes, if advertising revenues are removed, all that is left are subscription-only services – something that only large corporations are good at building.

In many ways search advertising is a good representation of the future of significant portions of digital advertising in that it aims to offer only services and goods relevant to our interests. Nelson (2007a), citing a survey conducted by Nielsen//Netratings, comments that although the majority of American web users say they see too many advertisements, they wouldn't mind having those advertisements better targeted to their needs. Ninety-one percent of those over-exposed to advertising would prefer using a search engine rather than being served display advertisements. Although digital media represent another set of media to add to the media mix for advertisers to utilize, it is also representative of new and perhaps more agreeable ways of soliciting consumers. Media planners have for years sought to understand more about their consumers and their media habits. Although they have had reams of data to work with, many will admit that educated presumptions play a part in deciding the medium to place their clients' advertising. Digital aims to take the guesswork out of the equation. As Castells observes, 'we are not living in a global village, but in customized cottages globally produced and locally distributed' (2001, p. 370). Digital advertising no longer seeks to broadcast *en masse*, but is increasingly customized for micro-targeted market segments. As opposed to traditional branded advertising that works on a broadcasting model with the knowledge that there will be a large of degree of wastage, much digital advertising aims to go further than the narrowcasting model and engage users on a more-or-less individual basis. In addition, much digital advertising is low in intrusiveness, a characteristic that has plagued wider digital and online advertising and high-involvement media.

However, in exchange for targeted advertising (requested and unrequested) we offer up data about ourselves. Anecdotal evidence from my students tells me they have mixed feelings about this. Although they relish the notion of not being bombarded with irrelevant advertising, they are unsure about having significant banks of data being held about them. Further, do behavioural profiles actually belong to the surfer? For example, many share computers in the home, in the office and in public spaces such as libraries and cafes. In addition, users may wonder whether they may be missing out on any services or products by being potentially so tightly segmented. Sheehan and Hoy (1999) also correctly ascribe negative perceptions of online advertising to user concerns over privacy, noting user reticence to provide informational data to advertisers.

Trust

With many online business models predicated on the delivery of advertising to highly defined audiences, users are right to be concerned about how their data is used and who it is sold onto and shared with. As described above, there are many discourses of anti-advertising that impact on the users' conceptions of digital advertising as a legitimate means of soliciting consumers, although this view over the years seems to have been worn down with the advance and acquiescence to businesses and the services they deliver online. One of the key determinants of co-optation to digital advertising is trust.

The need for trust occurs when we feel vulnerable. Given that the digital environment is a relatively new, chaotic ensemble of pages, spaces, protocols and processes both overt and covert, involving varying degrees of legality and stakeholder sincerity, marketers and advertisers have had a significant task building trust amongst prospective consumers. Lee (2007) offers a useful table on definitions of trust derived from a range of literature, broadly characterizing it as having to do with: a need to know what has happened; emotional interpretation of perceptions, information or knowledge; and proactive aspects of behaviour where users decide on what to do about a situation. Bakir and Barlow (2007) similarly offer a range of trust definitions and their application to media.

Although the advertising business (generally meaning those who make use of advertising agencies) may distance itself from the practices of adware, spam merchants, over-use of pop-ups and similarly intrusive and annoying practices, consumers do not make such discriminations. Instead they remain distrustful of irrelevant digital advertising and often find it intrusive, particularly if it is not relevant to them or activities they engaging in at a particular time (McStay, 2006). Schlosser et al. (2000) comment that trust levels are higher in the online advertising sector than the offline sector due to perceptions of online advertising as being informative. Rettie et al. (2003) similarly note that a large proportion of their study participants found online advertising trustworthy, although many of them considered online advertising to be a hindrance to other online activities. Cheong and Morrison (2008) highlight that consumers also tend to be more trustful of information about products generated by fellow users and they will describe both positive and negative information about products and services, although, as Pan et al. (2007) observe, people trust Google in that they click on abstracts in higher positions even when the abstracts are less relevant to the task. This means that ranking algorithms and lethargic searchers doubly punish alternative sites. Allsop et al. (2007, p. 398) note many users consider word-of-mouth as more credible than marketer-initiated communications 'because it is perceived as having passed through the unbiased filter of "people like me"' though this may be subject to the efforts of public relations (PR) practitioners and marketers to influence opinion leaders and attempts to create a two-step flow effect (Katz and Lazarsfeld, 1955).

Trust is important in a number of regards but particularly in reference to users' information and personal data. Through data-miners' collection of our online actions and behaviour, we turn over significant data on our preferences and ourselves. Rahul Lahiri from Ask Jeeves [now Ask.com] reflects that

> (Personalization) isn't an area where the technology isn't ready, where there's a need for a lot of innovation...The question is, are people willing to give up (more information) to get a better search engine back in return? Only time will tell. (cited in Hines, 2005)

In advertisers' endeavour to get closer to their target audiences they may in fact alienate or stifle their audiences. In attempting to create intimate relations with their audiences, it is likely that marketers and advertisers do not dispel distrust but instead amplify distrust by utilizing the same mechanism that users are distrustful of, that is, the surveillance of users' activity and the positioning of users as information providers. Cuneo (2008) writing for Advertising Age comments 'Customers are desperate to have a relationship where they are nurtured, cared about and recognized. Of course, you have to be careful not to recognize them too much'. She also quotes Bob Thacker, senior vice president of marketing and advertising at OfficeMax observing 'Personalization is the whole theme of this marketing era,' ... 'It's the end of mass communication as we know it.'

However, reality and theory may have diverged somewhat, at least for a few years yet. A survey of 700 chief marketing officers (CMOs), chief executive officers (CEOs) and top marketing executives conducted by Advertising Age reports that 82.9 per cent of respondents said they use no more than a moderate amount of personalization in their communications, and only 17.1 per cent said they use personalization extensively. Some 18.3 per cent said they spend more than 20 per cent of their marketing budgets on personalized communications, while 35 per cent said they spend less than 10 per cent, and 24.9 per cent said they aren't sure what percentage goes to personalization (Cuneo, 2008). Investment in personalized communication is not as high as one may imagine with only 55 per cent of respondents sampled planning to spend more than 10 per cent on personalized communication. The study cited these key challenges: inadequate systems and infrastructure; lack of customer data and insight; and cost and complexity. What appears to be working best are a number of traditional techniques: individualized emails and letters, targeted database marketing leveraging personal profiles and opt-in, permission-based marketing programs (ibid).

Trust is a corollary of risk, and a risk need not be some fixed outcome; it may have more to do with perception than technological and economic practices taking place. For Giddens (1990), trust is something that operates in the face of risk. Trust is a necessary characteristic of expert systems and symbolic tokens that are reliant on what he describes as the 'development of disembedding mechanisms' (Giddens, 1990, p. 53). Expert systems, as Giddens notes, are akin to being able to walk up stairs to a bedroom secure in the knowledge they will not give way or, to use a more contemporary example, surfing the internet with a virus guard on. They are a consequence of scientific revolutions and the resulting increase in technical knowledge. Giddens (p. 33) describes 'symbolic tokens' as making possible interactions unbounded by time and space, for example money. A more contemporary example is Paypal, the online money transfer system (McStay, 2007b). Disembedding mechanisms are social practices that extend outside the context of the local and instead reorganize social relationships based on processes such as economics and communications across greater expanses of time and space in the drive to further globalization. As O'Hara points out: 'Trust is the big issue of the 21st century' (2004, p. 23). If users will not engage in trusting relationships with digital service or advertising providers, it will be very difficult for digital economies to function. We depend on persons, and more importantly structures, upon which we have no intimate relationship. They are a consequence of scientific advances and the resulting increase in technical knowledge.

Luhmann correspondingly argues that we should expect trust to be increasingly in demand as a means of 'enduring the complexity of the future which technology will generate' (1979, p. 16). Jarvenpaa et al. describe that 'trust is a belief or expectation that the word or promise by the merchant can be relied upon and the seller will not take advantage of the consumer's vulnerability' (1999, p. 1). It is worth remembering that digital advertising is different from traditional advertising in that so many variables are measured as advertising is delivered. Users are expanding the amount of personal information shared with companies, for example address books, email accounts, their shopping habits, not to mention the cross-referencing and data gathered as users traverse sites that are signed up to advertisement servers such as Tacoda and DoubleClick. Such intensive data mining is redolent of Massumi who observes people in late-modernity harbouring a kind of low-level fear, not hysteria or paranoia, but rather a 'kind of background radiation saturating existence' (1993, p. 24). Where trust is ruptured ontological insecurity and existential angst ensues brought on by living with modernity's risk profile (Giddens, 1990).

Drivers of concern online: contagion

In contrast to traditionally secure media, such as television, press, cinema and radio, the online environment presents unique concerns to online users. Adding to concerns over perceived threats from attacks from organizations, individuals (perhaps digital bullies, paedophiles or hackers), there remains the constant threat of viruses, Trojan horses and worms.[59] Arguably, the threat of contagion and viruses carry similar discursive resonances as they did in the 1980s when computer viruses were first formulated. Ross (1991) posits that the first virus attack on the internet in 1988 aided in inculcating a hysteria that transformed computer culture. Intertextually this was conflated with fears over AIDS (Davison, 1991). Bardini (2006) extends the disease metaphor to describe the four phases of capitalism involving plague, tuberculosis, cancer and AIDS. He describes that 'plague is the archaic and thus the archetypical disease (Girard); tuberculosis is the plague that corresponds to the second phase of capitalism (mechanized capitalism) and cancer the third disease. In this situation growth, both economic and cancerous, capitalism is out of control and the usual limitations for growth are ineffectual (ibid). AIDS arrived in the 1980s as the fourth syndrome to charac- terize capitalism due to its viral capabilities and the way it gripped the popular imagination.

The relationship between disease and business can be carried further. The notion of high-risk contagion has also aided the devel- opment of anti-virus companies who have utilized the discourse of protection against unknown, unseen partners and unknown files. Popular viruses have seen huge profits for anti-virus companies and it is 'part of the virality of capitalism that accidents and break-ups can be turned into elements of its productive flows' (Parikka, 2005). This is as it should be with the introduction of any new technology as this entry into media ecology necessitates the possibility of its fail- ure and threats to its existence. This is equally applicable to national security, international commerce and the individual user (ibid). Kember argues that this scenario of protectionism has strengthened the ideology of privatization and that there has been a closing of bar- riers to the 'unknown' (1998, p. 103). Kember further suggests that the relationship between the organic (body) and the online persona share characteristics in that both process information and both are susceptible to disease. Concerns over contagion also facilitated the use of anti-advertising software through conflation between percep- tions of viral styled attacks and early advertising that appeared from apparently nowhere. Importantly both engendered a sense of being out of control.

Howcroft (1999) argues that cybercultural studies of the internet are often characterized by an axis of utopia and dystopia, involving the internet as a site of social revolution. To a large extent this is fuelled by what Lister et al. describe as the 'technological imaginary' and the way new technologies and new media are taken up within a culture and 'are hooked into, or have projected onto them, its wider social and psychological desires and fears' (2003, p. 163). Derived from an abundance of historical sources and discourses, the technological imaginary projects both utopian and dystopian imaginings of com- puter networks and the processes carried out through them. Furedi argues this point further stating that we are in a condition of perpet- ual fear unconnected to any particular problem. He maintains that 'risks hover over human beings' and have an independent existence and 'by turning risk into an autonomous, omnipresent force in this way, we transform every human experience into a safety situation' (2002, p. 5). Rather than risk existing as some form of recognizable loci that can be taken, considered and faced, risk instead maintains an omnipresent status over the online environment.

Direct risks from digital advertising are small although cyber-criminals have hacked pages on a publisher's site and inserted code behind a content page or advertisement, as happened with an infected advertisement served on MySpace.com (Burns, 2007c). In this case malware was disguised in an advertisement for DeckOutYourDeck. com and machines lacking appropriate Windows patches downloaded a Trojan, enabling pop-ups while browsing and recording surfing habits while trying to download additional malware.[60] The cost for entry is also low with criminals able to distribute software packages online to start infecting users with Trojans. Indirectly risk-accidents may occur through the data we offer up to advertisers and associated companies such as Facebook may come back to haunt us. For example, in November 2007, users discovered that Facebook's tracking system was compiling their purchasing history through vendors like Fandango and Travelocity. In addition, the Facebook Beacon system was sending users' friends lists of sites users had visited and what they had purchased.

Targeting: data aggregation and consumer perspectives

If we are not already there, then we are moving into a world predicated on data aggregation. Data aggregation involves aggregators gathering information for purposes of statistical analysis. For example, one purpose is to get more information about particular groups based on specific variables such as age, profession, income or interests. The information about such groups can then be used for website personalization to choose content and advertising likely to appeal to an individual belonging to one or more groups for which data has been collected. Processes of data aggregation are of course not restricted to advertising and marketing but also involving public records, health databases, criminal databases, credit agencies not to mention consumer research organizations. We live in times of data abundance.

Turrow (2006, p. 162, cited in Plummer et al., 2007) observes that although users describe positive aspects of behavioural targeting there was concern over the integrity of advertisers. Only 17 per cent of a sample taken agreed with the statement 'What companies know about me won't hurt me' whilst 79 per cent agreed they are 'nervous about websites having information on me'. A survey conducted by Harris Interactive records that 59 per cent of Americans sampled object to Microsoft, Google and Yahoo! tracking their online activities for marketing purposes (Russell, 2008). Although researchers from Harris Interactive flagged up that those companies with greater information on their preferences would be able to offer higher quality (more tailored) advertising, 59 per cent were still uncomfortable with targeted advertising through online data tracking. Researchers probed as to whether the American adults would alter their views after seeing a series of potential policy and security policies. These were based on the Federal Trade Commission's (FTC) current publication about the adoption of possible self-regulatory principles for online behavioural advertising.[61] These involved

1. *Transparency and consumer control*: this had to do with clearer disclosure on whether users have to use personalized advertising or not. Recognizing that many people do not read lengthy privacy policies this principle proposes that 'every website where data is collected for behavioral advertising should provide a clear, concise, consumer-friendly, and prominent statement that (1) data about consumers' activities online is being collected at the site for use in providing advertising about products and services tailored to individual consumers' interests, and (2) consumers can choose whether or not to have their information collected for such purpose. The website should also provide consumers with a clear, easy-to-use, and accessible method for exercising this option' (FTC, 2007).

2. *Reasonable security, and limited data retention, for consumer data*: this reflected Stakeholder concern that 'data collected for behavioral advertising may not be adequately secured and could find its way into the hands of criminals or other wrongdoers'. The FTC proposed that 'any company that collects and/or stores consumer data for behavioral advertising should provide reasonable security for that data with degrees of security relative to the sensitivity of the data (ibid). It was also proposed that companies should retain data only as long as is necessary to fulfill a legitimate business or law enforcement need' (ibid).

3. *Affirmative express consent for material changes to existing privacy promises*: this reflects 'changes over time in privacy policies and that before a company can use data in a manner materially different from promises the company made when it collected the data, it should obtain affirmative express consent from affected consumers'. For example, this would 'apply in a corporate merger situation to the extent that the merger creates material changes in the way the companies collect, use, and share data' (ibid).

4. *Affirmative express consent to (or prohibition against) using sensitive data for behavioural advertising*: this reflects stakeholders expressing 'concern about the use of sensitive data (for example, information about health conditions, sexual orientation or children's activities online) to target advertising, particularly when the data can be traced back to a particular individual'. They state that consumers may not welcome such advertising even if the information is not personally identifiable; they may view it as invasive or, in a household where multiple users access one computer, it may reveal confidential information about an individual to other members. The FTC propose that 'companies should only collect sensitive data for behavioral advertising if they obtain affirmative express consent from the consumer to receive such advertising' (ibid). For this last criterion, the FTC comments that it is looking for input on what classes of information should be considered sensitive and whether using sensitive data for behavioural targeting should be banned rather than subject to consumer choice.

The regulatory impact of this is explored more fully in Chapter 6. For the purposes of this chapter it is instructive to note that even with the inclusion of these four privacy policies, respondents were still broadly unsure about personalized advertising. Alan F. Westin, a collaborator in the report from Columbia University, commented that 'The failure of a larger percentage of respondents to express comfort after four privacy policies were specified may have two bases – concerns that web companies would actually follow voluntary guidelines, even if they espoused them, and the absence of any regulatory or enforcement mechanism in the privacy policy steps outlined in the question.' So potentially, in contrast to dystopian science fiction-based versions of reality, many users maintain a pragmatic approach to their online negotiations.

A 2009 survey carried out by TRUSTe (2009), a consumer privacy organization, records that two out of three US citizens sampled from a representative sample of demographic backgrounds are aware that their browsing information may be collected by a third party for advertising purposes. In addition, consumer dissatisfaction with behavioural advertising fell from 57 per cent in 2008 to 51 per cent. The report also states that 72 per cent of those surveyed said they found online advertising intrusive and annoying when the products and services being advertised were not relevant to their wants and needs. However users are also more concerned about privacy with users deleting their cookies more often than they were a year ago and 48 per cent saying they delete cookies on their computer at least once a week. This is an increase from 42 per cent in 2008 suggesting a high level of awareness on the part of the consumer that their browsing activity may be tracked.

It is an interesting and close correlation with the aforementioned study that describes 59 per cent of those sampled by Harris Interactive objecting to Microsoft, Google and Yahoo! tracking their online activities for marketing purposes. In addition, both reports conclude that transparency of what is monitored is paramount. Carolyn Hodge, TRUSTe's vice president of communications, reflects that it is obvious that users want 'customized experiences and relevant advertising from brands they trust' although she further observes that there will be a lot of mistrust about behavioural targeting methods unless those in industry do more to educate consumers about their activities. She cites Amazon.com as a company whose site uses behavioural targeting to deliver customized recommendations and works well (ibid). In addition to business practice and transparency, more clarity is needed about the law, particularly in the United States. According to a poll from the Consumer Reports National Research Center, more than seven in ten web users are worried about marketers tracking and analysing their online data, and many users mistakenly believe companies in the United States by law must let them know that their data is being collected or shared (Quenqua, 2008). This indicates a distinct lack of correlation between concern over data and the legal and technical processes that inform business and data controllers' use of our personal data.

Given the importance of legal infrastructures in modulating user and producer behaviour regarding digital advertising, the following chapter examines issues of policy and regulation.

- To what extent do internet-enabled mobile telephones generate telecocoons?
- How comfortable are you with the notion of a peer-surveillance society?
- To what extent do you agree that in attempting to create intimate relations with their audiences, it is likely that marketers and advertisers do not dispel distrust but instead amplify distrust?
- Within your own national or regional locale, to what extent are users concerned about browsing information being collected by a third party for advertising purposes? What types of measures are taking to prevent this, if any?
- To what degree does contextual cuing affect advertising targeted by behavioural techniques that need not be related to the context it is situated within?

6   Policy and Regulation

Whereas prior chapters have inquired into business, media, dataveillance and ways of conceiving user practices and perceptions, this chapter looks more closely at law and regulation that arguably lags behind technical innovation and social change. In particular, this chapter focuses on UK, EU and US regulations, directives and laws, highlighting perspectives on dataveillance in terms of coverage of privacy concerns. In addition to discussing governance on privacy and data protection this chapter also draws attention to the potential exploitation of law and advertising regulation. In these two cases it focuses on the UK examining regulation on advertising to children and controversial viral advertising imagery and content.

Technology and social change

We live in a period characterized by speed, velocity and rapid social and technological change. Technology and the business potential it unleashes have arguably moved faster than regulation. In addition, such innovation has also moved faster than wider society's understanding of dataveillance and the physical, electronic, social and ethical make-up of the digital environment and the people connected to it. The social theorist Bauman (2005, p. 1) describes contemporary life as 'liquid life', a development of modernity. This is 'a society in which the conditions under which its members act change faster than it takes the ways of acting to consolidate into habits and routines' (ibid). Progress is a train to be caught, preferably with upgrades. Without doubt modernity and consumerism have delivered many positive contributions to society but concurrently people have arguably developed an isolationist or atomized attitude against risk without obvious source (Furedi, 2002).

As described in Chapter 4, the development of data mining and the configuration of consumers and users as spending variables to be tracked, mapped and configured is a reality that has caught many unawares. Liquid life is then a precarian life lived under an auspice of uncertainty. This is often without loci and is characterized in relation to the beat of contemporary life, social change and technological "progress". Although users may not complain overtly about privacy, dataveillance and the mining of information, is this due to users and consumers not caring or has it to do with not knowing who to complain to, how to opt-out or perhaps a more general fatigue with the pace of digital life and development? Part of the problem is that technology advances faster than government safeguards. As Marc Rotenberg, of the Electronic Privacy Information Center notes, 'There is a rapid expansion of technologies for surveillance, identification, and border control and a much slower adoption of policies to safeguard privacy and security' (McKenna, 2008).

Privacy

Interest in privacy has a long, legal history; perhaps all the way back to fourteenth-century England and the Justices of the Peace Act in 1361 that provided for the arrest of peeping toms and eavesdroppers. Lanier and Saini (2008) offer a useful overview of privacy concerns describing that the right to privacy has to do with free expression in democratic societies. Whereas in totalitarian societies, privacy is compromised for the ideology and functioning of the State, for democracies to function citizens must be allowed to participate in organizations (including privacy of membership), and enjoy freedom of political choice (including secret ballots) and freedom from coercion by the State (including limited surveillance and intrusion) (also see Westin, 1967). These are undermined by denial of rights to privacy and the ability to control information about themselves and their affiliations.

As Lessig (2006) notes, the perpetual monitoring of behaviour is an inexpensive process and what needs to be decided upon is the degree to which we as citizens will allow this. This involves finding a balance between public and private interests. As argued in McStay and Bakir (2006), privacy is often viewed, even from a legal perspective, as a distinct consumer right (Goodwin, 1991) and a political right (Reidenberg, 2000). Westin similarly offers what has now become a canonized definition of privacy, that is, 'Privacy is the claim of individuals, groups or institutions to determine for themselves when, how, and to what extent information about them is communicated to others' (1967, p. 7). It is an issue that concerns regulators. Democratic governments around the world have unequivocally declared that protection of citizen privacy is essential to the robust development of e-commerce (United Nations, 2001). For the sake of brevity, this section focuses on the United States and the European Union – two regions with significant volumes of e-commerce yet different approaches to privacy regulation. In both regions, issues of transparency have been raised. Given the nature of these online marketing and advertising techniques, the academic literature focusing on users' rights in these areas sees privacy as a prevalent ethical issue – particularly from the perspectives of government policy-making (Caudill and Murphy, 2000; Miyazaki and Fernandez, 2000; Petty, 2000; Reidenberg, 2000; Beltramini, 2003) and corporate policy-making (Caudill and Murphy, 2000; Miyazaki and Fernandez, 2000; Maury and Kleiner, 2002; McRobb and Rogerson, 2004; Gordon, 2005; Palmer, 2005). Privacy issues are bound up with those of user control, knowledge (Caudill and Murphy, 2000; Culnan, 2000; Miyazaki and Fernandez, 2000; Petty, 2000; Sheehan and Hoy, 2000; Lanier and Saini, 2008) and transparency (Grabner-Kraeuter, 2000; Petty, 2000).

From the perspective of advertisers and marketers, adware and other cookies-based technology are legitimate business tools that enable customization and personalization of advertising. In addition, as Garfield (2008a) observes, privacy can be seen as a commodity that can be traded: celebrities trade it for fame, travellers for security and the rest of us for the saving of a few pennies or the chance to enter a competition. As with the broader advertising business model, it allows free or price-reduced content and services in exchange for advertising and a few personal details.[62] Use of such data collection techniques ensures a smoother web experience that serves involved parties: users, advertisers and site owners. These techniques allow online marketers to reach those who are interested in such communications (Petty, 2000; Wood, 2003) thus facilitating relationship-marketing (Culnan, 2000) intended to generate greater customer retention and satisfaction. Whilst information collected through cookies about users' preferences or browsing habits can be distributed widely and easily on the internet to other companies who can in turn use it to market other goods and services to these users (Milne, 2000; Stead and Gilbert, 2001, cited in Palmer, 2005), advertisers and marketers increasingly realize that intrusive communication with users damages their brands. Sheehan and Hoy (2000) find that important dimensions influencing users' willingness to provide information online are control, particularly where users regard information as sensitive (typically medical records, social security numbers and financial information); financial or informational compensation offered to users in exchange for their information; and long-term relationships, including how familiar users are with the entity collecting the information. The importance of relationships is highlighted through user initiation (Sheehan and Hoy, 2000). Whilst many online users distrust marketers that collect information through websites, users who receive unsolicited email from a company to which they have sent an email in the past or whose website they have visited, did not consider the practice an invasion of privacy, even if the unsolicited email had nothing to do with past communications.

Gordon (2005) notes that international legislation ranges in scope from requiring End User License Agreements (EULAs) from adware thus prohibiting automatic downloading to requiring public bodies to conduct privacy impact analyses when authorizing or prohibiting the use of invasive technologies. Indeed, as Baumer et al. note, the 2002 EU Directive on Privacy and Electronic Communications (European Commission 2002/58/EC) recognizes spyware as an invasive practice when it states that 'The use of such devices should be allowed only for legitimate purposes, with the knowledge of the users concerned' (2004, p. 404). However, for users, the wording of EULAs may be complex or unclear (Briskman and Smith, 2004) and many recipients of adware are unaware they have given consent (PC, 2004, cited in Gordon 2005). Although onus has been shifted to the consumer and user to understand what details they are releasing, Gordon's (2003) study of privacy-enhancing desires and behaviours of information security professionals (who presumably believe privacy is important and who are not technologically naive) from the United States, United Kingdom and the European Union showed that few always read privacy policies on websites or EULAs. Even in the more regulated region of the European Union, whilst the EU has demonstrated greater ethical concern for its users' privacy rights than the United States, there remain problems with assumptions about user competence or willingness to educate themselves and engage with safe online privacy practices. For example, Sherman (2008) conducted a test on privacy policies by putting policies through online sites that calculate readability scores. These were The Gunning Fog, SMOG (Simple Measure of Gobbledygook) and Flesh Kincaid Grade Level whose scores all gave approximate years of education necessary to comprehend the policies on a first read. Results indicate that the majority of policies require a university degree and many a post-graduate degree to comprehend them.[63]

UK user rights regarding privacy

The United Kingdom is undergoing tumultuous times in regards to privacy. Most recent is the proposal of the Communications Data Bill (2008) that will lead to the creation of a single, centralized database containing records of all emails sent, websites visited and mobile phones used by UK citizens. In 2009, this proposal was pared back and rather than data being centrally held, it is being compiled by communications providers. Quite reasonably one can argue that privacy is being eroded at an exceptional rate under the rubric of combating terrorism – a prominent popular discourse since 9/11. This has led some quarters to criticize the UK government for exploiting fear of terrorism to pass laws that infringe civil liberties. These come not only from civil-liberties groups but also from the former head of the UK security service MI5, Dame Stella Rimington, who accuses the government of using fear over terrorism to pass questionable laws. Yet, there are a range of Acts, Directives and regulations that currently protect UK citizens from potential misuse of their data.

The Freedom of Information Act (2000) is an important piece of legislation in that it gives individuals or organizations the right to request information from any public authority. With regards to private, as well as public organizations that collect data on UK citizens, UK citizens may refer to the Data Protection Act (1998) that sets rules for anyone keeping or processing personal information on individuals.[64] The Act works in two ways. First, it states that anyone who processes personal information must comply with eight principles, which make sure that personal information is

- fairly and lawfully processed,
- processed for limited purposes,
- adequate, relevant and not excessive,
- accurate and up to date,
- not kept for longer than is necessary,
- processed in line with your rights,
- secure,
- not transferred to other countries without adequate protection.

However, private and public organizations regularly break many parts of this act. For example, in November 2007, the Revenue and Customs department of the UK government lost two computer discs holding names, dates of birth, bank and address details of 25 million child benefit recipients. This is not an isolated incident. As King (2008), citing the BBC (2008) describes, other examples include the Ministry of Justice admitting in August 2008 that it had lost details of 45,000 people throughout the year, on laptops, external security devices and paper, and that 30,000 of them had not been notified. Prior to this, the Home Office announced it had lost the data of 3000 seasonal agricultural workers on two unencrypted CDs. In May 2008, the Department for Transport lost the data of 3 million learner drivers. Other data losses occurred at the Foreign Office, which lost 190 people's data in five incidents. In January 2008, the Ministry of Defence (MoD) said it had lost a laptop containing the details of 620,000 recruits and potential recruits, and some information on 450,000 referees for job applicants. In October 2008, the MoD again revealed that data on 1.7 million people who had enquired about joining the armed forces had been lost in the care of its main IT contractor, Electronic Data Systems (EDS). The BBC (2008b) also reports this data was unencrypted. In March 2008, the UK government also revealed that over 11,000 military ID cards had been lost or stolen in the past two years, while the UK Home Office launched an investigation in February after a buyer acquired a laptop on eBay that contained a disc with confidential information. As King (2008) also describes, as the government spends £12.7 billion (US$ 25.4) putting NHS patient health records onto a central computer, there have been a string of data losses from NHS hospitals. In June 2008, two NHS trusts lost unencrypted laptops containing 31,000 patient records and in May 2008, 38,000 patient records on tape were lost after being posted by the Isle of Wight Primary Care Trust. Private companies are not exempt either: Jamie Cowper, marketing director EMEA at data protection firm PGP, comments that 'I'd be surprised if nearly all companies aren't in some way contravening the Act as it currently stands, whether they realize it or not' (Leyden, 2008). For example, in August 2008, the BBC (2008a) reported how a computer containing bank customers' personal data was sold on eBay for £77. The machine contained information on several million bank customers and details of customers of three companies, including what was then called Royal Bank of Scotland (RBS) and its subsidiary, NatWest. The information is said to include account details and in some cases customers' signatures, mobile phone numbers and mothers' maiden names. A 2008 report from IT World notes that 88 per cent of IT administrators admitted they would take corporate secrets if they were suddenly made redundant. The target information included CEO passwords, customer database, research and development plans, financial reports, accounts, salaries, mergers and acquisitions plans and the company's list of privileged passwords (IT World, 2008). In addition, the survey found that one-third of IT staff still keep passwords on post-it notes whilst 35 per cent admitted to sending highly confidential information via email or couriers.[65]

The second area covered by the Data Protection Act (1998) provides individuals with important rights, including the right to find out what personal information is held on computer and most paper records (Information Commissioner's Office, 2008). This means that citizens can find out what is included on their electronically stored (and some paper versions) medical records, files held by other public bodies and files held by credit reference agencies. By letter, citizens can also use the Data Protection Act (section 11) to tell an individual or organization to stop processing information about them, if it is causing unwarranted and substantial damage or distress. The Act also means that citizens can stop unrequested direct marketing materials. This involves 'communication (by whatever means) of any advertising or marketing material which is directed to particular individuals' (Office of Public Sector Information, n.d., section 11).

There is an extensive list of where the Data Protection Act does not apply and data controllers are not obliged to observe citizen's rights. They mostly involve national security, situations where information is required by law, sensitive commercial data and interestingly information for the purposes of journalism, literature or art. Outside of the United Kingdom, yet within the European Community, this is also covered by the 95/46/EC Directive in section 5 (article 12) that describes rights of access. Member states should enforce data subjects' rights to obtaining basic information about how their data has been processed. Given the nature of distributed computing, this may present substantial difficulty for companies.

The European Union

The European Union, of which the United Kingdom is a part, requires each member state to have comprehensive statutory protections for citizens. This is born from a concern which began in the 1970s when countries such as Germany, Sweden, France and Denmark started to introduce legislation on data protection (Busch, 2006). As local national privacy protection varied this may have produced difficulty for electronic trade between member states. As a consequence wider

European legislation was created. Most relevant here is the 1995 EU Information Directive (European Commission 95/46/EC) that addresses the protection of individuals with regard to the processing of personal data and on the free movement of such data, and the 2002 EU Directive on Privacy and Electronic Communications (European Commission 2002/58/EC) concerning the processing of personal data and the protection of privacy in the electronic communications sector. Other relevant legislation includes EU Directive 2006/24/EC on the retention of data generated or processed in connection with the provision of publicly available electronic communications services or of public communications networks and amending Directive 2002/58/EC; and Directive 97/66/EC concerning the processing of personal data and the protection of privacy in the telecommunications sector. In addition, with regards to data protection, Article 8 of the 1950 European Convention for the Protection of Human Rights and Fundamental Freedoms states that

> Everyone has the right to respect for his private and family life, his home and his correspondence [and that] ... There shall be no interference by a public authority with the exercise of this right except such as is in accordance with the law and is necessary in a democratic society in the interests of national security, public safety or the economic well-being of the country, for the prevention of disorder or crime, for the protection of health or morals, or for the protection of the rights and freedoms of others. (CE, 2003)

The 95/46/EC Directive is important in that it pertains to ensure privacy for member states of the European Union. Directive 95/46/EC of the European Parliament and of the Council of 24 October 1995, on the protection of individuals with regard to the processing of personal data and on the free movement of such data, was implemented to standardize the requirements for the protection of personal information across all the countries that make up the European Union. As Bergkamp observes, the Directive has been heavily influenced by the concept of "informational self-determination" as endorsed by the German Federal Administrative Court (Bundesverfassungsgericht). This notion dictates that 'individuals should have a right to control "the image of his personality" that is presented to others through the processing of his personal data' (2003, p. 72).

Personal data, for example an address, credit card number, bank statements, criminal record and Internet Protocol (IP) address, is defined as any information relating to an identified or identifiable natural person ('data subject'); an identifiable person is one who can be identified, directly or indirectly, in particular by reference to an identification number or to one or more factors specific to his physical, physiological, mental, economic, cultural or social identity. (art. 2 a)

As Kuner (2003) describes, the most important part of this definition is that data should be related to an 'identified or identifiable natural person'. This involves a number of factors, for example who is doing the matching, what their technical capabilities are, what type of data is involved and what other data are available to aid the matching (ibid). For example, it is much easier to identify and track a static IP address rather than one that is dynamic (an address that is allocated for the period of their internet session). In regards to identification, and 'identifiable' persons, this refers to a set of data which, taken together, could make it possible to match a set of data to a person, or at least make it easier to identify a person. This stands in contrast to a demographic or some other segmentation that offers no insight into who an individual or set of individuals may be. Although deep digital analysis does not necessarily state the person's name, with reasonable effort, it is possible to link this description with a specific person. In addition, since much information flows freely across the internet, a question arises as to whether this is public information not requiring protection. Data protection in Europe instead rejected this view deeming it as covered by protection law. Kuner (2003), for example, observes that under the Italian Data Protection Act (1996) the collection of email addresses gathered for the purposes of sending unsolicited commercial email is legitimate only if the sender has received consent from the addressee.

Data control in Europe

Another point of contention has been the use of cookies, small text files placed on users' computers as they navigate the internet. These are probably the most common forms of identifying oneself to a website. They are not only used for the purposes of authentication but also serve purposes of personalization and timesaving in regards to re-entering usernames and passwords. As Bergkamp states, information used in a cookie may be deemed personal data in two cases:

> (1) if it contains personal data such as the user's name and address, or email address; or (2) if the web site that receives the data already has personal data about the specific user at its disposal, and is able to cross-link the data' [for example if the hypothetical site bought data from a list broker or direct marketing services company]. (2003, p. 75)

This would mean that direct or identification becomes possible. Under the Directive on Privacy and Electronic Communications (2002/58/EC), member states should ensure that users are provided with clear and comprehensive information about the processing of cookies and similar tools to allow the choice of opting out. In coming years however, the future of privacy and the notion of personal data will come under pressure as more and more objects, tools and hardware go online. This is due in large part to Internet Protocol Version 6 (IPv6) that allows items such as cameras, refrigerators and other domestic objects online. Article 2b of the Directive defines processing of personal data as

> any operation or set of operations which is performed upon personal data, whether or not by automatic means, such as collection, recording, organization, storage, adaptation or alteration, retrieval, consultation, use, disclosure by transmission, dissemination or otherwise make available, alignment or combination, blocking, erasure or destruction. (art. 2 b)

A data controller is defined as an entity who may be a public authority, agency or any body which is alone or working jointly with others who determines the means and processing of personal data (art. 2 d). The term data processing or processor 'shall mean a natural or legal person, public authority, agency or any other body which processes personal data on behalf of the controller' (art. 2 e). This means that data processors have a less significant role and data controllers are therefore liable for data protection violations and processors. Again, guidance offered by national versions of the data protection act is vague when it comes to determining when a company can be deemed a data controller (see Kuner, 2003, p. 62). Defining who controls the data is a complicated process given the range of actors involved. Such a network involves the telecommunications providers; access providers supplying storage and transmission; information providers; content service providers and of course individuals making use of these services.[66]

In regards to electronic commerce the storage of personal data constitutes data processing. Data may only be processed if unambiguous consent has been given (art. 7). In addition, data should only be collected for clear and unambiguous purposes. This is the purpose limitation principle (art. 6 1 b) that attempts to set boundaries for data use: (1) the data controller must specifically inform the data subject of the purposes for which the data are being collected, and (2) once it has been properly collected, it must not be used for the purposes incompatible with the original purposes. So, for example, data gathered from online registration forms should not be used for the sending of email advertising. However, as Kuner (2003) also observes, the notion of an 'incompatible purpose' is an unclear one and national laws that enforce the Directive have different interpretations.

There are five cases where consent is not required, with the third being most relevant here. First, consent is not required if processing is necessary for the performance of a contract with the data subject or is done at his request in connection with preparing to enter into a contract. Bergkamp (2003) uses the example of a service provider where, in order for certain services to be performed, the email address and the name and phone number are provided. Second, processing without consent may occur if it is in vital interests to a person, for example in medical life or death situations. Third, and most contentiously, consent is not required for the purposes of the 'legitimate interests pursued by the controller or by the third party to whom the data are disclosed, except where such interests are overridden by the interests for fundamental rights and freedoms of the data subject' (art. 7 f). The notion of "legitimate interests" is highly unclear and is interpreted differently by national legislation. The expression is not defined in the Directive, although Recital 30 of the Directive states that 'Member States may determine the circumstances in which personal data may be used or disclosed to a third party in the context of the legitimate ordinary business activities of companies and other bodies'. Although marketing and advertising would fall into this category, the Recital notes that:

> Member States may similarly specify the conditions under which personal data may be disclosed to a third party for the purposes of marketing whether carried out commercially or by a charitable organisation or by any other association or foundation, of a political nature for example, subject to the provisions allowing a data subject to the processing of data regarding him, at no cost and without having to state his reasons.

This then requires the data subject, or user, citizen or consumer, to opt-out of having the data shared. The fourth scenario where consent would not be required to process data is where it is necessary for the controller to comply with legal obligations. The fifth involves tasks carried out in the public interest.

The Directive also casts an interesting light on end user license agreements (EULAs) and the nature of opt-in/opt-out processes. The Directive states that the data subject's consent 'shall mean any freely specific and informed indication of his wishes by which the data subject signifies his agreement to personal data relating to him being processed' (art. 2 h). In addition, as stated in the second half of the Directive, it also requires that the 'data subject has unambiguously given his consent' (art. 7 a). As observed above, if security specialists do not read EULA's before clicking "I accept", "Agree" or "Continue" then is it fair to expect the rest of us to? Although the Directive is technically adhered to, it is arguable that the spirit of it is not. As such, this is a restrictive definition in that it requires the data subject – user, citizen or consumer – to be clearly aware of what is being consented to. Furthermore it also means that processing of the data going beyond that disclosed to the data subject is invalid. In Europe, consent to EULA's and similar opt-in situations may be rendered invalid if it is shown that the terms and conditions were long and opaque and/or buried away in the site so as not to give reasonable opportunity to review and understand them before accepting. There is no specific advice contained within Directive 95/46/EC on opting-in and opting-out of information sharing. Instead the general Directive only provides data subjects with a right to opt out of certain types of processing. In the United Kingdom, the IAB (2009) created a set of "Good Practice Principles" for businesses to sign up to. These companies include AOL, AudienceScience, Google, Microsoft Advertising, NebuAd, Phorm, Platform A, Specific Media, Wunderloop, Yahoo! SARL (SARL represents how the company is registered in Switzerland). These are self-regulatory principles that extend beyond consent as defined by Directive 95/46/EC.[67]

This Directive also informs the aforementioned Data Protection Act in that it stipulates the data subject's right of access to data (art. 12) in a timely fashion and that it should be understandable by laypersons. It should include types of data and what it is being used for. Other legislation that addresses co-optation, opt-in and opt-out concerns is the e-commerce Directive (2000/31/EC) that stipulates that member states adopt an opt-out regime with respect to unsolicited emails for direct marketing purposes. This is to ensure that legitimate commercial communication is identifiable and unambiguous as soon as the recipient receives it. This engenders trust and transparency and aids in the filtering from illegitimate communications that have plagued advertising and marketing activities.

The United States

In contrast to the European Union and United Kingdom, the United States has a market-dominated policy for the protection of personal information and only accords limited statutory and common law rights to information privacy, narrowly targeted by sector. This approach seeks to protect privacy through self-regulatory practices developed by industry norms, codes of conduct and contracts rather than statutory legal rights. In the United States, a long-standing area of the privacy debate is the right to be left alone. Warren and Brandeis (1890) groundbreaking article, *Right to Privacy*, raises alarm at the encroachment of yellow (sensationalist) journalism. In combating this they sifted through existing legal rights deriving a deeper principle lodged in common law that reflects the general right to be left alone. From this assessment new remedies to protect privacy could be derived (Solove, 2004). However, the US Constitution does not address privacy directly although it offers some protection. As Lanier and Saini (2008) describe, although most US citizens believe they have a right to privacy, the US Constitution does not explicitly grant this right or its protection, although the US Supreme Court has argued that the right to privacy is implicit in the First, Fourth, Fifth, Ninth and Fourteenth Amendments. The US Supreme Court however does not count every privacy infringement as a violation of a US citizen's constitutional rights. Importantly, the US Constitution only protects against state action, and many databases belong to the private sector. However, as much of the data fed to data miners and managers are derived from government census data and similar, constitutional protection may serve as a useful tool for dealing with the infractions. Acts include the Privacy Act of 1974[68] that regulates the collection and use of records by federal agencies, giving individuals the right to access and correct information in these records. In a contemporary setting this means that the right to privacy may translate to the right to be free from unwanted marketing solicitations (Miyazaki and Fernandez, 2000; Petty, 2000; also see Lanier and Saini (2008) for a complete literature review on US consumer privacy) such as pop-ups, and the right to avoid cookies and other data-mining practices. Consumer privacy has been defined as

> [T]he consumer's ability to control (a) presence of other people in the environment during a market transaction or consumption behavior and (b) dissemination of information related to or provided during such transactions or behaviors to those who were not present. (Goodwin, 1991, p. 152)

The concept of control in Goodwin's definition of privacy has been used in other such definitions, leading to user knowledge also being incorporated (for citations, see Milne, 2000; Brown and Muchira, 2004). Correspondingly, much of the privacy debate has centred on the issue of control over personal information: users should be protected from personal information being collected (for example, via cookies) and disseminated in databases without user consent or perhaps even knowledge (Caudill and Murphy, 2000; Culnan, 2000; Petty, 2000; Sheehan and Hoy, 2000; Yang et al., 2003). Issues of transparency have been raised: as Grabner-Kraeuter (2000) notes, many users are sceptical or suspicious about unclear processes of e-commerce. The common practice whereby marketers sell their information lists to other marketers compounds the problem from users' perspective of knowledge and control (Petty, 2000; Sheehan and Hoy, 2000; Baumer et al., 2004). This has raised a range of users' concerns including profiling, and the fact that users might not be informed when data that specifically identifies them as individuals are collected or disseminated (Caudill and Murphy, 2000; Petty, 2000).

The Cable Communications Policy Act (CCPA) of 1984[69] requires cable operators to inform subscribers about the nature and uses of personal information collected. In general, cable service providers must obtain prior written or electronic consent from the subscriber before collecting any personal information. The law prohibits any disclosure that reveals the subscriber's viewing habits, and it is enforced with a private cause of action (a claim or legal complaint). The statute, however, applies only to cable operators and it has a broad exception where personal data can be disclosed for a "legitimate business activity". As Solove (2004) describes, in 1986, Congress updated electronic surveillance laws when it passed the Electronic Communications Privacy Act (ECPA). The ECPA extends the protections of the federal wiretap law of 1968 to new forms of voice, data and video communications, including cellular phones and email. However, this was amended, and weakened to some extent, by some provisions of the USA PATRIOT Act (2001), an Act brought into being after 9/11 for the stated purpose of fighting terrorism in the United States and abroad. Amongst an exceedingly wide-ranging set of powers it gives the US government, the Act increases the ability of law enforcement agencies to search telephone and email communications (see Ewing, 2005 for a full exposition of this controversial law).

An interesting case example of the difficulties of the ECPA in action is exemplified by a case in 2001 involving DoubleClick and Privacy Litigation.[70] Here a group of plaintiffs profiled by DoubleClick contended that DoubleClick's placing and accessing of cookies on their hard drives constituted unauthorized access in violation of ECPA. The court concluded that the ECPA did not apply to DoubleClick because its cookies were permanent and ECPA restricted unauthorized access only to communications in "temporary, intermediate storage". In addition, DoubleClick did not illegally intercept a communication in violation of the ECPA because DoubleClick was authorized to access the cookies by the websites that people visited. Other relevant public and private US Acts include the Telephone Consumer Protection Act of 1991; the Health Insurance Portability and Accountability Act of 1996; the Federal Communications Act, 1934, 1997 (Wireless); Omnibus Crime Control and Safe Street Act, 1968; Bank Secrecy Act, 1970; Right to Financial Privacy Act, 1978; Privacy Protection Act, 1980; Computer Security Act, 1987; Family Educational Right to Privacy Act, 1993; Electronic Communications Privacy Act, 1994; Freedom of Information Act, 1966, 1991, 1996; Driver's Privacy Protection Act, 1994, 2000; Fair Credit Reporting Act, 1971, 1997; Cable TV Privacy Act, 1984; Video Privacy Protection Act, 1988; Health Insurance Portability and Accountability Act, 1996; and the Children's Online Privacy Protection Act of 1998 that regulates the collection of children's personal information on the internet when under the age of thirteen. The Gramm-Leach-Bliley Act of 1999 permits any financial institution to share non-public personal information with affiliated companies. However, the Act does state that people can opt out if they wish, though this is not simple and may lead to inaction on behalf of the consumer (Janger and Schwartz, 2002).

More broadly Solove (2004) reflects that federal laws are a start in addressing privacy concerns but do not address the underlying asymmetric power relationship. He argues that cards are stacked in favour of companies who hold our information and opting out is not easy or straightforward. Goodwin (1991, in Lanier and Saini, 2008, p. 16) identifies four sources of conflict with consumer privacy rights:

> 1) conflicts between consumer privacy and desired service levels, 2) conflicts between consumer privacy and other consumer and marketer rights, 3) conflicts between the consumer privacy and the cost of privacy protection, and 4) conflicts between consumer privacy and other societal values.

US laws are also "sectoral" dealing with privacy in some areas but not others. This again derives from US fears of government intervention in private activities and a much deeper reticence to regulate industry than in Europe. This leads to 'an approach that is reactive rather than anticipatory, and fragmented rather than coherent. There may be lots of laws, but there is not much protection' (Bennett, 1992, in Solove, 2004, p. 29).

US-based websites are not required by law to inform users about placing cookies on users' hard drives as long as cookies are not combined with personally identifiable information (Baumer et al., 2004). US law does not require general websites or online service providers to offer users the opportunity to consent to the collection of personally identifiable information, except in several specified domains (such as concerning children, medical and financial information). In contrast, EU law requires that users be notified when personally identifiable information is collected about them and the 2002 EU Directive extended the notice requirement to the use of cookies and other tracking mechanisms. In general, however, those attempting to use personally identifiable information for purposes other than the transaction for which it was collected must obtain an affirmative opt-in from users (Baumer et al., 2004).

Adware also raises specific consent and transparency issues given that much adware is bundled with other free software applications useful to users (often freeware or shareware) or downloaded covertly ('drive-by downloads') (Gordon, 2003; Briskman and Smith, 2004). Adware generates pop-ups, which infringe users' rights to be left alone and their rights to control over their desktop, particularly when pop-ups cover parts of the website users wanted to view. Pop-unders may not cover the intended website but still require users to close the window in to remove it from the desktop, forcing them to view advertisements they might not want to see. Recently, legislation to help combat spyware (including adware) has been introduced worldwide. In the United States, since May 2005, at least 27 states were considering or had passed spyware legislation. At the federal level, two spyware bills were introduced in 2004 and 2005, and three others were at more advanced stages of the legislative process (Bodden, 2005; Crawford, 2005; Edelman, 2006).

Self-regulation versus legislation in the United States

The American system of *laissez-faire* economics is predicated on a flexible system of self-regulation. Privacy is conceived as an interest that can be negotiated away whereas a contractual waiver is not necessarily effective in Europe where privacy is conceptualized as a right and not a point of negotiation. The US Department of Commerce (2005) states that

> The concern is that privacy issues differ across industry sectors, and that 'a one size fits all' legislative approach would lack the necessary precision to avoid interfering with the benefits that result from the free flow of information.

As Bergkamp (2003) describes, the United States does not have the same kinds of concern over privacy from business as Europe and is instead more concerned about state intervention. He further observes that the European Union believes that the self-regulatory approach largely used by the United States does not offer adequate levels of protection.

Safe Harbor

To this end the EU and the US Department of Commerce have agreed to abide by the EU Directive's "adequacy" requirements. These are called the Safe Harbor Principles, approved by the European Union in 2000, that help US companies avoid experiencing interruptions in their business dealings with the European Union or facing prosecution by European authorities under European privacy laws (Export.Gov, n.d). These are principles that bridge these opposing views on privacy policy and abide with the arguably more stringent European approach. As Busch (2006) describes, the US reaction to the EU's 1995 data privacy directives was surprising and perhaps nonchalant, taking for granted that data flows would be unimpeded through the exemption clause of article 26 of the Data Protection Directive. Discussion began in 1998 with the United States pursing a strategy of independent auditing through which seals would be awarded by agencies including TRUSTe and BBBOnline. However, applications were low, reinforcing the EU Commissions' scepticism of self-regulation. David Aaron, the American lead negotiator, suggested a set of principles that American companies would consider "adequate" (ibid). This meant that the United States would not have to pass comparable privacy legislation, yet opening up data flow between involved companies satisfying the European Union. US companies can opt into the programme as long as they adhere to the seven principles outlined in the Directive. As the US government webpages on export advise (ibid), these principles must provide

- *Notice* – Individuals must be informed that their data is being collected and about how it will be used.
- *Choice* – Individuals must have the ability to opt out of the collection and forward transfer of the data to third parties.
- *Onward Transfer* – Transfers of data to third parties may only occur to other organizations that follow adequate data protection principles.
- *Security* – Reasonable efforts must be made to prevent loss of collected information.
- *Data Integrity* – Data must be relevant and reliable for the purpose it was collected for.
- *Access* – Individuals must be able to access information held about them, and correct or delete it if it is inaccurate, unless the burden or expense of providing such access would be disproportionate to the risks to the individual's privacy.
- *Enforcement* – There must be effective means of enforcing these rules.

However, the EU Privacy Working Party has criticized the Department of Commerce (DOC) for not checking beforehand whether an organization meets the required criteria. Instead, in line with the spirit of self-regulation, organizations can self-certify.[71] US organizations that register with this programme, having self-assessed their compliance with a number of standards, are "deemed adequate" for the purposes of Article 25 of the Directive that states that personal data may only be transferred from the countries in the European Economic Area (EEA) to countries which provide adequate privacy protection. In addition, the Federal Trade Commission (FTC) has been somewhat weak in enforcement of its privacy policies and is only of use when a company makes a promise about privacy.

Since 1995, the FTC has monitored US self-regulatory activities in regards to online privacy. In May 2000, it issued an Online Privacy Survey to US Congress.[72] It states that 'Self-regulation alone has not adequately protected consumer online privacy, and as a result, legislation is now needed to supplement self-regulatory efforts and guarantee basic consumer protections, according to Privacy Online: Fair Information Practices in the Electronic Marketplace' (FTC, 2000). The report concludes that self-regulatory efforts alone 'cannot ensure that the online marketplace as a whole will emulate the standards adopted by industry leaders', but states that industry initiatives should continue to play an important role within any statutory structure, and 'widely-adopted seal programs could be an important component of that effort' (ibid). Examples include TRUSTe, CPA WebTrust, PrivacyBot, ValidatedSite.com, International Bureau of Certified Internet Merchants, Better Business Bureau Online Privacy Seal, Trust Guard, SiteTrust Network, Trust Report and Website Certifications.

In addition, Safe Harbor principles do not apply to US companies holding the personal data of US citizens. Individual states therefore began to address the issue of privacy, mainly by focusing on data breaches. Of particular significance is a 2003 Californian disclosure law. This is the California Security Breach Information Act (SB-1386)[73] that requires organizations that maintain personal information about individuals to inform those individuals if the security of their information is compromised. The Act stipulates that if there is a security breach of a database containing personal data, the responsible organization must notify each individual for whom it maintained information. Specifically it states that

> a state agency, or a person or business that conducts business in California, that owns or licenses computerized data that includes personal information, as defined, to disclose in specified ways, any breach of the security of the data, as defined, to any resident of California whose unencrypted personal information was, or is reasonably believed to have been, acquired by an unauthorized person.

A majority of other states have followed California's lead and passed breach disclosure laws of their own.

Online behavioural advertising: self-regulatory principles

The traditional position of US policy has been one of self-regulation although there is some federal coverage under 47 USC 551, the Cable TV Privacy Act of 1984, in that 'A cable operator shall not use the cable system to collect personally identifiable information concerning any subscriber without the prior written or electronic consent of the subscriber concerned' (Cornell, 2008). Recently there has been a significant push for privacy laws to be passed. Yet, former US presidents such as Al Gore and Bill Clinton have openly stated that self-regulation is the preferred modus operandi in regards to internet technology and that the private sector should lead in addressing privacy concerns. Responses to proposed law have been mixed but support has come from surprising quarters.

Joe Barton, the senior Republican on the House Energy and Commerce Committee, wrote to Google asking for details about the search engine's privacy practices since it acquired competitor DoubleClick. In 2008, Google responded asserting that it would support creation of a federal internet privacy law.

> Google supports the adoption of a comprehensive federal privacy law that would accomplish several goals such as building consumer trust and protections; creating a uniform framework for privacy, which would create consistent levels of privacy from one jurisdiction to another; and putting penalties in place to punish and dissuade bad actors. (Bartz, 2008)

Sceptical of Google's endorsement of a federal privacy law, Marc Rotenberg, executive director of the Electronic Privacy Information Center said that when companies push for a "comprehensive" law, they often want something that would pre-empt more stringent state laws. 'We do not want the states to have their hands tied', said Rotenberg, citing California and New York as examples of states with tough privacy laws (ibid). At the time of writing, the FTC is investigating the possibility of creating self-regulatory principles on online behavioural advertising.[74] This is in response to the acknowledgement that the advertising industry has invested, and will continue to invest, large sums of money in behavioural advertising. This hearing, held in November 2007, involving consumer representatives, industry members, academics, technologists and other interested parties, under the banner of "Ehavioral Advertising: Tracking, Targeting, and

Technology" derives from the outcome of three days of public hearings held under the auspice of, "Protecting Consumers in the Next Tech-ade" in 2006. In calling for comment and observation, the FTC has offered a definition of their conception of online behavioural advertising:

> ... for purposes of this discussion, online 'behavioral advertising' means the tracking of a consumer's activities online – including the searches the consumer has conducted, the web pages visited, and the content viewed – in order to deliver advertising targeted to the individual consumer's interests. (FTC, 2007, p. 2)

A range of issues and concerns emerged – in particular, the lack of consumer awareness of the exchange of free web content and services for personalized advertising. Both business and consumer groups pertained to value transparency and consumer autonomy. It was also recognized by all parties that there are at least some justified concerns about consumer data collected falling into the wrong hands or being used for unforeseen purposes. Given the agreed importance of these issues, the FTC now seeks to establish governing principles and, at the time of writing, is in the process of inviting comment from interested parties. As articulated more fully in Chapter 4, these five proposed principles involve greater clarity on transparency and consumer control, and clearer disclosure notices to the US public about whether individual consumers want personalized advertising; reasonable security and limited data retention; consent for changes to existing privacy promises where businesses have a legitimate need to change their privacy policies; the need for consent to – prohibition against – using sensitive data for behavioural advertising; and finally a call for additional information on using tracking data for purposes other than behavioural advertising. Randall Rothenberg, president and CEO of the Interactive Advertising Bureau (IAB), commented that

> Anti-consumer advocates are out to stifle the industry, including the FTC, which wants complete regulation of cookies themselves and could require opt-in stipulations for all online ads. As last week's hearings suggest, they feel the time for fact-finding is over, it's now time to regulate. (Kaplan, 2007)

In response to FTC proposals, a wide range of responses have been generated from a wider range of interested parties.[75] AdShuffle, an advertising server for advertisers and website publishers, unsurprisingly calls for flexibility of regulation citing an undisclosed number of people who enjoy the benefits of targeted advertising. Lanier and Saini (2008) dispute such utilitarian arguments as firms often benefit more than consumers from the use of this information, 'which may cause firms to ignore or incorrectly estimate the utility of their actions in order to fulfill their egoistic needs' (2008, p. 17). Second, 'the fact that consumers are often unknowledgeable of a firm's information practices denies them their deontological rights of respect and autonomy' (ibid).

Google also offered a rationale for behavioural advertising and their support for self-regulation. Google highlights the need for differentiation between personally identifying information (PII) and information that is not personally identifying (non-PII); the need to have a narrower definition of "behavioural advertising"; and the necessity of drawing a distinction between first-party advertising and third-party advertising (Google, 2008a). Google states that online advertising is a critical building block of free expression on the web as a generalized principle and for businesses of all sizes also. They comment that advertising is vital for the well-being of the internet economy more generally. Their letter strikes an interesting tone through the privileging of freedom online and the capacity for online advertising to provide bloggers with independence from traditional networks. Highlighting discourses of self-determinism they also cite the ability of Chris Anderson's "Long Tail[76]" and the 'ability of small businesses to prosper in ways that would not have been possible a decade ago' (ibid). They also highlight the fact that the advertising model has provided a range of content for users, as well as small businesses, that otherwise may have been impossible to offer for free.

With regards to privacy, Google, already the subject of an FTC anti-trust investigation in 2007 after acquiring DoubleClick (a company that delivers advertising across a wide range of web publishers) states that user trust is paramount and essential to building the best possible products. Responding to FTC concerns over transparency, they refer the reader to the Google Privacy Center (www.google.com/privacy). They also observe that they offer options to speak "off the record" on their instant messaging services and that many of their search services do not require personally identifying information at all. Google highlight that the current FTC definition of behavioural advertising is so broad that it encompasses any collection and any use of information. In addition, the definition sits uncomfortably with some of their search advertising products, and it does not distinguish between first-party advertising and third-party advertising, where Google allows other advertising publishers to deliver advertising across their network. Instead they suggest, and ask for, three levels of information privacy and to treat 'PII in one way, non-PII in another way, and non-PII that are closer to identifiability in a third way' (ibid).

Facebook also seeks a stronger distinction between personally and non-personally identifiable information. They came under fire for their Beacon advertising system in 2007 for an aggressive tracking system that compiled users' purchase history through vendors including Fandango and Travelocity and sent "friends" lists containing purchase behaviour. In February 2009, they also received criticism and petitions over changing terms and conditions regarding data retention if a user tries to leave. This would have given Facebook perpetual ownership of a user's contributions to the service. Such action has led Fuchs to describe Facebook as 'the platform that makes use of intellectual property rights and data surveillance most extensively' (2009, p. 43). Facebook states that most data collected is of a self-disclosed personally identifiable form and that users have control over who has access to that information. In addition, they declare that advertisers do not have access to users' profiles, although Facebook will deliver advertising for the 'expressed attributes of a profile' (Facebook, 2008).

Google also draws attention to the fact that the web has changed significantly since its inception and is difficult to assess in terms of unique webpages. They observe that

> In a Web 2.0 world, any web page could have any number of third party applications embedded in it – each one providing a different service, collecting different data, using the data in multiple ways, and providing advertising based on disparate criteria. (ibid, p. 6)

So, for example, users of Facebook and MySpace may have the same third-party applications embedded into both profile pages. This would call into question – who is the first-party advertiser, the application provider or the page provider? In addition they also describe that the first principle of being able to opt out if a user requires leads to a scenario where a user would have to give personal identifiable information to be registered as having opted out. Google also suggest that it may be 'inappropriate to mandate that choice be offered in all circumstances' if users are well informed of privacy policies and there is a competing site that users can access. They further state that 'we see no reason for specific types of choice to be mandated with respect to all (PII and non-PII) for the purpose of behavioral advertising (as defined by the proposed principles)' (ibid, p. 7). Rather than prescribing what companies do, their emphasis, rather, is on transparency of what companies actually do with the data. With regards to principle 4 that seeks to regulate sensitive data, Google requires more clarification on what constitutes sensitive data. They record concern about this particular principle, arguing that it would 'preclude legitimate contextual advertising practices, which are viewed as positive by consumers' (ibid, p. 9). Google use the example of HIV as a search term saying that users would be surprised not to see advertisements for clinics or other resources and that searches conducted when not logged in (or "authenticated") reveal nothing about the searcher's health status.

Deep-packet inspection

Phorm, formerly known as 121Media, is a company that had some of its products classified as spyware and has caused controversy in the United Kingdom and the United States through teaming up with Internet Service Providers (ISPs) to deliver advertising. This involves deep-packet inspection in which webpages requested by users are scanned and reviewed by ad-targeting software to improve advertising relevancy. Without informing consumers, ISPs in the United Kingdom and the United States have secretly turned on and trialled their targeting systems that intercept web traffic with minimal reference to it in their terms and conditions. In the United Kingdom, another set of trials have begun with British Telecom (BT), although this time on an opt-in basis. Customers are presented with a page offering safer browsing, fewer irrelevant ads and privacy protection. They are asked to either switch on BT Webwise or click the much smaller No Thanks option.[77] Representatives of AT&T, Time Warner Cable and Verizon, three of the four largest ISPs in the United States, have also stated to the Senate that they will seek permission before tracking online activities.

The system works by scanning web pages accessed by users for keywords that are then used to target advertisements. Companies such as Phorm have equipment at associated ISPs that will track activities through port 80 – the primary port used by the web system – although not to secure websites. Arthur (2008) describes that systems capture the URLs of sites visited, search engine searches, plus enough of the header data from the page to categorize it into one of a number of clusters, and that a cookie with a unique number is set on a browser when a user starts using it. Systems operate through the profiling of IP addresses as allocated by ISPs. Assuming the non-disclosure from the ISP to real world identity, this allows anonymity.

Phorm is representative of a range of interested companies including NebuAd, Project Rialto and FrontPorch that intends to use software installed in the networks of ISPs that scans particular keywords of webpage requests. This in turn generates a profile upon which targeted advertising can be delivered. Service providers Knology and Cable One acknowledged that they recently ran tests using deep-packet-inspection technology provided by NebuAd[78] to see whether it could help them serve up more relevant ads, but their customers were not explicitly alerted to the test. According to the UK's Information Commissioner (2008a), Phorm has asserted that it does not have, nor would it ever want or need, access to any information held by the ISP which would enable it to link their user ID and profile to a living individual. In addition, the ISP does not create lasting records of browsing habits in this context and does not seek to link living individuals to that information as it is profiled and sent to Phorm. Also maintaining an office in the United States, Phorm (2008) comment that they maintain three 'pillars of privacy'. These include not knowing whom the user is, the inability to know where the user has been online and that the user has the ability to turn the service off.

Answering calls for a response to FTC proposals, they also state that maintaining a one-size-fits-all regulatory policy would be burdensome and request that an opt-in approach not be implemented as this would be ineffectual for industry and consumers alike. They claim that this would be both an unworkable and non-consumer friendly standard as they would be forced to repeatedly contact consumers regarding their online privacy policies. The use of service provider data raises questions as to why service providers themselves have not attempted to extricate value from internet traffic. At present, broadband providers are not involved in advertising although there is potentially huge revenue to be generated through monitoring of online activities and the creation of behavioural profiles.

AOL (2008, p. 3) comments that proposed regulation on consumer notification also raises difficulties in terms of who the notices should be pitched to and that there is difficulty in satisfying 'the granularity requested by technologists, the legal accuracy and comprehensiveness demanded by regulators, and the ease of use needed by an ordinary user' who may quickly glance at privacy information while checking the weather online or accessing email. Instead they intend to use flash animation featuring an interactive penguin as a means of informing non-specialists as to their privacy policies. Whereas interested companies, media owners and advertising networks call for self-regulation, other parties have noted the dangers of allowing companies to police themselves. This is a fair point, for example, AOL in 2006 managed to release data to the web that included 20 million web queries from 650,000 AOL users. Should criminals or interested parties want to mine this data, it would not take long to find out the real name behind the user ID number and a variety of personal details.[79]

A case against behavioural advertising

The Worldwide Privacy Forum states that they 'have no complaint about legitimate advertising; our complaint is with intrusive and difficult-to-detect (or nearly impossible to detect) profiling of consumers that is part of certain kinds of advertising practices' (2008, p. 2). With regards to comment from companies described above, they accept that advertising is healthy for the online economy and maintain that advertising is not the concern, but rather the deep and detailed profiling of consumers. To this end they recommend that a 'much improved balance' (ibid) may be found in online and other digital advertising that do not rely on behavioural tracking activities. This then allows the support of free content, the protection of consumers and the non-necessity for regulatory enforcement.

The World Privacy Forum, seeing self-regulation as unlikely to be successful, instead calls for a mandatory scheme. One of their major concerns is the ubiquity of consumer profiling and ingratiation into online activities, business practices and business processes. Their gripe stems from the fact that this sort of regulation 'rewards the worst actors' which results in a large degree of corporate snooping. They argue that if self-regulation is going to be the way forward then it should be one with pressures of direct consumer enforcement, as opposed to industry self-enforcement. They seek regulation that is transparent and allows the public access to consumer complaints, without any amendments or adulteration. In addition, they seek for an independent audit of any enforcement scheme. Companies should also provide a yearly report to the FTC of their targeting activities, to be relayed in an aggregated form. Importantly they also call for widespread publicity for complaint mechanisms. This is likely to be one of the more uncomfortable recommendations. It states that 'any regime must require the regulated companies to publicize the chosen complaint mechanism. For example, there needs to be a *direct* link to an FTC complaint form, along with the notice of the privacy practices of the company, on appropriate web pages' (ibid, p. 4). This is to ensure greater feedback opportunities and offer consumers the ability to navigate that feedback. They also seek much clearer regulation on disclosure of what information is being collected, who is collecting it, why is it being collected and which other businesses will be using or receiving this data. Their recommendations include web 2.0 materials that involve embedded applications and interactions with third parties and also clarity on data used for establishing a price point on an item, for example where potentially a wealthy customer could be charged more for a service or product. This information needs to be disclosed to the consumer so they can find the best possible offer regardless of profile designators. They also seek clearer policies on secondary data and that expressions such as "business partners" are avoided. The World Privacy Forum has also explicitly called for separate rules on sensitive medical information. They argue there is a risk that a rush towards advertising using medical records or other healthcare information will terminally undermine consumer willingness to adopt greater use of information technology for medical information.

Genetic segmentation and profiling

In this case more precise definition of sensitive medical information is required: for instance, although cancer is treated as sensitive, genetic records are not. This presents situations that are not merely hypothetical. For example, data miners may offer genetic testing at low-cost or free to consumers. The profit would stem from the sale of a consumer's genetic profile to marketers and advertisers. Data gathered would be relevant for the period of a person's life, offering insight into all aspects of a person's development, maturity, orientation, life stages, taste development, leisure and perhaps psychological schemata. Whereas data mining and extraction have focused on geography, mobility, motivational profiling, life stage, class and other designators, there opens up the very real possibility of advertisers and marketers using genetic profiling as a means of targeting consumers. Bio-technological developments found their first commercial applications in the 1980s through genetically altering organisms to do things such as clean up pollution. However, technical, scientific and legal obstacles, not to mention ethical and risk concerns slowed development (Castells, 2001). In the 1990s, this found new expression in cloning and the ability to isolate genetic defects. Although a direct link should not be derived just yet, it is interesting and perhaps alarming to see that Google has invested $3.9 million in 23andMe, a company founded by Anne Wojciki, wife of Sergey Brin (co-creator of Google). The company mission statement found on their homepages claims '23andMe's mission is to be the world's trusted source of personal genetic information'. They offer services that allow their customers to 'unlock the secrets of your DNA today with 23andMe'.[80] Knome, a high-end personal-genomics service, is the first to sequence the entire genome at nearly three billion bases for the first private client at $350,000. In 2008, the first customer received a silver box containing an eight-gigabyte USB drive detailing his or her genome sequence (23andMe, Navigenics, and Decode instead only offer analysis of hundreds of thousands of genetic variations, to predict risk of disease or assess ancestry and other traits (Singer, 2008)). This is a service currently accessible only to the financially able although scale of provision, competition from other companies such as Illumina and lower sequencing costs will reduce prices. Prices continue to drop rapidly with Complete Genomics now offering a complete human-genome sequence for $5000 (Singer, 2008a), though unlike Knome, Complete Genomics do not offer personalized analysis for this price.

Although one may wonder who would sign up for such a Faustian deal, one only has to consider data we already readily give away online, for example, surveys about diabetes and other conditions. The temptation to gain information on genetic futures with little immediate financial expense may prove highly tempting, particularly if the service is not offered via national health services. In addition, existing privacy and oversight mechanisms may be irrelevant because of limited applicability to parts of the US healthcare enterprises. Furthermore, existing federal or state law is not likely to be of use. According to the Worldwide Privacy Forum, 'no existing regulation is likely to limit the maintenance, use, or disclosure of the information' (2008, p. 7). They also express concern over consumer perspectives and the lack of disregard for them. They highlight Google's example of HIV and advertising (described above) stating that although users of a search engine would expect search results on HIV and its effects, they do not necessarily expect to see (other) advertisements. They also do not expect that their search will be added to their personal profiles, perhaps used to assess health status and interests in the future. This is not to isolate

Google or even suggest that it would do this, but rather to say that there are fraudulent actors who may seek to benefit. Ultimately, the Worldwide Privacy Forum argues that 'Companies with a strong commercial interest in maximizing advertising dollars should not be the sole deciders about what constitutes medically sensitive information' (ibid) given the range of other interested parties including those from the medical community, patient groups and representatives, health providers and other interested individuals and groups.

2009 updates

In light of comments from industry and other interested parties and individuals, in February 2009, the FTC released an update report laying out new principles to govern behavioural advertising. Although vague in parts and "work-in-progress", proposed amendments include the recognition that potential principles should cover data that 'reasonably could be associated with a particular consumer or with a particular computer or device' (FTC, 2009, p. 25). These include clickstream data that could potentially be combined with the consumer's website registration information. It also includes

> individual pieces of anonymous data combined into a profile sufficiently detailed that it could become identified with a particular person; and behavioral profiles that, while not associated with a particular consumer, are stored and used to deliver personalized advertising and content to a particular device. (ibid)

Furthermore, the FTC also agreed with industry observers that "first party" data monitoring is expected from consumers and does not need additional regulation. These include, for example, personalized recommendations. Instead, consumer harm is more likely to come from 'practices involving the sharing of data with third parties or across multiple websites' (ibid, p. 26). This is due to consumers potentially not understanding why they are receiving advertisements from unknown marketers. Furthermore, they may not know who to contact to complain, or how to avoid the practice.

As to whether it should cover PII or non-PII, the FTC revised its definition so to account for consumer choice and that proposed regulation should cover the collection of data for online behavioural advertising if the data reasonably could be associated with a particular consumer or with a particular computer or device. In regards to privacy disclosure and giving consumers information about what advertisers are doing with data, it was recognized that existing policies are long and difficult to understand. Advertisers are being 'encouraged' to innovate more understandable signposts and disclosure tools. Revised principles for data retention involve covering all data that may be associated with a person or device, although this should be scalable according to sensitivity of data. Data, however, should only be stored 'as long as is necessary to fulfill a legitimate business or law enforcement need' (ibid, p. 38). Moreover companies cannot use data in a manner that is 'materially different from promises the company made when it collected the data without first obtaining the consumer's consent' (ibid, p. 40).

The FTC staff also changed the principles to exclude contextual advertising where an advertisement is based on a single visit to a web page or single search query. Where advertising and data collection occurs outside of the traditional website context, advertisers and marketers are told that they should develop easy-to-read and prominent methods of disclosing to the public what is occurring. Companies also need to be clear about their data users and inform consumers if they intend to use data for different purposes from which the data was originally intended.

Spam and data protection

In addition to concerns over legal marketers and advertisers are illegal advertisers. Spam is an annoyance for users, a bane for forum administrators and moderators, and a worry for those involved in web publishing and advertising as it challenges the legitimacy of digital advertising, particularly through email. This is in marked contrast to traditional formats that maintain higher trust levels. From available 2006 data (Sophos, 2006) the European Commission lists the worst twelve countries as a source of spam (see Table 6.1).

As discussed in Chapter 3, the Worldwide Web Consortium (W3C) defines spam as involving 'the mass electronic distribution of unsolicited email to individual email accounts, aliases, or mailing lists and archives' (Hernandez, 2007). The illegitimate child of the direct marketing industry, Matwyshyn (2006) observes that spam dates as far back as the 1970s when an employee of Digital Equipment Corporation sent a mass message over ARPAnet advertising his company's opening

Table 6.1 The dirty dozen spam producing countries

Position	Country	Percentage
1	United States	21.6
2	China (incl. Hong Kong)	13.4
3	France	6.3
4	South Korea	6.3
5	Spain	5.8
6	Poland	4.8
7	Brazil	4.7
8	Italy	4.3
9	Germany	3.0
10	Taiwan	2.0
11	Israel	1.8
12	Japan	1.7
13	All others	24.3

of offices in California to computer researchers. She also notes that it was through USENET that the first large-scale email harvesting by spammers began to occur. In addition to unwanted advertising, in recent years we have seen the advent of phishing that deceives recipients into believing that the unsolicited email originates from a trusted source (for example, banks and financial institutions). Spammers and virus writers have also joined forces who prey upon the unwitting and non-security savvy to gain access to domestic computers and their resources, as well as data.

Estimates signal that around 80 to 95 per cent of email traffic is unwanted spam. Levels fall and rise, with 2008 seeing a massive two-thirds drop as McColo, a web-hosting firm that served as host to a number of "command and control" centres for botnets,[81] closed down. The end of 2008, however, saw spam rising to previous levels. By infiltrating an existing botnet, Kanich et al. (2008) managed to establish that spammers they sampled make a sizable profit despite only obtaining one response to every 12.5 million emails sent. Through analysis of three spam campaigns comprising over 469 million emails they describe how much spam is successfully delivered, how much is filtered by popular anti-spam solutions, and, most importantly, how many users "click-through" to the site being advertised (response rate) and how many of those progress to a "sale" or "infection" (ibid, p. 2). Their findings also reveal that their conversion rate was well under 0.00001 per cent and that of these, all but one were for male-enhancement products costing around $100. Though a profitable enterprise, such organizations are sensitive to new defenses and require large-scale economies to develop and maintain suitable botnet software.

Spam in United Kingdom and Europe

Spam presents a challenge to legitimate email marketers and advertisers and has impacted on consumer trust in commercial communication through email. Europe has an EU-wide "ban on spam" adopted in 2002 as part of the Privacy Directive (2002/58/EC) although this has been difficult to enforce. Within the United Kingdom, a new rule titled the Companies Act 2006, formerly the Company Law Reform Bill, was introduced on 1 January 2007 stating that the name of the UK Registered company entity, the company registration number, the place of registration (that is, England and Wales) and the registered office address be included on every email marketing campaign (IAB, 2007).

Another important piece of British legislation is the UK Privacy and Electronic Communications Regulations 2003[82] that monitors electronic mail. Electronic mail refers to emails, SMS (text), picture, video and answer-phone messages. The Information Commissioner's Office[83] (2008b) states that electronic mail marketing messages should not be sent to individuals without their permission unless all these following criteria are met:

1. The marketer has obtained your details through a sale or negotiations for a sale.
2. The messages are about similar products or services offered by the sender.
3. You were given an opportunity to refuse the marketing when your details were collected and, if you did not refuse, you were given a simple way to opt out in every future communication.

The regulations say that organizations must have prior consent to send unsolicited marketing material by electronic mail to individual subscribers, unless they have obtained the details during the course of a sale, or negotiations towards one, and they give users the opportunity to object in every message. However, in relation to spam rather than legal promotional email, laws and Directives have little power or reach. The Information Commissioner's Office states that 'Most bulk 'spam' is sent from outside the United Kingdom. If you have a general problem with spam sent from overseas, then there is little help we can give' (ibid).

Spam in United States

Under the CAN-SPAM Act of 2003 (Controlling the Assault of Non-Solicited Pornography and Marketing Act) in the United States, businesses must also include the valid physical postal address of their organization. Its main provisions are as follows:

1. It bans false or misleading header information. Your email's "From," "To," and routing information – including the originating domain name and email address – must be accurate and identify the person who initiated the email.
2. It prohibits deceptive subject lines. The subject line cannot mislead the recipient about the contents or subject matter of the message.
3. It requires an advertiser's email to give recipients an opt-out method.
4. It requires that commercial email be identified as an advertisement and include the sender's valid physical postal address. The sender's message must contain clear and conspicuous notice that the message is an advertisement or solicitation and that the recipient can opt out of receiving more commercial email from the sender. It also must include the sender's valid physical postal address.

Additional fines are provided for commercial emailers who not only violate the rules described above but also

- "harvest" email addresses from websites or web services that have published a notice prohibiting the transfer of email addresses for the purpose of sending email;
- generate email addresses using a "dictionary attack" – combining names, letters, or numbers into multiple permutations;
- use scripts or other automated ways to register for multiple email or user accounts to send commercial email;
- relay emails through a computer or network without permission – for example, by taking advantage of open relays (types of email accounts that allow anyone on the internet to send email through it) or open proxies (types of servers that are accessible

by any internet user and allow anonymity as users can conceal IP addresses) without authorization.

The law allows the US Department of Justice (DoJ) to seek criminal penalties, including imprisonment, for commercial emailers who do – or conspire to

▸ use another computer without authorization and send commercial email from, or through, it;
▸ use a computer to relay or retransmit multiple commercial email messages to deceive or mislead recipients or an internet access service about the origin of the message;
▸ falsify header information in multiple email messages and initiate the transmission of such messages;
▸ register for multiple email accounts or domain names using information that falsifies the identity of the actual registrant;
▸ falsely represent themselves as owners of multiple Internet Protocol addresses that are used to send commercial email messages.

A report published by the FTC in December 2005 for Congress[84] notes that since the CAN-SPAM Act was enacted, spam volume has fallen (although levels have subsequently fluctuated). In addition, it has created a framework for lawful commercial email, legitimate marketers and "etailers" (electronic retailers) who are largely complying with it. Accordingly, the majority (89 per cent) of companies are honouring opt-out preferences.[85] The FTC confirmed this through carrying out a study with the top US "etailers" testing whether (1) commercial email from these etailers contained clear and conspicuous notice of the recipients' right to opt out of receiving future marketing messages; (2) commercial email from these etailers provided recipients with an opt-out mechanism; and (3) the etailers honoured opt-out requests made by FTC staff.

Advertising to children: the shift to online

This chapter so far has focused on privacy, information gathering, information flows and spam in Europe and the Unites States. It now turns its attention to online advertising and marketing in relation to children. In the United Kingdom, in particular, regulators have tightened regulation to children in offline media such as traditional televisual formats. Calls have come from a range of sources – including the UK group Which? – for tighter regulation on online advertising to children. They argue that food and drink companies should be banned from marketing unhealthy snacks and drinks to young children through new media such as social networking sites and text messaging. In 2008, they released a report[86] commenting that they have seen an increase in the targeting of the teen market through the use of social networking sites. They also highlight the global nature of the web and that although many brands are reducing their child-focused website content, many of the global and US sites still feature games and appealing downloads. They also state that enforcing age restrictions in mobile marketing is more difficult to monitor on mobile phones than the web.

Advertising to children in the United Kingdom has always had a large degree of regulation although not as much as other European countries such as Sweden where advertising to children under 12 is banned altogether. With regards to television, Gunter et al. (2005, p. 1) highlight a range of issue and concerns. For example, does advertising promote the trying out of unsuitable products? Does it promote a materialistic attitude? Does it encourage "pester power"? More broadly there is concern that children are exploited, particularly in the case of branded goods and associated branded lifestyles. Another key area of concern is the rise of obesity levels amongst children that has been attributed to intensive advertising of fast food and similar products. Marketers and advertisers have, however, responded to these claims by describing that a sedentary lifestyle is to be blamed. With regards to the content of commercials, the use of popular characters, both real and fictional, are believed to lead to children's inability to distinguish between advertisements and programmes. This is perhaps the crux of the argument: at what age can children differentiate between an advertisement that intends to persuade in some fashion and programming that seeks to entertain or inform? UK regulation via Ofcom has focused on the under-16s whilst US coverage is for individuals less than age of 13 under the Children's Online Privacy Protection Act of 1998. This Act involves types of digital information that can be collected from children online and how such information may be used. In the United States, the FTC (2009a) is turning its attention to examining advertising literacy and children examining what experiences of the commercial world and what consumer education will benefit them.

Oates et al. (2003) explored children's perceptions of advertising through the use of focus groups concluding that their perceptions of advertising through television are not well developed and this raises implications for the regulation of television and advertising. Written before the formation of Ofcom (the UK communications regulator established through the UK Communications Act in 2003) they observe that the Independent Television Commission regulations (who used to regulate advertising on UK television through its Code of Advertising Standards and Practice) were not adequate. The debate revolved around the notion of understanding and what this means regarding children and advertising. Oates et al. (2003) describe that advertising agency descriptions of the term revolved around differentiation, in that children can differentiate between advertising and other programming. Supporters of a ban of advertising to children claimed that very young children, three or four years of age, do not understand that there is a source behind the advertisement that intends an audience to purchase. They found that 'Children's understanding of advertising is less developed than previously thought and by no means all of the children at age 10 years expressed understanding of its persuasive intent. None of the 6 year olds demonstrated this understanding' (2003, p. 69). In addition, they found that age was not a reliable variable and that experience of shopping, handling money and the relationship between a product advertised and the product in reality often led to disappointment. Another key element of the advertising to children debate is the role of the parent. Furnham (2002) argues that that learning how to handle advertisements is educative and a useful part of growing up and that the banning of advertisements may hinder social development. Furthermore, rather than extend regulations, Furnham suggests that the most effective way of helping children to negotiate advertising and the economic sphere with its persuasive imperatives is through their parents.

Whilst this argument has obvious appeal, it perhaps fails to account for media usage in domestic settings. Regulation of television advertising for food and drink products high in fat, salt and sugar have tightened up in the United Kingdom since the February 2007 Ofcom ban including airtime on programmes and channels aimed at children aged under 16. According to the UK government's Food Standards Agency, advertisements for chocolate bars, crisps and fizzy drinks should be treated like sex, swearing and graphic violence and banned from television before 9 p.m. This has arguably sped up a migration to the internet that, as described in Chapter 2, is already extremely popular with the targeting of youth audiences. For example, the confectionary brand, Skittles, paid a six-figure sum to set up a profile on the social networking site Bebo that has attracted more than 11,000 "friends". In an interview with the *Guardian*, a Bebo spokesman described these "friends" as "brand ambassadors". Bebo users have to declare they are at least 13 although it is commonly known that much younger children use the social network site. Other popular brands, including McDonald's, Starburst and Haribo, have arguably switched to the internet to target children since new rules from the media regulator Ofcom have made it difficult to advertise during children's television programming (Smithers, 2008). Ofcom has little influence or jurisdiction online, stating that internet content is not regulated in the same way as television or radio programmes and that Ofcom has no responsibility for anything online, including websites, emails and multimedia content available through mobile phones.

This is not to suggest that regulators are entirely ineffectual as, for example, the 2008 banning of an online advertisement for a Carling beer football game on a free games website called Mousebreaker demonstrates. This was banned by the Advertising Standards Authority (ASA) for irresponsibly targeting under-18s, with research showing that 29.7 per cent of users of Mousebreaker are less than 16 years old. More broadly, a report published by the ASA reveals that where the self-regulatory rules apply in digital media, there is a high compliance rate. Of the 551 advertisements surveyed by the advertising watchdog, only 16 seemed to breach the Committee of Advertising Practice (CAP) non-broadcast advertising code representing a compliance rate of 97 per cent (ASA, 2008). This has led the ASA to claim that digital advertising is no longer the "wild west" of non-broadcast media.

The ASA (a self-regulatory body) covers online marketing and advertising to children, but it does not cover anything classed as "editorial". The non-broadcast Codes of Advertising Practice[87] (CAP) that the ASA uphold maintain that it does not cover editorial or 'website content, except sales promotions and advertisements in paid-for space' (see section 1.2, CAP, 2003). Many traditional definitions of advertising involve the following account where advertising is 'the nonpersonal communication of information usually paid for and usually persuasive in nature about products, services or ideas by identified sponsors through the various media (Bovee and Arens, 1992, p. 7). Online and wider digital blur the distinction between editorial and media therefore opening up and arguably exploiting loopholes. If greater regulation is to be created, it is in the recognition that the dynamics of advertising media have changed and that the distinction between content and media has changed. Whereas in the past the separation between media, content and advertising was relatively clear (allowing for exceptions such as advertorials), this is now highly unclear.

Editorial, as referred to in section 1.2 of the CAP, may be anything on a brand's own website. This allows McDonald's site to feature a Kids Zone section,[88] inviting children to play a range of games such as versions of Space Invaders where McDonald's logos are shot at. This also reflects another change in advertising and marketing, the greater use of pull-based media formats. Whereas traditional advertising is by-and-large push-based advertising, much commercial communication, particularly to children, is of a pull-based variety, particularly the virtual environments described in Chapter 3. Although no official sponsoring takes place on sites such as Habbo now, they have carried sponsorship in the past with Fanta placing a campaign there. Other examples of non-paid for communications include the use of Windows Live Messenger (formerly MSN messenger) by brands such as Xbox who created identities called MeeGos to target potential customers, who are urged to download branded "buddies" to their friends list.

The concern here is over the commercialization of childhood. Although regulations are tight, even the IAB (2008), the trade representative of the online advertising industry, admits the regulations are not futureproof and need updating up for all actors concerned. They state that

> the commercialisation of childhood is, without a doubt, a controversial issue. It is sometimes viewed as taboo within the marketing world. However, the bottom line is that we all have to aim for greater control. Action is required whilst we still have some say on the eventual outcome.

In March 2008, the IAB (UK) held a debate on the virtues and practice of advertising to children. Industry representatives Damon Westbury, Laurent Ezekiel and Mikhail Goldgaber cited examples of memorable advertising from childhood including Coca Cola's 'First Love[89]' and then Lego's 'Its a new toy, everyday[90]', as they claimed advertising would be a missed commodity of childhood if it was banned as children share these as memories. Their argument follows one similar to Furnham (2002), reflecting the notion that children should be exposed to the realities of the world from an early age.

Critics including Claire O'Brien of CDA (an interactive content consultancy) explain that online is still in its infancy, and in its current form should not be the testing ground for brands to advertise to children. Harbouring concerns over children and digital environments, a new watchdog is to be launched called the UK Council for Child Internet Safety (UK CCIS). This follows a report published by the Culture, Media and Sport Committee on harmful content on the internet and in Video Games[91] and is also recommended by the Byron review[92] (a review from the clinical psychologist Tanya Byron into risks faced by children from the internet and video games). These are employed to protect children from harmful content. The UK CCIS seeks to establish a public awareness safety campaign; establish measures to protect children and young people, such as taking down illegal internet sites; promote responsible advertising to children online; and establish voluntary codes of practice, with an examination of how websites handle videos or messages posted by users.

Exploiting loopholes: the case of viral

In addition to the examination of children and online advertising, viral advertising has come under the scrutiny of regulators with the ASA stating that some have 'the potential to offend or bring advertising into disrepute' (ASA, 2005). Of particular interest are viral video executions that both aim to court controversy and have created legal problems for their creators. As unpacked in Chapter 3 with a range of textual examples, viral can be described as commercial publicity passed on by users through pre-existing social networks. Viral video advertising is deemed a non-broadcasting format although it is expected to abide by broadcasting codes of honesty and decency. The ASA's position on obscenity and advertising is largely dictated by the Obscene Publications Act 1959 that defines obscenity and separates it from works of art, primarily as a means of protecting literature. This Act made it possible for publishers to escape conviction if they could show that a work was of literary merit. This meant that texts such as D.H. Lawrence's (1928) *Lady Chatterley's Lover* and its usage of words such as "fuck" and derivatives were acceptable in an artistic context. Although the 2008 ASA report cited above claims that all 551 examples of digital advertising collected was compliant with the Codes of Advertising Practice (CAP), the report also contained a curious clause noting 'that many of the virals we did not include in the survey for remit reasons pushed the boundaries of taste, decency or social responsibility and would have breached the Code'.

Although it is not covered in the Codes of Advertising Practice, the CAP comments that the ASA will deal with each complaint on its merit. The CAP states that it

> recognises the limitations on the application of the Code as set out in clauses 1.1 and 1.2, including those in respect of all editorial content and private correspondence and much commercial information on websites. But advertising virals are not excepted from the Code merely by having originated on a website or by being forwarded-on by consumers. (CAP, 2006)

The CAP also reminds advertisers that a range of other regulations can be brought to bear. These include the Electronic Commerce (EC Directive) Regulations 2002, the Privacy and Electronic Communications (EC Directive) Regulations 2003, the Communications Act 2003 and the Video Recordings Act 1984. It has also come to the attention of regulators in the United Kingdom with the Consumer Protection Against Unfair Trading Regulations (CPRs) having come into force on 26 May 2008. Cynics in some quarters are hailing the death of viral video marketing. As iMedia Connection note, the main area that will be affected is guerrilla-marketing techniques that involve 'falsely claiming or creating the impression that the trader is not acting for the purposes relating to his trade, business, craft or profession, or falsely representing oneself as a consumer' (Button, 2008). Viral advertising thus remains embroiled in debate over its legality. Although viral may be covered by the letter of the regulation, monitoring it is a much harder activity, particularly in regards to authorship.

The role of viral is further explored in the next chapter, in regards to notions of creativity. Creativity is unpacked from a range of perspectives, particularly in terms of the discursive formation of advertising agency notions of creativity. It also explores tension and potential in the relationship between technical innovation and creativity, and the creative opportunities that current and nascent digital media offer.

▸ To what extent do you agree that in network societies, privacy should be subject to self-regulation?

▸ Ideologically, technologically and legally, what is your position on opt-in versus opt-out debates?

▸ What in your view constitutes sensitive data?

▸ To what extent is current privacy debates a war of PR, articulation and definition?

▸ What public responsibilities, if any, do internet service providers have?

▸ Genetically targeted advertising: Frankenstein-type science fiction or a logical extension for information hungry market researchers?

▸ What should a privacy disclosure notice consist of and how would you strike the balance between detail and readability?

▸ To what extent should we be concerned about digital marketing to children: does it represent the commercialization of childhood, or should children be exposed to commercial realities of the world from an early age?

7　Creativity, Science and the New Consumer

It is worth flagging up at the outset that this is not a "how to" chapter. For a book on how to produce creative digital advertising have a look at Barry (2008) that contains useful techniques such as how to approach interactive advertising, in addition to traditional media. This chapter, rather, aims to offer some definitions of what creativity in advertising is, inquire into manifestations of creativity and advertising in the digital environment, and consider the impact of new technologies on digital advertising. As such this chapter considers the relationship between creativity and technological innovation.

A brief review of the history of advertising

Many early advertising practitioners championed a scientific approach to advertising. This approach grew out of Taylorism, scientific management approaches to managing production and consumption and a need to professionalize and delineate an agency's function. Around the turn of the nineteenth century, advertising businesses were steeping themselves in the marketing concerns of their clients and gradually freeing themselves of their ties to the press from which the origins of the advertising business derive. Leiss et al. (2005) describe that by 1917, 95 per cent of national advertising in the United States was handled by agencies. In 1923, Claude Hopkins wrote that

> The time has come when advertising has in some hands reached the status of a science. It is based on fixed principles and is reasonably exact. The causes and effects have been well analyzed until they are well understood. The correct method of procedure has been proved and established. We know what is most effective, and we act on basic laws. (Hopkins, 1998, p. 213)

The practice of advertising here is a process of trial, error, review, the learning of principles, application, more feedback, refinement and the use of data through tools such as coupons and other methods of enabling feedback to understand what works and what does not. Hopkins describes that his agency ascertained the cost of advertising, which promotional materials worked and which did not. This involved analysis of headlines, settings, sizes, pictures and the disallowance of guesswork. He further states that 'no wise advertiser will ever depart from those unvarying laws' (ibid, p. 216). They, of course, did. Many of the most famous practitioners seek, and have sought, to inspire consumers, their clients and their colleagues. As widely chronicled (Berger, 2004), the 1960s saw a shift in gear in advertising that has widely been dubbed "the creative revolution". Without doubt, this had to do with a wider cultural post-war shift taking effect in art, architecture, literature, photography and elsewhere. This involved declining interest in the old markers of status and instead a 'new dynamic of "cool" and authenticity' (Leiss et al., 2005, p. 316). In addition, the 1960s also saw the explosion of mass media. In this period the advertising agency Doyle Dane Bernbach (DDB) famously challenged the car buying US public to "Think Small" in a period where bigger was still commonly perceived to be better. It asked its audiences to think about social conformity and look at the funny little German Volkswagen car with fresh eyes. Although it may be easy to see advertising's involvement in counterculture as mechanisms of assimilation in action, Leiss et al. (2005) suggest that Bernbach shared an affinity with many of the youth movements.

This is not to suggest that earlier advertising had not been "creative". Although earlier decades are stereotypically characterized by the dominance of the unique sales proposition (USP), there are many examples of advertisements that do not fit into the reason-why approach and have more to do with what we consider as contemporary advertising. However, as noted above, the 1960s initiated a new way of making and looking at advertising. In the United States, DDB set in motion a sense of wit and irreverence in advertising to be found in innovative layouts, tight copy and a dedication to the product or service. In the United Kingdom, this shift culminated in work produced by Collett Dickenson Pearce (CDP) who in the late 1960s and 1970s produced a range of advertising still memorable for brands including Heineken with campaign lines such as "Heineken refreshes the parts other beers cannot reach" living well beyond its birth date of 1974 (Tungate, 2007). Other countries such as Thailand, Germany, Sweden, Brazil, Argentina, Australia, New Zealand, India and South Africa, amongst many others, are all now producing globally recognized and award-winning creative work.

Around thirty-five years from the 1960s that saw the mass adoption of television as a mainstream media form, advertising from the mid-1990s has experienced tectonic shifts in media usage. Despite being an extremely young sector, digital advertising itself is rapidly changing.

Whereas only a few years ago digital media options included only banners and pop-ups, there is now a plethora, many of which are described in Chapter 3. When asked how well the advertising community is adapting to change, Randall Rothenberg, CEO of the Interactive Advertising Bureau, a trade group, responded, 'Badly. The structure of the agency business has not kept pace with the needs of marketers' (Taylor, 2008). Despite being an industry obsessed with the nebulous term, "creativity", the advertising business has been slow to make engaging online digital content. Part of this situation stems from the fact that digital is attractive primarily as it tempts its advertisers with greater accountability, or return on investment, as required by Hopkins. Creativity has thus arguably taken a backseat whereas search-based advertising has grown exponentially, for example. However, advertisers and their agencies now have an extraordinary range of digital channels to solicit consumers with, and there is creativity to be found in the planning of media vehicles used to engage consumers. In some cases the media option is inextricable from the creative endeavour due to the novelty of some new technological platforms and the way that they engage people. Equally fundamental is the recognition that online and wider digital media should not be thought of as another form of broadcast media. Since the formation of an identifiable advertising business around the turn of the past century, in many ways little has changed. Copy moves in and out of vogue and much advertising has become more surreal in how they tell the story of their brands. There remains among many, however, the mass media mindset where audiences are an entity to be persuaded and sold to. There are many distinct qualitative and textual differences between digital and traditional media. People use them differently and have different expectations. For instance, whereas in television there is an unspoken contract that it is acceptable to disrupt television viewing every 20 minutes or so, this simply does not hold in a digital environment. Although digital has its fair share of push advertising, more strategic advertisers and their agencies are looking to pull-based advertising that engages, gives and demands something of a potential, or existing, customer.

Creativity: central but poorly understood

What is creativity in advertising? This is a long-standing question that needs addressing. It is a hazy term that suffers much abuse in the advertising industry and other creative industries that sit so close to the centre of economic action, particularly in small countries such as the United Kingdom. Trevor Beattie, sometimes cast as the enfant terrible of British advertising, comments that the best creative agencies and practitioners should be 'able to help a client company satisfy its stakeholders' interest for earnings, whilst also creating a strong demand for its products' (Yeshin, 2005, p. 282). Johar et al. (2001) similarly observe that organizational theorists consider creativity as something that gives businesses competitive advantage, aids in the generation of new and useful produce and allows companies to respond to environmental opportunities.

In addition, creative work acts as advertising for the agency and the benchmark by which they are judged. It is also the criterion that tells a client that an agency can do more than the next with the same level of budget. Creativity is thus important both externally and internally. Within an agency, creativity may be appreciated at differing levels and with different degrees. Tensions and battles between scientific empirical-based approaches and belief in unverifiable creative ideas were played out in copy tests of years gone by. This in large part stems from the diverse range of personalities working in an advertising agency. A scientist, or at least a researcher with social science inclinations, working for an agency will see things very differently from a creative director, for example. Raymond (1978) describes that each of the interested individuals, the creative team, management and scientists, all lay claims to "the real world". The problem stems from different types of proof needed for each belief. He observes that

> The creative artist in advertising *knows* when he communicates effectively because he simulates the receipt of that communication within himself and finds that it works. The manager *knows* when he has made a correct marketing decision – with or without the help of evidence – when he observes its presumed effects on the earnings of his firm. The scientist *knows* when he has developed a usable theory or prediction because he exposes it to rigorous tests by which it could be falsified, and it has passed these tests. (1978, p. 59)

Although it is difficult to crystallize, many agency staff feel it is clear what uncreative advertising is. Advertising that solely operates on the basis of conversion to sales appalls many in the advertising business. However, as Stafford and Faber (2005) bear out, although intrusive advertising may be irritating, it does not mean that it is ineffective.

Sullivan (2008) agrees, noting that sometimes the most grating execution will stimulate sales and also arguing that creative advertising may change the way people think about a brand. Wilmhurst and Mackay (2002, p. 187) observe that creativity is a matter of expressing clearly defined ideas in a compelling way to attract and interest specified people in known situations and motivate them to react in a particular fashion. Although the application is difficult to discern, stereotypes of practitioners, definitions and formal properties are not. The consensus from digital agencies as well as traditional agencies is that there remains the need for "Big Ideas". These are ideas that underpin advertising that translate across media, including digital, however different its properties may be.

In James Webb Young's (2003) *A Technique for Producing Ideas*, first published in the 1940s, Young observes that ideas for advertising are 'nothing more nor less than a new combination of old elements' (2003, p. 15) and that the ability to bring old elements into new combinations depends on the ability to see relationships. Creativity then has to do with the generation of new ideas or new associations between old ones. It is born from an understanding of cultural discourses and the often-arduous process of reconfiguring these in a unique fashion. This is not to suggest that creative output is an entirely contrived artefact: it is often the case that creative materials are founded upon collisions of ideas, frisson, accidents and juxtaposition. Traditional offline advertising creativity draws upon a huge array of discourses and genres (Kraidy and Goeddertz, 2003). These include film, illustration, typography, art, music, literature, photography, fashion, architecture, environmentalism, gender, sexuality, subcultures and ethnicity amongst sources, not to mention practices unique to digital culture. These discourses, or genres, are employed as methods of codifications to aid in delivery and acceptance of brands' values (Hackley, 1999).

Creativity, as applied to the generation of ideas to create advertising with, is hard to pin down. In reference to traditional advertising formats, Jones (2004) suggests that creativity and the hallmarks of successful advertisements are found in three ingredients. These include, first, mention of properties of the brand, in both functional and non-functional terms; second, the introduction of a new idea at the symbolic level, for example diamonds and love, cigarettes and masculinity or perhaps more surreal additions to campaigns as with Absolut vodka or the croaking frog of Budweiser; production values provide the third ingredient including the perfection of body copy, camera work, quality of illustrations, typography, lighting and other aspects relating to production. These last elements however will in no way mask an inadequate advertising idea.

Strategy

As Bell (1992) points out, creativity in advertising is slightly different from creativity found in other spheres due to the constraints of marketing objectives, budgets, the advertising brief, hierarchical approval of creatives' work (copywriters, art directors, creative directors and others involved with the creative department within an advertising agency) and collaborative constraints. Johar et al. (2001) similarly note that creative creations in advertising should work and that anything else is miscreation. An advertisement then is not considered a creative success in the real world unless it achieves a client's communication objectives (Kover et al., 1997).

In advertising, the role of a creative department within an advertising agency is to give form to the strategy for the advertisement – strategy consisting of the target market, how the advertisement should speak to the target market (for instance, tone of voice), and the media best suited for reaching that target market (McStay, forthcoming 2009). Strategy can also be described as that which 'sets out the underlying plan and objectives for an advertisement or an advertising campaign, and it is related to all the other elements in a manufacturer's blueprint for its brand' (Jones, 1999, p. 156). Key factors may include a client background document and a strategic brief. This will describe the target market, the intended message and the communication objective. It may include elements such as campaign lines or slogans, an emotional tone (or tone-of-voice), brand equity position, format (for example, problem-solution), end benefit demonstration, and/or slice-of-life platform (Johar et al., 2001).

Strategy is also the part of the process of advertising that points and directs creative components and processes in the right direction. In addition, advertising strategy differs significantly from agency to agency and may take on different meanings depending on who is using the term (ibid, p. 160). However it manifests, strategy is important to the final outcome as well written, precise strategy helps creatives understand limits on what can and cannot be said in the advertising, and it helps to channel creative energies towards imaginative expressions and solutions to an advertising problem. In essence it is the "what do we want to communicate" versus "how are we going to communicate it". As such, creativity is perhaps the visual and aural component of the strategy made manifest.[93] For many management teams, creativity is accountable to sales and tangible benchmarks of attitudinal persuasion that clients and agency management can agree upon (Mehta, 2000). Another way of understanding effectiveness is not to consider sales as the direct function, but rather the end product of an outcome of a change in consumer behaviour (Bullmore, 1999).

Researchers repeatedly note the paucity of literature on creativity in both online and offline advertising sectors (Boyd, 2006; Cunningham, et al., 2006; El-murad and West, 2004; Plummer, 2004; Romeo et al., 2004; Sasser et al., 2007; Smith and Yang, 2004; Till and Baack, 2005; Zinkhan, 1993). Only a handful of researchers have investigated creativity in advertising empirically (Boyd, 2006; Johar et al., 2001; Koslow et al., 2003; Till and Baack, 2005; Sasser et al., 2007). Smith and Yang (2004) also note that major reviews of the conceptual space of creativity lack any significant reference to advertising (citing Amabile, 1996; Sternberg, 1999). Although this is starting to be redressed with the expansion of the discourse on the cultural and creative industries from the UK government (House of Commons, Culture, Media & Sport Committee, 2007) and, correspondingly, academia (for instance, see Bilton, 2007), few books on creative industries significantly examine advertising (Hartley, 2007; Hesmondhalgh, 2006; Negus and Pickering, 2004).

The creative practitioner

Koslow et al. (2003) describe that within the advertising industry itself, there are highly differing views as to what constitutes creative advertising. Outside of the industry there is even more disagreement. Stone et al. (2000), for example, found that while 70 per cent of the advertising that consumers remembered and liked was categorized as creative by trained judges, 47 per cent of strongly disliked advertising was also categorized as creative by the judges. In contrast to awards and recognition, creatives argue that effectiveness criteria have little to do with how advertising works and that it is the "creative" (execution over strategy) element that gains the brand greater exposure. El-murad and West (2004) also observe that despite the most systematic and scientific approaches towards developing award-winning creative ideas, the evidence suggests it is a random process (2004, p. 188). As Koslow et al. (2003) describe, creatives working for agencies highlight advertising that is artistic over advertising that is "on strategy", as preferred by account managers with strategy involving the matching of advertising messages to target markets and their motivations to try a new product or remain with an existing brand. The most valued advertising by both creatives and management is that which manages to stay on strategy, yet maintains a high degree of divergent creativity – as described below (Koslow et al., 2003).

Within the hermeneutic and everyday environment of agency life, divergent and relevance factors are often fought over. Creativity is often synonymous with divergence whereas relevance draws parallels with uncreative, "safe" advertising. As account executives are directly answerable to clients there is often a tendency for account executives within an agency to err towards campaign ideas and executions that rely upon relevance in contrast to divergent thinking. Kover et al. (1995) similarly note that within agencies there is a constant struggle between those who create the advertising (creatives) and advertising managers who insist that it be effective. Kneller (1965) similarly describes creativity as being exploratory, innovative and venturesome whilst uncreative thought is characterized by caution, being methodical and conservative.

Artistry and the myth of genius

Where this creative capacity comes from is a difficult question. It involves interplay between psychological and social forces. In Western societies creativity is often synonymous with the notion of genius. Weisberg (1993) describes this as the "myth of genius". This has its roots in religious art and thinking whereby people are vehicles for higher powers and original ideas. In less religious terms, creativity is something done by people who "think different" or "think outside the box". It is ascribed a status as a different type of thinking that allows people to break conventional shackles and to connect previously unseen phenomena or ideas. Another stereotype of genius and creativity is the Rimbaudian notion of creativity that manifests through pain, mania and affective disorders. In this account of creativity, pain along with anxiety and sadness is deemed by poets such as Rimbaud and Baudelaire to signal an increased penetration of truth and creative endeavour (Kaplan, 1978). Interestingly there is little correlation between the output of work produced by artists and depth of mental affliction.[94] In addition, a large number of poets, musicians, artists and perhaps advertising creatives may exhibit manic behaviour because these occupations and lifestyles are assumed to be the refuge of individuals with such afflictions. This suggests that the clustering of such personality types may mean nothing more than that they can function in that field. Weiseberg (1993) further observes that to function as a chemist, for example, one needs to maintain an academic or industrial position that someone with such swinging moods and temperament may have problems holding down.

Thus the role of artist and advertising creatives are often blurred. White (2000, p. 13) comments that creatives 'are sometimes frustrated poets and artists manqués, and less disciplined than may seem ideal'. The genius-driven creativity that romanticism emphasizes is individual, subjective, irrational, imaginative, personal, spontaneous, emotional, visionary and transcendental (Weisberg, 1993). Notions of the creative as artist stem from foregrounding the individual before the collective. This is also expressed in the advertising industry press. As Nixon (2003) also points out, the UK's advertising newspaper, *Campaign*, frequently refers to creatives in the same manner as premier league footballers moving from agency to agency giving a sense that these agency folk are both privileged and of more importance than planners or account managers. This is born in part from the dramatic success that the London scene enjoyed in the 1980s through the expansion of Saatchi and Saatchi, and Bartle Bogle Hegarty (BBH). In terms of the creative department, Nixon also observes that creativity within advertising is valorized by 'newness, breaking new creative boundaries and establishing new genres' (2003, p. 89). In Nixon's study of agency life, in creative team's pursuit of newness, they coded themselves in generational terms in pursuit of the new thing that would win themselves industry-recognized awards and financial rewards. For advertising creatives, artistry is not without a competitive streak.

Advertising creatives are sensitive to situations that will serve as vehicles for artistic expression with possible universal significance. They tend to be observational people interested in fellow humans, trends, everyday minutiae, mini-life dramas and the ability to conceptualize these vignettes for advertisements and vehicles to express brand values. In addition, the most successful creatives do not rely on some magical process but rather are able and willing to generate a large number of approaches to a creative brief. The production of numerous ideas is more profitable than pursuing one doggedly and obsessively. The latter approach imposes unnecessary constraints. Johar et al. (2001) also empirically observe that which many practitioners intuitively know: it is not necessary for creative partners to get along and be alike as this results in the generation of ideas that are similar and may prove an impediment to the creation of numerous answers to a creative problem. Weisberg (1993) observes that criterion for calling something creative is that it be novel, or that there is a degree of transformation. For creativity to have any meaning in advertising, it must also have value and be appropriate to the demands of a situation or brief. To suggest otherwise could involve a situation of free association, irrelevance and an inability to address the problem at hand. In addition, what is perceived as creativity is often the end of a long process involving research, strategy, brand orientation and consumer insight that creative work is intended to illustrate. Weisberg observes that

> The creative achievement can be extraordinary because of the effect it produces, rather than the way in which it was brought about. As a rough analogy, the straw that breaks the camel's back is not extraordinary qua straw, but it is extraordinary because of the effect that it has on the camel. (1993, p. 10)

Whereas many quarters have struggled with ascribing forms of value to creativity, fortunately in advertising that task is somewhat easier, where there are a variety of benchmarks including client sales, more business from the client, colleague esteem and awards. Finally, in this regard it is misguided to conflate art and advertising. In advertising there is a problem to be solved or a task to be undertaken, as is the existence of a deadline (Bullmore, 1999).

Roles and new craft skills

All agency and industry representatives consulted for this book highlighted the need for traditional craft skills and understanding of the core fundamentals of producing ideas for advertising campaigns that are strong enough to work in digital in addition to traditional media forms. Tom Evans, founder of Mook, stresses that 'the role of traditional skills is still paramount and they [creatives] must be able to think in terms of strong ideas that may or may not be part of a wider integrated campaign' (Interview, 05/11/07). Neil Hughston of Saatchi and Saatchi Interactive describes that they have added a third element to the creative team. Whereas the 1960s and 1970s saw closer working relationships between copywriters and art directors, there is now a third element in the mix, the information architect or the developer. Other roles that may combine with traditional creative teams are designers, creative technologists, social media experts as well as planners. He describes that

> There are of course still the pure disciplines within that as there
> are within traditional advertising: so you will have a need for copy-
> writers, you will have a need for graphic designers, you will have
> a need for art directors, you will have a need for an information
> architect, you certainly will have a need for a very good techno-
> logical understanding. What we do here is marry technical very
> firmly to strategic creativity so with we have a three skill-set that
> wrap themselves around the business challenge set for them by
> a client and therefore develop an organising thought with media
> comm's next to it because if you involve media comm's understand-
> ing and know-how, you get a better informed creative brief and
> different things will spin out to create better work for the client.
> (Interview, 24/11/07)

In discussion of the future of advertising, the role of craftsmanship, art
direction and copywriting he also adds

> I'm quite determined and sort of manifest in my statement of trad-
> itional creativity and traditional agencies are by no means finished,
> and they are absolutely integral to the further development of
> creativity and interactive creativity in the interactive space. And
> one of the reasons for that is probably because filmic executions
> are becoming a lot more common and easy to do so why on earth
> wouldn't we work with TV producers to do something that, that sits
> on someone's laptop? Of course you would because you want to use
> their expertise. You need art director's knowledge of how to make
> commercials. (ibid)

This need for traditional art directional skills in digital is highlighted
well in the entries for the 2008 D&AD awards (titled Digital vs.
Antidigital) with many featuring video. For example the Black Pencil
Online Advertising Award went to Uniqclock[95] whose online video featured dance routines performed by models dressed in Uniqlo clothing.

McCann Erickson Brazil similarly won D&AD art direction awards
for online work for the Salvation Army.[96] This uses illustration, sound
and text to highlight the plight, rights and dignity of children living
on the streets in Brazil. The upmarket advertiser, Louis Vuitton,[97] has
also made interesting use of the web and traditional craft advertising skills by focusing on travel "journeys" taken by their celebrity
ambassadors, such as Andre Agassi, Steffi Graf, Catherine Deneuve,

Uniqclock

Mikhail Gorbachev and Keith Richards who describe their favourite cities. These are represented through sound, photography, video, original score and other content. Although digital media presents unique advertising opportunities, many traditional craft skills are still required to express these ideas. To suggest that these will wane as digital becomes a pre-eminent platform is to both misunderstand the broad base that digital offers and also the necessity of traditional skills of visualization and representation found in traditional art direction and graphic understanding. Digital media does, however, bring closer together the roles of creatives and media planners to best leverage advertising opportunities digital platforms provide.

Science versus romanticism

Competing with advertising and media agencies, both traditional and digital, are the technology giants. Whereas creativity traditionally has to do with the maverick, the latest incarnation of technologically determined advertising involves technology behemoths such as Google and Microsoft who arguably care little for advertising practitioners' preoccupation with creativity. Campaign performance and understanding of audiences, context and behaviour are more important for them. They instead foresee advertising as an enterprise based on relevance for consumers (Smith and Yang, 2004) and clearer returns on investment for advertisers. The drive and incentive to refine advertising into a science harkens to a period known as the "Wanamaker era" in the 1870s when the Philadelphian merchant John Wanamaker, who was a large advertiser and owner of a large in-house advertising department, famously commented, 'I know half my advertising is wasted. The trouble is, I don't know which half' (Economist, 2006, p. 69). What this means is that although large amounts of money are spent on advertising, it is difficult to work out which parts of the advertising programme are working and which aspects of a campaign are do not.

New media, new science?

The digital advertising business appears to be undergoing a revolution of sorts. Whilst new media are characterized by the promise of revolution and the "Next Big Thing", there do seem to be tectonic shifts occurring in the way that advertising operates. Philosophically there appears to be a stark contrast between the artists and the scientists. Media owners such as technology giant, Google, embody the science of mapping and the algorithm. Frank Wilczek quotes the German physicist Heinrich Hertz regarding Maxwell's equation on electromagnetic theories of light:

> One cannot escape the feeling that these mathematical formulae have an independent existence and an intelligence of their own, that they are wiser than we are, wider even that their discoverers, that we get more out of them than we originally put into them. (in Langville and Mayer, 2006, p. 30)

The belief of Larry Page and Sergey Brin in the abstract power of mathematics holds sway (Battelle, 2005). This sentiment derives from the wider enlightenment project, modernity, and the power of number and reason. Claude Hopkins further describes that 'where they long exist, advertising and merchandising become exact sciences. Every course is charted. The compass of accurate knowledge directs the shortest, safest, cheapest course to any destination' (1998, p. 215). As discussed in Chapter 5, this ties in with wider discourses of administration, controlling and managing complex tasks. Cindy Gallop, a former chief executive of the New York office of the advertising agency BBH suggests that Google 'clearly wants to replace the advertising industry in its totality' (Pfanner, 2008). Many agencies and their executives fear that the technology companies want to extend their remit into the traditional sphere and 'transforming, as they see it, a business built on creativity to one controlled by the sterile algorithms of computer programmers' (ibid).

Perhaps agency fears are based on a more fundamental philosophical concern: the death of creativity? This applies not only to their search programmes but also to their optimization services that test a website's effectiveness for free. Creativity has always been a quintessentially human endeavour, so for agencies to have their modus operandi challenged by young technology upstarts who have so easily leveraged dominance in advertising through applied mathematics is not only threatening but also deeply galling. Despite this, traditional practitioners and digital agency practitioners agree that good ideas are paramount and this must still be the foremost driver of any advertising campaign. In interview, Amy Kean of the IAB stressed that agencies (and their clients) have been guilty of following media trends and the next new "Big Thing", possibly losing focus of the core advertising messages. Instead she calls for a deeper understanding of the properties of each medium and its communicative capabilities (Interview, 10/12/07). These capabilities involve moving beyond conceptualizing users as passive entities and understanding them as communities to be engaged with.

Artificial intelligence?

Many attitudes towards digital are redolent of the original Luddites who destroyed mechanized looms in textile factories in the nineteenth century. A more contemporary, although aligned, question is this: can the role of the creative be replaced by digital technology? In the utilization of media that are essentially dynamic, programs and software respond and interact with users in new, and perhaps personalized, ways. In 2004, Burger King released an advertising campaign entitled "Subservient Chicken[98]" developed by the agency Crispin Porter and Bogusky.

The advertisement is considered as one the most successful viral campaigns to date. This involved a person dressed in a chicken suit who would respond to virtually any query or command given in a text bar below the main televisual frame. Although the kooky chicken was interesting, what was most gripping was the amount of responses it offered to outlandish and eventually rude queries. It was driven by a solid creative idea of being able to "Have it your way" and executed in an unusual fashion that made use of new technology. Daniel Solana, Creative Director and founder of DoubleYou, observes that

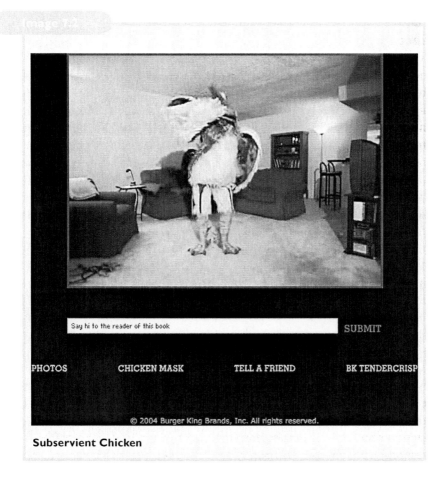

Subservient Chicken

digital advertising objects are defined and generated by means of programming codes. He comments that 'They [advertising items] are completely different in nature. They are not static, unalterable ads, to be consumed. This is organic matter that can evolve and develop in response to the consumer's interaction. They behave' (Wiedemann, 2006, p. 180). Although all media have properties that both limit and expand opportunities of what is achievable, few media can pertain to artificial intelligence, or at least the mimicking of it. Ubiquitous networked computer technologies are still at a very early stage and it would be churlish to suggest that coming avatars or advertising objects will not be able to pass the standard interpretation of the Turing (or Cartesian) test. As the semantic web comes online and rules of inference that allow automated reasoning become the norm, systems that reflect humans' wide-ranging needs will become more normalized.

Interactivity

Perhaps because of ambiguity surrounding the word creativity, perhaps because of the lack of advertising focus in academic thought on creativity and perhaps because of a drive to understand one of the most obvious features of digital channels, it is interactivity rather than creativity that has received the most intense academic scrutiny among digital advertising scholars. The interest and will to interactivity and immediacy is not a new phenomenon to Western culture; it is in fact a defining characteristic, at least in the sphere of representation. Bolter and Grusin (1999) point to the well-cited example of Alberti's window being central to understanding immediacy along with televisual media. Leon Battista Alberti, the fifteenth-century Italian Renaissance artist, was central to the development of three-dimensional representations on two-dimensional canvasses. Alberti (1972 [1435]) stated that "On the surface on which I am going to paint, I draw a rectangle of whatever size I want, which I regard as an open window through which the subject to be painted is seen" (in Bolter and Grusin, 1999, pp. 24–25), in other words, importing viewers into the artist's space and creating a portal whereby the viewer is confined by the representation presented to them. As Manovich (2003) points out, it is no accident that the two key formats for computer display are portrait and landscape. These techniques still hold sway in the age of computer representation and have done so through the advent of painting, photography, film and television. Immediacy is still contrived through aesthetic interlays of transparency, linear perspective, erasure and automacity, which as Bolter and Grusin (1999) rightly point out is still very much at work in the digital arena. So, on many levels the interactive aspect of new media is not that new. Many of the visual tropes are the same as those that have been played out in other visual media. This checking of the historical rear-view mirror serves well to illustrate that digital advertising and the modalities of representation it facilitates have unique characteristics, albeit derived from not only televisual media but also wider techniques of representation.

Interactivity and advertising

Interactive advertising when done well builds richer, deeper and engaging relationships, but then the same can be said of successful advertising campaigns in that they foster long-lasting brand relationships often characterized by trust and goodwill. It is characterized by high levels of engagement that extends beyond the advertising. For example, the telecommunications company, Orange, teamed with the organizers of UK's Glastonbury festival to play a GPS-enabled form of "Spot the Bull"[99] created by POKE. Another example from POKE (winner of Creative Agency of the Year 2008 at the Interactive Marketing and Advertising Awards), involves a balloon race across overlays on thousands of sites across the internet with players navigating as they go.[100] Such creations are emblematic of interactive approaches to media where consumers, to some extent, can take control of media, marketing and advertising. Crudely put, it is the eventuality of media innovation, manufacturing and marketing that for the past 100 years has become more involving and personalized. Matt Freeman, CEO of Tribal DDB Worldwide, puts the scenario thus:

> Digital media allow the consumer to become a part of the campaign. The most powerful new medium we have discovered is not digital, but rather consumers themselves. (Wiedemann, 2006, p. 8)

This observation bears some truth. Investigating the impact of personal factors, Jee and Lee (2002) describe that interactivity has much to do with an individual's need for cognition, product involvement, product expertise and internet skills and experience. Johan Tesch, of Lowe Tesch, offers a similar sentiment noting that the advertising industry has tried to communicate with someone lying half asleep on their sofa; this person is now awake (ibid, p. 48). Disregarding for one moment issues of dataveillance and the extent to which consumers are aware of how advertising is served to them, as described in Chapter 4, consumers are much more active in how they deal with advertising in online spaces. Cho and Leckenby (1997) state that interactivity plays a crucial role as a criterion for advertising effectiveness on the internet. They argue that the higher the levels of interactivity in an online advertisement, the more favourable the user finds the advertisement and the brand itself. Accordingly this leads to high purchase intention. Lombard (2001) notes that although the purpose of online advertising is the same as offline, that is to persuade consumers to buy a particular product or service, the media environment into which the advertising is placed is changing. He also states that through this, the nature of advertising is changing too and the tools with which we understand the process of consuming advertisements needs to change. Lombard (2001) understands interactivity to be defined by the user's ability to influence the form or content of the advertising message. He looks to interactive advertising to present advertising content that increases a sense of telepresence, which in turn involves engaging with the brand on a more intimate level than has been possible with traditional media. However, as Manovich points out, there is nothing radically new in these conceptions of interactivity. He comments that

> All classical, even more so modern art is 'interactive' is a number of ways. Ellipses in literary narration, missing details of objects in visual art, and other representational 'shortcuts' require the user to fill in missing information. (2003, p. 56)

Manovich (2003) instead points to the users' experience of these interactive objects. He notes that there is a danger in privileging the physical action of pressing buttons and using hyperlinks over the psychological aspect of these processes. Whilst pre-interactive TV (one-to-many (broadcasting), one-to-few (narrowcasting)) offered an arguably passive role in media consumption, computer media and the consumption of advertising content online is an active one, that is, where the user is necessarily part of the process of one-to-one media in providing feedback. Interactivity is a term that suffers from lack of clear explication in both the theoretical sense and the operational sense. Steuer (1992) and Kiousis (2002) both offer clear working definition of interactivity[101] for the graphical user interface GUI and computer mediated communication (CMC):

> [...] the extent to which users can participate in modifying the form and content of a mediated environment in real time. (1992, p. 84)

> With regard to human users, it additionally refers to the ability of users to perceive the experience to be a simulation of interpersonal communication and increase the awareness of telepresence. (2002, p. 379)

As Liu and Shrum observe, although user–machine interaction is important, it is also essential to recognize user–user interaction and user–message (and content) interaction. Interactivity can thus be defined as 'the degree to which two or more communication parties can act on each other, on the communication medium, and on the messages and the degree to which such influences are synchronized' (Liu and Shrum, 2005, p. 105). Telepresence, or the capacity of being at a location other than where the physical body is located, is a fundamental component of the interactive experience. Manovich (2003, p. 165) also defines telepresence as providing the ability to control remote physical objects in real time through its image. Li et al. (2005) argue that a sense of presence can be generated when users interact with virtual objects or virtual environments. They state that 3-D advertising – for example, through the inspection of an image of a camera or other item where a user can see all sides – offers a media richness and vividness analogous to being able to pick up and inspect the real object. Although quite different from breathable reality, advertising opportunities are richer than those offered by print, television, radio or 2-D advertising online. Li et al. (2005) also recognize that consumers inspecting products may be looking for different attributes and functions from an item. This necessitates creative awareness of the nature of interaction and sensitivity to the psychological and ergonomic engagement. Use of virtual experiences may also help create the real.

Nike, for example, has developed their iD series[102] that allows customization of their trainers and apparel. Users and consumers can choose the colour of their "swooshes" and others aspects of a trainer, insert words, view them from many angles, magnify and zoom out and email specifications to Nike for design and production. As Liu et al. (2005) note, virtual experiences offer marketers and advertisers the capacity to engage users with unique shopping experiences and interaction far more powerful than currently available in offline media.

Interactivity involves perception of interactivity as well as actual processes that hardware, bandwidth and applications facilitate. According to McMillan and Hwang (2005) the nature of this perception revolves around the expectation that interactive advertising is more like face-to-face personal advertising, as opposed to one-way broadcast styled advertising. For marketers and advertisers, creating and maintaining dialogue is therefore of utmost importance at both strategic and creative levels. Another point of separation between traditional and interactive advertising is that while advertisers have traditionally maintained control over content and timing, interactive advertisers and marketers must relinquish some of this control to users. Users do not want to be exposed to advertising; they want to engage with content of relevance and interest. Art directors and copywriters now have other concerns to attend to in addition to aesthetics, layout and attracting attention for the few seconds that consumers give to traditional advertising; they must also develop a sensitivity to notions such as ongoing dialogue, loading speed and generating interactivity resulting in high-level brand involvement.

Another aspect of interactivity is that users must learn codes and practices of the content or medium. Interactive content asks that users learn and engage in deeper cognitive processes; for example, Nikeplus. com that operates under the strategic insight of *The Human Race*. Here users are asked to upload data generated from a shoe sensor and wristband containing a USB data stick. This charts distance, calories burnt, speed and other information about a user's run. This can be mapped via Google Maps and users can also make use of forums attached to the main site and a range of other site add-ons including personal trainers. New Balance, a sports-shoe competitor, has also created a Facebook application in the form of a running game that encourages users to challenge their friends to a virtual race. As Liu and Shrum (2005) also describe, interactive advertising that requires such engagement is not without pitfalls. Novice users may experience apprehension or anxiety at having to engage with other users via a computer. They advise that companies proceed carefully and do not lapse into techno-determinism and the implementation of interactive tools where they are not needed or warranted.

Creativity in web 2.0 and beyond

In post-World War II years, many people in advertising believed that exposure equalled persuasion and that the mass media, particularly television would be all-powerful (Krugman, 1999). This, to some extent, was true; many large advertisers have created and maintained brands perhaps unachievable without broadcast advertising. Conversely, broadcast advertising breaks are not treated with the same degree of appreciation by consumers as their creators and sponsors. Bauer and Greyser (1968, in Brown et al. 1999), also observe that the average consumer – presumably of those living in wealthy economies – is exposed to around 1500 advertisements per day. Recent guesstimates place this at 3000. Perhaps more important than this figure is the filtering process of selective perception that occurs; out of the 1500, only 76 will be perceived, and only 12 will elicit a response. Whilst these numbers should be taken with a pinch of salt, intuitively they make some sense.

George Gallup (1974), founder of the Gallup Organization, a consumer and citizen research organization, observes that advertisers and associated promotional organizations should focus less on the selling than the serving of a need to know about products and services. Somewhat pithily, he comments that advertising agencies are staffed by people who have been able to see everything but themselves. He observes that

> Certainly, as we move from the concept of selling to that of serving, from hawking to that of helping meet the real needs of the consumers, then the advertising profession will inevitably gain in public esteem, product improvement will be given more attention, and advertising will itself become more effective and will perform a more important function in our free-market society. (ibid, p. 11)

In theorizing and reflecting upon digital and future advertising, it is worth configuring these in terms of relevance, personalization and the engendering of involvement. Advertising will increasingly become personalized and although this is in many ways inevitable (and has been for some time), consumers will quickly opt-out or click-away should it become too intrusive. Whereas advertising has traditionally beamed directly into our homes and media with little or no consultation with users or consumers, one of the significant issues for the future is how to gain permission and how to create compelling content for users.

Advertising strategists and creatives thus need to think much more broadly about media and how to entice consumers into permission-based activities. No longer is advertising – if we can still call these kinds of promotion advertising – representational in nature. As Rapp and Collins (1990) presciently described around twenty years ago, marketers and advertisers need to think further than making first contact with consumers and also how to manage the communication process in the longer term. Accordingly this requires creativity of a different order and that creativity should not be stacked towards mass media displays but also to everything that happens after initial consumer interest is obtained.

Advertisers and marketers instead are tasked with delivering ideas that are engaging technologically, in terms of content and at the level of the brand. In web 2.0 creating relevance through high-involvement digital media sets the creative bar high. Writers and art directors must understand their target audiences well and offer content that strikes the correct tone and emotional resonance. It must also respond to daily events, breaking news and the wider milieu in which the brand and users operate. The prizes are deep brand loyalty, brand evangelism and, of course, repeat custom. In this scenario, through selective exposure, consumers are also more likely to expose themselves to traditional broadcast and cinema advertisements that reassure them of the wisdom of their buying decisions and where they have allocated their loyalty.

As broached in Chapter 3, media and technological advances are rapidly expanding the avenues of communication that advertisers and their agencies have at their disposal. This in part also reflects changes in consumer media habits but more broadly reflects the sheer diversity in media innovation. As James Hilton, co-founder and executive creative director of advertising consultancy AKQA, describes 'the people coming into and out of college don't look at things in terms of media or marketing. They look at what is cool' (Haycock, 2007). Although techno-determinism brings with it problems, new technology also brings with it new opportunities, particularly if an advertiser is among the first to use it. A 2009 campaign by the fizzy drink company, Fanta, allows users of Nokia phones to play virtual tennis through augmented reality. Users print off a tennis court from a Fanta website and then can play tennis through their mobile phones using the printed court.[103]

Similarly a mobile/print advertisement for Wellington Zoo by Saatchi and Saatchi was the first New Zealand advertisement to use augmented spatiality to promote their Close Encounters Tours. These tours allow the public to come face to face with the zoo's animals and get inside their enclosures. They used new technology to bring to life how close to the animals people can get on these tours.[104] When people viewed the pattern on the print advertisement through their mobile phone they saw a virtual 3-D animal they could explore from any angle. This campaign highlights the potential for interrelationship between traditional media and digital tools. Software mash-ups, convergence, user-generated platforms and content, growth of the internet beyond the desktop and other developments all offer means of communicating with consumers that make traditional platforms such as television, cinema, radio, poster and press seem archaic. And they are: a screen only controllable by channel changing is quickly beginning to make little sense. However, as media platforms they will not disappear of the media register anytime soon. The book is still with us and has been for over 500 years. Nonetheless, it is senseless to look at digital media as fringe media.

Michael Roth, CEO of the Interpublic Group, predicts that creativity would thrive in the digital space: 'Technology isn't going to bury creativity. It is going to enhance creativity' (Teinowitz, 2008). DDB West's Liz Ross said a change in marketing thinking is required. 'Consumers

Sony Rec You I

are the new media, and they know it', she said. 'You have to market with consumers, not at consumers. Ultimately it becomes a collaborative process' (ibid). Sony, for example, commissioned a video called "Color Tokyo". This video allowed allows users to "colour" a Sony building located in Ginza, the cultural centre of Japan, from wherever they are.[105]

Also in Japan, the agency GT Tokyo/Dentsu created a multiplatform campaign for Sony Walkman where visitors to the "Rec You" (Record You) site upload a still image that is then photo-realistically animated to sing, bob in time to a section of Verdi's Requiem "Dies Irae" and wear a Walkman. The site then sends users a movie of their singing self. Users then join a huge online group of singing heads presented through a range of platforms including banners, blogs, YouTube that may also be distributed via mobile. In addition, users may receive text messages stating when they will appear on national television. Utilizing an innovative approach this D&AD award-winning campaign has a viral character thus requiring much less media expenditure, though it also involved traditional above-the-line, out-of-home and television advertising. The head-banging motion to strident European classical music also presents an interesting frisson and slight disjuncture that only serves to intrigue further. The UK's popular singing competition X Factor and their sponsors, The Carphone Warehouse, commissioned CHI & Partners to create an interactive audition microsite.[106] This encouraged viewers to sing into their mobile phones for a chance to become stars of The X Factor sponsorship idents on the television programme itself. Users and viewers could then go online and see the X Factor brand character, Mowbli, animated to their own vocals. Users could also act as judges, voting on other performances. Again, the lack of media expenditure, the use of non-tokenistic interactive tools, highlights enterprising and engaging use of digital advertising media.

Traditionally advertising is an exercise in synthesis and the distillation of clear unique ideas to communicate with a member of an audience in an extremely short period. This again has changed: audiences, if the commercial content is interesting enough, will spend as much time as they want with it. Whereas creative advertising has been about encapsulating ideas, one-liners, mnemonics and the like, advertising now has the potential to build virtual scenarios, environments, tactile spaces, brandscapes, narratives, games, experiences in both virtual and real spaces, and where virtuality and reality collide or work in synchronization as with locative media. This is not to suggest, however, that advertising no longer needs clear ideas quickly identifiable by consumers, or catchy elements. Burgess (2008), for example, notes that much successful viral advertising possesses textual hooks or key signifiers that cannot be identified in advance but are rather identified and taken up after it has been released into the wild and undergone repeat viewing. These hooks are then taken and plugged into other 'forms, texts and intertexts – they become part of the available cultural repertoire of vernacular video' (ibid, p. 105). Although it is debatable as to whether creatives have any idea as to what will be taken up and what will not, it is true to say that viral opens up possibilities for playful creativity and contributions to professional and user-generated video (and other content) lexicon. Interesting advertising ideas in the digital sector stem from an interest in digital and wider culture. As opposed to technologically determined advertising or the use of technology because it is the latest tool, digital should still reflect, and sometimes create, cultural trends.

Participation

Jan Leth, Co-Chief Creative Officer of Ogilvy New York, describes new media advertising as an opportunity for dialogue akin to live performances in that it requires audience participation (Wiedemann, 2006, p. 272). He also comments that

> Most ads, online or off are unappealing. Advertising has gotten away with this because we weren't in a consumer-controlled world. But we are now, and uninspired marketing, lacking insight and differentiation will begin to fail miserably. Creativity has never been more critical. (ibid, p. 273)

For advertisers, the notion of greater involvement of consumers as a creative strategy has been met with some trepidation, particularly as it requires a letting-go of some control of a brand. The reward is that users may feel more empathy towards a brand than one-way broadcast advertising could ever hope to deliver. It is worth observing the difference between user-generated content (UGC) and word-of-mouth. One refers to content *generated* by users, the other content that is *conveyed* by users (Cheong and Morrison, 2008). As described in Chapter 2, user-generated content is a practice and environment in which consumers produce, design, publish or edit content with consumers sitting at the centre of a UGC advertiser's strategy planning process (Krishnamurthy and Dou, 2008). Utilizing a user-generated approach requires that advertisers ask users to create content (or advertisers create content to sit alongside UGC). Although the practice may not be widespread, it is emblematic of strategic changes in communication with audiences.[107]

Such letting-go requires bravery on the part of brands, although the breaking down of boundaries between producers and consumers may only serve to foster deeper relationships. Bruns phrases this relationship in terms of 'produsage' (2006, p. 2). These 'produsers' engage not in a traditional form of content production, but are instead involved in *produsage* – the 'collaborative and continuous building and extending of existing content in pursuit of further improvement' (2006, p. 2). Examples abound online in the form of Second Life, Wikipedia, Slashdot, distributed journalism and other enterprises that involve both community and creativity. In this view, users (or produsers) are invited to collaborate and use other participants' content as with Google Earth or Nikeplus.com where users may plot circuits and runs. As with open source computing, this form of *generative advertising* builds and creates a palimpsest: a repeatedly overwritten, multilayered document. Ideally, and as Bruns (2006) discusses in relation to gaming, the relationship between users and companies would be one that ideally involves integrity and sincerity on behalf of businesses and agencies, and the harnessing rather than the hijacking of creative endeavour. A 2008 advertorial from Dare, an interactive marketing agency, in the UK's industry newspaper *Campaign* similarly highlights the potential for generative strategies suggesting that agencies should not focus so much on broadcasting, but instead arm users with tools to become evangelists, immaterial labourers and myth-makers on their behalf.

Interactive storytelling

A large portion of advertising created by agencies has to do with creating empathy for a brand and much of this is done through creating myths and stories to be attached to products and services. As Johnson (2008) in discussion of Bruner (1991) observes, the narrative forms and stories we tell are the way in which we relate accounts and explanations of things that have happened to us. As such, we create reality, or at least some of our social reality, through the telling of stories. Randazzo observes that 'Madison Avenue is in the business of mythmaking, of creating and perpetuating the myths that reflect and shape our values, sensibilities, and lifestyles' (1993, p. 1). This is to condense the maximum amount of meaning into a given period of attention. Bastholm (2008) comments that although many industry commentators claim digital does not tell branded stories in the same way the 30-second spot does, stories are potentially instead told in a different way. Whereas advertisers and their agencies hoped that audiences would become interested in their monologue, digital pertains towards opening up dialogue with users, sometimes by any means possible. For example, when EA (Electronic Arts) found that someone on YouTube spotted a glitch in their Tiger Woods golf game, they – via their agency Wieden + Kennedy – uploaded a video response of Tiger walking on water inside the game, with the idea being that Tiger really is that good. This gained both respect from users and millions of views worldwide.[108] Creative strategies have to be reconsidered from the ground-up. Rather than digital being the bolt-on component, digital strategies that make full use of digital potential are conceived both in creative and technical terms. This means that technological innovation and creativity go hand in hand. Rodgers (2007) describes how interactive agencies such as AKQA, Deep Focus and R/GA continue to play with interactive capabilities of the medium building in-house studios, scripting interactive storylines upfront, shooting in high-definition for ultra-high speed internet connections and booking time with "talent" early in the campaign planning process. One way for creative digital advertisers to reach consumers is by stories and ways to make the individual (the user or consumer) the hero or success of the story in some way.

One particular format that has been readily taken up is transmedia storytelling (Jenkins, 2006).[109] In many ways this shares formal similarities with integrated approaches to marketing where communication about brands are relayed across a broad array of media, including offline. Advertiser usage of transmedia storytelling intends to facilitate brand involvement at a much deeper level. Important aspects of the narrative may be dispersed and fragmented across different media texts. Transmedia storytelling has proved successful with film, probably most significantly in Larry and Andy Wachowski's Matrix universe. There is significant scope for advertisers to work across a range of platforms and environments providing that content is engaging enough. So rather than transmitting the same idea across several media why not work with the properties (for example, technological, social, viewing scale, static, filmic, indoors and outdoors) and use these to create brand communications far more interesting than use of the traditional media mix? Individual executions will still have the power to act in stand-alone capacity.[110] Similar to the BMW example described in Chapter 3, Coke has also engaged in transmedia storytelling promoting the "Coke side of life" as developed by Wieden + Kennedy Amsterdam. In contrast to branded entertainment that leverages the narrative and metaverse created by another project, Coke is building a world that readily translates across media. For example, see the television advertisements for Happiness Factory 1[111] and 2[112] and the global website[113] that allow users to get to know the characters better and play games. Key characteristics follow traditional storytelling in that worlds or settings should be immersive, characters should be engaging, the story should have an arc of some sort and the story should not date. Such a strong emotional base with an internal logic of story and actors facilitates access through different media, loyal fans and the capacity for engaging non-linearity, audience inter-activity and open-ended meaning.

Getting creative with locative

Pre-empting the current vogue and interest in locative media, Virilio's (1997) view of interactivity marks the move away from 3-D concepts of space, for example shapes, forms, streets and buildings we can touch with hands that are still governed by constraints of time. Instead, he points to a communicational paradigm whereby electronic pathways facilitate real space. Saatchi & Saatchi New Zealand created a Bluetooth-based campaign utilizing interactive outdoor posters for the New Zealand Army. These challenged passers-by to a mission to find an army operative in their vicinity within 30 seconds. The operative was hidden on a nearby standard poster site, camouflaged in jungle, forest or snow. When the participant located the camouflaged operative, they "texted" back his or her co-ordinates. If they succeeded, they were sent a congratulations message and directed to the NZ Army recruitment website. If they failed, they were directed to the NZ Army Force 9 training site, where further games and challenges awaited.[114] In Japan, Profero, a digital marketing agency, created a mobile campaign for Diageo/ Guinness using GPS-enabled and non-GPS enabled (through use of cell-ID technology) mobile phones to allow users to find the nearest Guinness serving establishment through Guinness "Navi". This allows consumers to find a place that serves Guinness amongst the thousands of places that do not. It gives users maps with pubs marked by Guinness icons where users can also see photos, opening times, reviews of the bar and number of seats, as well as a phone number to contact it directly. AKQA created a mobile out-of-doors campaign for Visa Signature, a US upmarket credit card, that allows users to text in a code at stores and outside popular restaurants to hear "Savoury Sound Bites" recordings from the chef and advice from wine experts. In these examples and more, advertising produces meta-layers of urban and spatial information adding an extra dimension to urban experience.

Mobile generally has received less creative treatment than its online sibling has. However, award-winning work tends to focus on interactive delivery rather than push-based advertising. For Tohato, a spicy snacks manufacturer who launched two similar products at the same time, Japanese advertising agency Hakuhodo produced a war game featuring two armies led by each of the characters, Ultra Tyrant Habanero and Satan Joloquia, basing these around the two products. Purchasers could participate by buying one of the products to choose a "master" and, through scanning the QR code (a 2-D bar-code) on the package with their mobile phones, join an online "army". Hakuhodo commissioned systems that enabled players to get stronger by summoning friends or winning points. For more examples of creative mobile usage, see the Webby Awards.[115]

For both digital on the move and plugged-in hardware, there is room for both works characterized by divergence, unusualness, being left of field and also those less mediated such as search. The speed of technological change means that advertising unavoidably involves an element of technological determinism. New hardware, platforms, software, mashed together software, environments and more mean that media in some cases will hold sway over the message. Novelty in some cases is no bad thing. Although the internet has been around for some time now, the platforms it has given birth to, particularly since the advent of web 2.0, are multiplying very quickly. The trick, however, for agencies is not to follow the crowd in a vain attempt to earn media kudos or real estate but rather to socialize with users in a sincere, straightforward, inventive and hopefully fun fashion.

▶ Is it time to rethink the premise of a Big Idea; is it dogmatic notion that made little sense first time around?

▶ To what extent is creativity the outcome of the chain of advertising production versus individual inspiration?

▶ Does creativity without romanticism make sense?

▶ Can an algorithm be creative?

▶ What is creative interactivity?

8   Conclusions, Ethics and Future Directions

This chapter explores some of the ethical ramifications of digital advertising, makes concluding points on themes raised in this book and offers some suggestions of what lies beyond the digital horizon. It does so by utilizing discussion raised in October 2007 with Kalle Lasn, editor of the crusading magazine, and author of *Culture Jam: The Uncooling of America* (1999).[116] Adbusting or culture jamming is the flip side of corporate driven consumer culture. As a verb and cultural process adbusting is anti-consumerist and aims to disturb the cultural logic of brands and their precession of signification, as popularly described in Naomi Klein's (2000) *No Logo*. *Adbusters* is perhaps most well known for its spoof advertisements of brands such as Calvin Klein's Obsession.[117] As what can loosely be described as a situationist movement it rallies against what it sees as the encroachment of branded versions of reality into everyday life. It describes itself as a not-for-profit, reader-supported, 120,000-circulation magazine concerned about the erosion of our physical and cultural environments by commercial forces. It portrays its readership as a global network of artists, activists, writers, pranksters, students, educators and entrepreneurs who want to advance the new social activist movement of the information age. *Adbusters* sells to the United States (comprising two-thirds of its circulation), Canada, United Kingdom, Australia, Taiwan, Portugal, Austria, Belgium, Germany, Italy, Norway, Sweden, Spain, Switzerland, Lebanon, Guam, India, Singapore, Mexico, Panama, Brazil, British West Indies and New Zealand, and it is currently trying to enter more countries in South America. Its small circulation figures belie its influence. It has a significant readership amongst the graphic design and creative advertising communities and represents a bastion of anti-corporate culture, which is, of course, a great source for advertising ideas and consumer insight. Given that Kalle Lasn is a key proponent of adbusting or culture jamming that seeks to engage citizens, users and consumers, organizing this concluding chapter around participatory principles seemed like a fitting way to end a book on digital advertising. This also allows me to summarize some ethical ramifications of digital advertising and look to the future.

On-demand fluidity

Perhaps an unexpected and little known fact about Kalle is that he used to work in the advertising business, a career which began in 1965 in Tokyo, Japan. Although *Adbusters* is very clear on its stance on corporate advertising, during interview Kalle Lasn warmed to the discussion of people working in agencies describing them as some of the 'most creative people on earth' hoping that individuals would turn their attention from 'crack marketing' to 'social marketing' (Interview, 20/10/2007). Whereas *Adbusters* is vociferous in its stance against the use of traditional advertising (particularly television) and marketing by corporations I was keen to hear what Kalle Lasn had to say about digital advertising, particularly with regards to personalized service-based advertising. As described in this book, a more personalized advertising environment should, in theory at least, be a less cluttered and relevant one.

Adbuster's critique of the business and practice of advertising involve advertising as a generator of "mental pollution". This involves culture conceived of as a "mental ecology" and advertising as a corporate pollutant. I was interested to find out whether advertising lower in mediation (as with search) is a positive development. Not only is it lower in mediation but it is also tailored to user interests. In response to opening questions about the changing advertising scene he comments that

> Advertising hit the wall about ten years ago. It got to the point where we just didn't want more than 15 minutes an hour of television ads, and they were hitting the wall because they were all kinds of messages from the top and you took them whether you like them or not, it was sort of an Orwellian kind of thing. Well I think that...in a sense there's more_____kind of a world of cyberspace in a sense it gave advertising another huge shot in the arm. Over several years there's all kinds of new gentler, sometimes even clandestine, ways of getting to people....
>
> Nike for example have a way of coming at you more personally. I don't mind the personal part of it, I mean if I had a choice and I was actually thinking of a holiday in Mexico then I guess I wouldn't mind – you know somehow while I was in cyberspace – somebody giving me some alternative that may help me out to buy a cheaper ticket or whatever. In some sense I don't have a problem with it, but in another sense I have a huge problem with it because it's just more power to the people that I've spent the last 20 years of my life trying

to take power away from [laughs]. (Interview, 20/10/2007)

These comments are surprising given *Adbusters*'s general attitude to marketing and advertising. The magazine, website and book (Lasn, 1999) that underpins the culture jamming philosophy is very clear on top-down advertising, but less clear on digital advertising. It would appear that advertising that is relevant, timely and of service is acceptable, even to advertising's greatest critic.

The search format is currently emblematic of relevance-based advertising. The digital advertising of today and tomorrow reflects well conditions in broader consumer societies. Leiss et al. (2005, p. 568) suggest that the current cultural milieu of consumption we are in is the outcome of around 120 years of advertising, marketing and consumerism. From their perspective, consumers from the 1990s onwards use brands, products, goods and commodities as stage-props to their lives. As Chaudhuri and Majumdar (2006) describe: pre-capitalist feudalist social structures engendered ostentatious behaviour amongst its nobility; in modern-capitalist societies the nobility and upper middle classes used trophy objects such as diamonds as a means of signalling power, ostentation and uniqueness (see Veblen, 1899). In this scenario, work or industry was seen as something base and unworthy of powerful gentleman. In postmodern societies many consumers, driven by the need for self-expression and the construction for self-image, use images and experiences as a means of signalling uniqueness or social conformation (Leiss et al., 2005).

This has led to a scenario where many people in advanced economies use the purchasing of goods as a social function and where, often, consuming becomes more important than the use or practical value of the goods themselves.[118] As such there has been a shift from the privileging of production, to consumption and then onto the self as a customizable entity. Although much of the produce may be mass-produced, the way users and consumers configure these is unique, or at least they are encouraged to believe they are artisans of meaning creation. In this media environment, reflexivity and understanding of intertextual references are prized (Lash, 1990). As consumption moves into the symbolic realm, such practices need not be overtly expensive. By 'adopting abstract interpretations and ascribing complex cultural meaning to products, those with "higher" taste but less money would aim to compete with those with money but no matching taste' (Chaudhuri and Majumdar, 2006, p. 5). Such a milieu is born of a pluralism found in postmodernism and diversity generated from the triumphing of pop over high modernism. As the intersection for art, commerce, intertextuality, historical and playful referencing, cultural fragmentation, hybridity and diversity, advertising is emblematic of the excavation and surface treatment of texts and meaning. Leiss et al. state that

> New technologies are essential for the success of this phase: animation, graphical design software, digitized and edited images, higher-resolution imagery, composite (collage) scene construction, rapid-fire editing for scene transitions, easy access to musical accompaniment, and a re-mastering of the earlier heritage of cultural property for an infinite supply of 'retro' designs, ... (ibid)

Whereas reflexivity in the content of advertising is nothing new, use of media and the engaging of users to create it are. Media forms such as the internet, as well as other digital media, are characterized by fluidity. They place users and consumers as directors of their own lives in terms of media content, form and the brand messages they interact with. Media is on-demand. However, this is a double-edged sword and the children of MySpace are squarely configured within the cultural logic of branding.

This is reminiscent of Bauman's (2000, 2005) discussion of liquidity and liquid life where consumption becomes a dominant activity. Lazzarato also observes that 'we live among goods and services that we buy, in houses, among furniture, with objects and services that we have grabbed as "possible" in the flows of information and communication within which we are immersed' (2004, p. 190). Similarly, emphasis on pull-based search media signals a shift to what Bauman describes as a 'consumerist syndrome' (2005, p. 83). Consumption here not only means products and items but also lifestyles. As permission-based media become more common and advertisers and their agencies develop engaging content, relationships with brands will become deeper and customers more loyal. It is worth putting this in context: whereas brands originally maintained a benchmark of trust and quality, brands are increasingly becoming the cultural air we breathe. In addition, the lack of representation found in much digital advertising also gives rise to a sense of self-determination about our relationship to advertising and marketing. So in this period we see the return of individuality. We are no longer so much confined by the drumbeat of manufacturers and instead engage in bricolage obtained through the much-vaunted Long Tail (Anderson, 2006b).

Jhally (2000, in Johnson, 2008) warns that internet-based advertising may facilitate a vortex of self-absorption. Due to advertising being an activity that addresses us as individuals, Johnson envisages a deepening scenario of self-involvement and the self-construction of identity through brands. She argues that advertising promotes the worst in people, for example greed and selfishness as opposed to caring, generosity and compassion. To quote Johnson

> The Internet is like a vortex drawing more and more time from more and more alternatives into its center. As the Internet becomes increasingly used by advertisers for brand-extension programming, a society already preoccupied with self-orientation and 'me-me-me' moves a little further away from productive, collective society. (2008, p. 235)

This is an extreme position, and perhaps pragmatically wrong. Although brands play a significant, and perhaps unhealthy, role in how we relate, read one another and construct (or constrict?) our own identities, the notion that online and digital media exacerbate this is untrue. Digital media are demonstrably social media and rather than promoting the worst, they may mediate admirable human characteristics. In contrast to the notion of users as atomized and isolated individuals, recent digital media rather have fostered both online and offline sociality. Locative media and wider digital may deliver services that facilitate social engagement, learning and creative expression. Whilst it may be uncomfortable to have such core human values represented and mediated through brands, to take such an oppositional stance misses the real concerns regarding ethics and power – namely, concerns over data flow and to a lesser extent the use of digital to advertise to children.

Adbusting, risk and digital advertising

Kalle Lasn observes that he does not have a problem with advertising per se, but rather how it has been used and the centrality it plays in today's social and media economy. He adds that

> No, I don't think there's anything intrinsically problematic with that. I think advertising is…is part of human nature. And the way that advertising has existed through the ages, I don't have a huge problem with that; but somewhere around the 19, somewhere after

the Second World War, a lot of things went...we didn't know at the time, but a lot of things sort of went off the rails around that time. (Interview, 20/10/2007)

For Lasn, the over-profusion of advertising involves an ecological risk. Whereas risk was once ascribed to the heavens and acts of God, risk is now often a human-created event (Lupton, 1999). Capitalism as an outcome of industrialization became the central belief system organizing society, as opposed to religion as a central mode of doctrine, thus making risk a man-made phenomenon. Smart (1993, p. 15) also argues that since World War II, this sense of agency in turn fostered a greater sense of selfhood and a wider sense of 'living in new times', a sense of taking control of one's own destiny. Giddens (1990, p. 7) sees this sense of the new as having 'double-edged characteristics' in that the acceleration of production not only offered greater comforts but also furthered the production of social, physiological and environmental risks. Lasn's concerns revolve around the centrality of consumption to advanced economies. One of *Adbusters*'s largest campaigns is the global "Buy Nothing Days". Here consumers are urged to opt out of consumer society, even if only for twenty-four hours. This is counter-pointed by governments quite baldly stating post credit-crunch (2008) that it is our duty as citizens to spend and consume. Accounts of consumerism take on an extra dimension when one considers the encroachment of commerce and consumption into the home. Although home purchasing has existed for some time with home lifestyle catalogues, this has entered overdrive with the ascension of internet home shopping.

The creation of data-doubles (as described in Chapter 4) consuming in what was once the private sphere of the home exposes us to both outsiders and unruly insiders (Nissenbaum, 2001). Although we employ software and systems to protect us from viruses and malware, there is little or no defence against unruly inside members of the online world who Nissenbaum argues are 'chipping away at trust just as surely as the allegedly amoral hackers' (2001, p. 12). Here, breaches of trust involve the collection of data as a means of extra income generation and concern over what may be done with this data in the future. This lack of trust stems in part from a distrust of market forces that characterized early usage of the internet and to some extent the web where countercultural discourses abounded. This, combined with discourses of contagion, and media formats that can be infected provides a fertile environment for distrust of both business and unseen forces who wish to do us harm. Yet, few users of home catalogues ever contracted malware.

Perceptions of risk not only stem from cyberculture and dystopian discourses but also from management practices emerging from modernity and the will to rationality that found expression in the seventeenth century. Kalle Lasn's and *Adbusters*'s perspective stem from a sense of heady modernity out of control. As discussed in Chapter 5, despite innovations in management and organizational techniques, this was at the price of what Weber (1994) describes as rule-based and rational control characterized by the "iron cage". The cognate freedoms lost are also those that Kalle Lasn perhaps considers as quintessentially human traits. From an *Adbusters*'s point of view, the 'clandestine ways' (Interview, 20/10/2007) of constructing reliable consumers involve data, personalization and an increasing lack of mediation. Arguably, whereas traditional advertising and corporate behaviour represent visible actions, the lack of visibility in digital (and refined targeting) represents a technical power Kalle Lasn is uncomfortable with. Moreover he wonders where such techno-power will eventually lead. This found expression in market research and the advent of commercial digital data mining beginning in the 1960s.

In its initial formation, audience research was used to bend audience demand to fit with production and distribution. This, however, soon gave way to segmentation and supply fitting types of demand, although those with an interest in promoting heavier consumption may in some part shape demand. Demographics was the first comprehensive system of segmentation employed and is an *a priori* method of segmentation in that it makes future plans on the basis of past behaviour. With the advent of computing power, segmentation and consumer habits became more predictive in nature. Despite current excitement in the potential of digital, the fetish over computational potential is nothing new and old as modernity itself. More specifically the use of computers to find deep patterns of behaviour was well underway by the 1970s and although the connectivity of the internet was not popularized, computers and algorithms were employed to make sense of and predict consumer behaviour.

As locative media develop into a mainstream form of audience research, the capacity to target by location and in real-time may become more common. This is dependent on regulation. Such developments also require significant trust on behalf of users and citizens. It is quite possible that in advertisers' endeavour to get closer to their target audiences, they in fact alienate their audiences. For businesses whose remit is to increase personalized advertising, marketing and customer relations, this proves a difficult obstacle. As Cuneo (2008) observes, although personalization fits a neat trend beginning with wide-scale broadcasting, many top executives in relevant communications industries spend only moderate amounts on personalized communications with consumers and users.

Opting in or out?

Contemporary digital life thus involves a combination of technological developments, regulatory interests, social usage and perhaps most influentially, social perceptions of technological change. This is an inheritance characterized by high velocity to which we spend our time trying to keep up or make par. The speed of technological development and its integration into cultures has proved faster than citizen and public awareness. In some cases development has occurred that regulation can attend to, particularly in regard to privacy. For companies and some users this is a commodity to be traded. We do this through entering competitions, by obtaining money-off vouchers or similar rewards for information. We also give privacy away to streamline our digital lifestyles through the use of cookies and other labour saving preference tools. However, as Lessig (2006) points out, the argument involving user control over disclosure assumes people and users are not being monitored in their routine online activities. This makes the notion of user control a difficult one. For example, on entering online public space, users give up rights to privacy in the same way that we give up a certain amount of privacy when entering offline spaces.

Although the sheer amount of data collected may be startling and the notion of a panoptic-influenced environment a worrying one, this may not be the main effect of an aggregated environment predicated on both non-co-opted and co-opted data sharing; it may be something more insidious yet profound. The cumulative effect of this is that data controllers and managers may not only get to know our habits well but perhaps also create them. As discussed in Chapter 4, if this appears far-fetched, one only needs to look at the original remit of the advertising industry that was to construct specific categories of consumer (Smith, 1956; Arvidsson, 2004; Leiss et al., 2005). Under the guise of manipulation, Lessig raises the possibility of a scenario where our tastes and preferences may be manufactured. He observes that

...profiles will begin to normalize the population from which the norm is drawn. The observing will affect the observed. The system watches what you do; it fits you into a pattern; the pattern is then fed back to you in the form of options set by the pattern; the options reinforce the pattern; the cycle begins again. (2006, p. 220)

This line of thinking presents an interesting feedback situation of mutual resemblance, disciplining procedures and offers advertisement-servers a means of tinkering with processes of aggregation so to create audiences in their own image. This is also surprisingly uni-directional and offers users little capacity to consciously articulate feedback. It sits distinctly at odds with web 2.0 pretensions to autonomy and user-centricism.

Solove (2004) argues that the United States promotes a *laissez-faire* system that is asymmetric where favour lies with businesses and opting-out is difficult. Many companies, including super-sized businesses such as Google, state that advertising is paramount for the expansion of businesses both small and large. In addition, it also fosters alternative news sources such as blogs and independence of small news sources from large media conglomerations, not to mention free user services. They also highlight the difficulty in measuring user data and exposure to advertising, noting that many web 2.0 styled applications (for example, those found on Facebook and MySpace) work across a range of sites and sources. Applications and chunks of code may be lifted and placed in different web contexts proving highly difficult in some cases to trace and chart how they are being used. As such, gaining opt-in verification proves difficult. US government – in comparison to Europe – is not keen to intervene, currently preferring to leave private business matters alone. To facilitate flow of personal data between the United States and the European Union, the Department of Commerce, in consultation with the European Union, created Safe Harbor Principles to meet EU "adequacy" stands for privacy protection. In both the European Union and the United States, concern revolves around whether users are fully aware of what they are opting into when signing up for deals and trading privacy for prizes or some other advantage. We do not know what the outcome will be of data creep and what the culmination and cross-referencing of data may facilitate in the future, especially in light of growing interest from ISPs in generating revenue from advertising in both the United Kingdom and United States.

The World Privacy Forum calls for mandatory regulation due to the premise that self-regulation rewards the most unscrupulous of businesses. They have also called for explicit rules on sensitive medical information. Although conditions such as cancer are currently covered, other information such as gene-based information is not. Given the growth of genetic profiling this is not such an outlandish notion as it may first appear. The potential for marketing on the basis of genetic code and a person's disposition to conditions raise cyberpunk-styled spectres of "megacorps". However, in the long run, the mapping of behaviour and activities for purposes of commercial communication extends to the human genome itself. Whereas digital involves representations of behaviour, thoughts and activities, DNA moves closer to the core of who we are, what we do and why we do it. In addition, it raises the proposition of DNA markers or keys as unique identifiers. Whereas motivational research dealt with symbols and abstractions as a means of understanding psychological drives, genomic mapping is potentially a much more reliable means of understanding a person's life trajectory and the challenges and possible outcomes that may lay ahead at various life stages. Although from a critical point of view this appears an unlikely Faustian deal, most of us regularly offer up private detail for prizes. Although this book has at times been somewhat critical of pre-millennial cybercultural rhetoric as having more to do with science fiction, cybercultural literature has been right to note that digital (as in the electronic conception of the word) is not the end-game but rather a step towards bio-technological information processing (see, for example, Kroker and Weinstein, 1994). In the case of advertising and marketing this involves aggregation at deeper and deeper levels that may well include genetic mining, as well as mining of demographics, psychographics, locative and internet histories and real-time activities.

Adbusting and web 2.0

In addition to thoughts on digital advertising, representation and dataveillance, I was also keen to explore perspectives on web 2.0 and advertising. Web 2.0 finds enthusiasts both in the business community and with those who seek to challenge traditional media structures with a decentralized bottom-up approach to knowledge and media production; for example, through collective annotation, user-generated content and participatory culture. I asked Kalle Lasn whether he imagined that these kinds of platforms might lead to a reclaiming of media back from conglomerations where users create their own content as opposed to receiving a diet provided by corporations. The notion of user-generated media content and the open use of digital platforms is a particularly pertinent one for *Adbusters* given its history of not being able to buy terrestrial or cable advertising space. In response he comments that

> Yeah, I've always felt that I was pretty despondent until the digital revolution sort of uh, started taking, creating this huge whirlwind. Um I think there's a real potential there. And I think that web 2.0, I think that's kind of a nice development. Um...*but* at the same time I remain scared that the same thing will happen to cyberspace as happened to television you know. When I was young then, my high school teacher told me that television is going to create a global relation and television is the biggest communications breakthrough that human kind has ever had and everything's just gonna be fine from now on; we're gonna be able to talk to each other and all the rest of it, and bit by bit by bit I watched television, this most powerful social communications medium of our time, I watched it being turned into a mass merchandising tool. And I'm afraid that the same thing is happening to cyberspace now. (Interview, 20/10/2007)

Merchandizing takes on a different guise to what we have seen prior to web 2.0 as it involves greater audience and user engagement. In web 2.0 received understanding tells us that advertising messages should be a collaborative process, one that involves interactivity or what Bruns (2006) describes as 'intercreativity'. Where many digital users are actively engaged in fan culture, producing their own videos, writing blogs and similar producerly activities, it would appear obvious that brands offer consumers the ability to get involved with the creation of their advertising. This, in turn, generates a secondary sense of brand empathy, inculcation and belonging to consumer society. What many brands have managed to achieve is the leveraging of sociality, communities and social relations online and the appropriation of these values as their own.

Immaterial labour, advertising and web 2.0

Although digital media provide a sense of freedom and lack of dependency on traditional media or mass marketing for entertainment, this is somewhat illusory. Under the cultural logic of participation, we inherently accept a contract with big business by playing with their tools to explore our own freedoms. For this there is a cost, albeit one we may be happy to pay. As Bassett (2008) puts it, we 'participate from within, rather than disrupt from without'. At the most extreme, from a highly critical perspective, digital tools may provide a somatic function. In addition, we are also pressed to work, consume, experience and expand to accept growing channels of sensory intake. As Bassett also observes, we do not 'entirely control the rhythms of convergence and fragmentation that organize our embodied engagement and participation in informational culture'. Although digital and web 2.0 discourses pronounce freedom, they also involve an enticing yet tiring invitation to produce immaterial labour (Lazarrato, 1996). Fuchs expresses a similar sentiment describing this labour as a form of surplus labour. Importantly, he also recognizes that without this, 'production and accumulation will break down if this labour is withdrawn' (2009, p. 31).

For brands and advertisers used to controlling every aspect of their brand and the public perception of it, web 2.0 also represents a letting go although to suggest brands such as Dove, Herbal Essences, Cadillac and M&M's are adrift on consumer whims would be naïve; they are managed too well for that. Only the best user-produced content receives maximum exposure, for example making it on to Superbowl airtime as with Doritos and user-generated advertising in 2007. Such strategies involve immaterial labour 'that produces the informational or cultural content of the product or service' (Lazzarato, 1996, p. 132). This stands in contrast to the passive audience as commodity that informs the traditional media content/advertising model. Lazzarato refers to both labour that involves the generation of immaterial types, for example aesthetic, cultural, social or emotional, and those whose labour is unpaid. Lazzarato adds that 'immaterial labour constitutes itself in forms that are immediately collective, and we might say that it exists only in the form of networks and flows' (ibid). In addition, the data trails we leave behind are other forms of immaterial labour and translate readily into fiscal reality in the form of information for marketers and interested parties. In this view consumption is a form of work and labour in that they contribute to the creation of values, as well as data products, on which the pre-eminence and hegemony of capitalism and more particularly digital media providers offer.

Although the term participatory media at first reading indicates choice, as any user of digital media knows these forms become increasingly, and surprisingly, authoritarian. If one does not participate one is by definition excluded and the compulsion to maintain communities, self-created profiles and the generation of content stems from users themselves. Writers of blogs know they must keep regular entries as do avid Facebook users who must maintain their own personal brands.

Whereas traditional advertising seeks to co-opt audiences into prescribed lifestyles, digital marketers and advertisers now promote a greater and deeper sense of subjectivity, yet contradictorily bound to processes of consumption. As Arvidsson puts it: 'The core functionality of immaterial labour is thus its capacity to produce sociality' (2006, p. 11). Whereas brands and advertising create options, lifestyles and represent a language of posture and gesture, advertising funded digital media offers something else. Digital services such as Google, Facebook, MySpace and a variety of other lifestyle brands involve the reorganization of approaches to knowledge and sociality, and how we find out about and consume music and other desirable content. They not only graft themselves onto our daily practices but also in many ways reorganize them.

Advertising, the semantic web and ubiquitous computing

Many technology commentators are predicting and awaiting the development of what is commonly dubbed web 3.0, or the semantic web. This version of the web is about integration. Whereas applications we use online and offline are mostly standalone, this incarnation of the web creates common formats for integration and combination of data drawn from diverse sources. This then has implications for data integration, classification, discovery, cataloguing and the use of agents to act on our behalf in sorting all of this. It might simply be best to think of the semantic web as having a highly effective personal assistant. In a hypothetical situation involving the setting up of physical therapy sessions, Berners-Lee et al. (2001) explored the use of semantic agents some years ago describing how they may act on our behalf. They described a scenario where a brother and sister arrange their mother's physical therapy sessions. The daughter's semantic web agent controlled through a handheld device retrieved her mother's medical information about medical treatment from a doctor's agent, looked up lists of treatment providers suitable for her insurance level, found therapists within a suitable geographic radius and excellence rating, and then made a match between available appointment times (supplied by the agents of individual providers through their web sites). Having knowledge of calendars, financial and insurance records, the agents subsequently reorganized the brother's schedule and confirmed their insurance plan.

As with traditional media, it is quite likely that if we use a free digital agent we may be exposed to more advertising (in a highly service-based, relevant and personalized fashion) than if we subscribe to a service. As with current debates over opting in or out of information sharing, those who choose not to share their information may well be at an informational and perhaps fiscal loss in a truly digital economy and culture. Presumably, in the same way that banks know the majority of consumers will stay with them for life, agent services will also be fighting hard for our custom and cognate advertising and marketing revenue. The semantic web, as an extension of the current one, will bring greater structure to the meaning of content. Behind the scenes computer programs can manipulate a meaningfully written programming language that reduces chances of ambiguity.[119] Whereas webpages are normally written to order the structure and organization of a page, semantic programming structures for computers are meant to process. In addition it is written to be readable and used by a wide variety of applications.[120] Its programming language, Resource Description Framework (RDF), acts as a common model that binds together different languages. This makes managing content much simpler. Relevance and semantic understanding of user preferences and search queries will become more pronounced. Whilst a semantic web (or web 3.0) has been promised for some years now, the likelihood is that it will arrive in a gradual and unannounced fashion, yet eventually be more profound than expected. The semantic web will certainly have interesting ramifications for optimization and the creation of display predicated on context and behaviour.

Where next?

As has hopefully become clear by now, new relationships between media and audiences have formed in parallel with the advent of popular use of internet and digitally based media. These involve deeper than hitherto seen practices of data mining, personalization and a variety of platforms for users to express themselves on. As with traditional media forms, audiences still translate to capital. Central is not only co-opted knowledge about users but also the capacity to leverage this information in a meaningful way. As our own experiences of digital advertising tell us, there is still some way to go in the refinement of relevance. It is perhaps also here that digital advertising reveals its age and lack of maturity. With regards to the future of digital media, Kalle Lasn presents an interesting analogy, best re-presented in his own words:

> I see the electronic environment like a sort electronic beach, where we're panting for breath on the electronic beach just like

we were panting for breath thousands and thousands of years ago on the other beach because we had not learned how to breathe. I don't think we've learnt how to be in the electronic environment yet and I think that we're panting for breath and we're going crazy for ___ maybe future generations will learn how to negotiate electronic space in such a way that maybe they'll fly within it. I'm not sure I don't want to live in that kind of a world, but for the moment I see any kind of a further move from the physical to the virtual as being a...as being a fundamental mistake. A sort of a mistake on a level of...pushing this whole, you know this whole human experiment on planet earth. Pushing it into some sort of a cul-de-sac. (Interview, 20/10/2007)

It is difficult to ascertain the degree of metaphor involved here. Reminiscent of cybercultural discourses that see networks as engendering place, Kalle Lasn discusses the digital environment in terms of ecology where we may live. Although environments such as Second Life and more recent incarnations of virtual worlds offer interesting opportunities to explore online spaces, practices of full immersion are someway off for the majority of us. However, as discussed in Chapter 3, virtual environments continue to become mainstream, with commercial environments such as Webkinz (as well as other brands and products aimed at children) now making large sums of money on the strength of their real and virtually created brand, once valued at $2 billion (Kushner, 2008). In addition, although full immersion is not yet realizable, haptic developments involving how we touch, interact and apply pressure to digital tools point to new ways in how we may manage avatars and relate to others online. Touch is far more natural than manipulating a mouse or keyboard. As Manovich (2006) describes, many coming versions of human/computer interaction involve 'treating the whole of physical space around the user as part of a human-computer interface (HCI) by employing physical objects as carriers of information'. This scenario involves wearable computers and buildings and spaces that monitor users' interaction with them. It also involves wireless and electronic paper that can be flexed, folded and display digital information, and, of course, advertising.

Understanding Kalle Lasn's quote more literally, the electronic beach is also one to be found in real geographic space. As Schari (2007) describes in his account of the geospatial web, the virtual and the real are no longer separate. The tagging of places and digital cartography is an increasing practice that is certain to develop alongside the rise of mobile internet access and freely available mapping services such as Google Maps and Earth, and Microsoft Virtual Earth 3D. In this scenario, any point in space will be linked to a 'universe of commentary on its environmental, historical and cultural context, to related community events and activities and to personal stories and preferences' (ibid, p. 6). It also presents opportunities for advertisers to either present narratives of place, or engage users to tell and show their branded stories of place and happenings (for example, sponsored music festivals). The wider internet and the social and business opportunities it offers are immense and it is fair to say that despite the intensity of literature on new media structures since the 1970s, we are only at the beginning of an era characterized by networks and ubiquitous computing. The augmentation and layering of the physical with the virtual receives extra stimulus from the advent of cloud computing that potentially brings concurrent risk and accidents, as well ease and convenience. This scenario aligns well with the growth of the semantic web and a decrease in human intervention. As the semantic web comes online and we continue to employ geospatially aware agents, or personal assistants, to sift and sort social and technical arrangements, advertising will become increasingly personalized, timely and geographically relevant. The challenge for advertisers, technologists, law makers, regulators and creatives is thus to engage with citizens, users and consumers, to create truly opt-in participatory relationships that benefit all parties though freedom and the capacity to choose.

Questions for further discussion

▸ To what extent are consumers self-determined artisans of meaning creation?

▸ If human values of sociality are mediated by branded communication platforms, are authentic online relationships possible?

▸ To what extent are popularized web 2.0 discourses of participation a disguise for the production of immaterial labour?

Notes

1. Viewable at http://www.zen77094.zen.co.uk/vintagebroadcasting/itvlaunch.htm
2. For an excellent technical account of the history of television (along with other electronic media) see Orlik et al. (2006).
3. For more on the history of computers see Frauenfelder (2005) or the Computer History museum at http://www.computerhistory.org/
4. For more on the development of the internet have a look at the Internet Society (www.isoc.org/) and Orlik et al. (2006). Also have a look at the World Wide Web Consortium (W3C) for a full exposition of the origins of hypertext, Tim Berners-Lee, the first web browsers and the web.
5. These are Arc UK (Publicis Groupe), Digitas (Publicis Groupe), Draftfcb (Interpublic Group), Euro RSCG 4D Digital (Havas), Golley Slater Digital (Independent), Greenroom Digital (Interpublic Group), Ogilvy Interactive (WPP), R/GA London (Interpublic Group), Six and Co (FullSix International), Tribal DDB London (Omnicom), Weapon7 (Omnicom) and Wunderman (WPP).
6. The COI works with government departments and agencies to produce information campaigns on issues that affect all UK citizens – from health and education to benefits, rights and welfare.
7. See http://www.wpp.com/WPP/Companies/ for a list of WPP's 252 companies.
8. Name changed and simplified to Razorfish.
9. On organizing a half-day conference with Web 2.0 in the title, the not-for-profit organization IT@Cork were sent a Trademark Infringement letter by lawyers on acting on behalf of CMP Media, a company working with O'Reilly Media. It stated that IT@Cork should 'immediately cease and desist from utilizing Web 2.0' as the title of their event. The letter in full can be viewed at http://www.tomrafteryit.net/oreilly-trademarks-web-20-and-sets-lawyers-on-itcork/ (last accessed on 20/10/08).
10. A portmaneau of folk (as in user-generated) and taxonomy. It refers to social bookmarking, tagging and users indexing content.

11. Viewable at http:// www. uk.youtube.com/watch?v= NLlGopyXT_g

12. The interview with Tim Berners Lee and IBM's developerWorks can be accessed at http://www-128.ibm.com/developerworks/pod-cast/dwi/cm-int082206.mp3.

13. Because the internet enables advertisers to track responses to online advertisements, some reason that advertisers should pay for their internet ads on the basis of responses or performances. Conversely, others argue that such pricing and measurement methods would dismiss banner advertising's brand-building value and force web publishers to assume accountability for the creativity and effectiveness of messages (Shen, 2002).

14. See IAB unit guidelines at http://www.iab.net/iab_products_and_industry_services/1421/1443/1452

15. Direct response is an advertising technique that urges the audience to respond in a particular manner, usually to buy a product and provides the audience with the means to do so. This is in contrast with branding which aims to inculcate a longer-lasting relationship with an advertiser.

16. See link for the first ever Spam mail and responses to it at http://www.templetons.com/brad/spamreact.html

17. See <http://www.youtube.com/watch?v=ODshB09FQ8w for the Monty Python sketch on Spam.

18. For more information see DMA's 2007 Email Marketing Best Practice Guidelines at http://www.dma.org.uk/DocFrame/DocView.asp?id=230&sec=-1.

19. URL stands for Uniform Resource Locator, a string of characters that represents a resource on the internet.

20. For a full exposition of the technical composition of PageRank, see Brin and Page (1998).

21. For specific tips on how to optimize a site have a look at www.highrankings.com/forum/.

22. To see what pages looked like in years gone by have a look at The Wayback Machine provided by the Internet Archive at http://www.archive.org/web/web.php.

23. See the IAB for a full account of al online video formats at http://www.iabuk.net/en/1/videomarketing.html

24. See MySpace and the 'Channels' tab for more mini-episodes.

25. As Rosen (2000, 20–22) notes, DFJ's investment in Sabeer Bhatia and Jack Smith, the creators of Hotmail, soon paid dividends in the form of moving from zero to twelve million users within eighteen months of operation.

26. For wide range of examples of viral advertising see Kontraband at http://www.kontraband.com or the Viral Chart at http://www.viralchart.com/vcom.php

27. Although humour is by far the most common creative strategy, other campaigns are released virally before they make it to television – for example, Sony Bravia's "Balls" or Dove's viral "Evolution". Respectively these can be found at http://www.youtube.com/watch?v=oP5J4W5GQ3w and http://www.youtube.com/watch?v=L_aDpmfAzxI

28. Viewable at http://www.youtube.com/watch?v=p-CQkG5N5Eo

29. Stephen Brook (2005a) writing for *The Guardian* states that claims to being a spoof advertisement are potentially dubious arguing that the "advertisement" was shot on 35mm film and would have cost circa £40,000 to produce.

30. Viewable at http://www.youtube.com/watch?v=aZ-fyst4–7w. Also see the AdWeek blog http://adweek.blogs.com/adfreak/2005/01/vw_suicidebombe.html for discussion amongst advertising professionals and interested laypersons.

31. See Home Office video at http://www.youtube.com/watch?v=VFGVzt7c5bY

32. See Evolution video at http:// www.uk.youtube.com/watch?v=4VGBL-SiqD0 and a somewhat puerile, yet funny, spoof version at http:// www.uk.youtube.com/watch?v=7-kSZsvBY-A

33. Cadbury's Gorilla viewable at http:// www.uk.youtube.com/watch?v=-ZB6S1C9qWM

34. More detail about The Well can be found at http://www.well.com/

35. The enforcer for UK's advertising regulations is the Advertising Standards Authority. See http://www.asa.org.uk/asa/focus/background_briefings/Children.htm for more on codes to be adhered to by advertisers.

36. See http://www.entry-hamburg-hafen.de/86/

37. See Haffner (1997) 'The Epic Saga of The Well' http://www.wired.com/wired/archive/5.05/ff_well.html for an in-depth 22,000 word account of the WELL, the first digital virtual community.

38. For more on the history of virtual communities see Rheingold (1993) or the online version of his now appropriately titled seminal text, Virtual Communities. This can be legally accessed at http://www.rheingold.com/vc/book/

39. See http://www.immersence.com/

40. See http:// www.secondlife.com/whatis/

41. See http://www.youtube.com/watch?v=85npyAgtCQ0 for video on Pontiac and Second Life.
42. A portmanteau of branding and landscaping, brandscaping refers to interior design and architecture that reflect a brand's values (Klingmann, 2007).
43. Full list of games at http://www.mmorpg.com/gamelist.cfm/show/all
44. See http://www.dyson.co.uk/about/games/
45. Data transmission capabilities for third-generation phones are up to 14.4Mbit/s on the downlink and 5.8Mbit/s on the uplink.
46. Errki Huhtamo's citation is derived from an article he wrote for Vodafone Receiver. This is an excellent resource on mobile media containing soundbites and short articles from artists, thinkers and commentators. It can be found at http://www.receiver.vodafone.com/
47. For an in-depth look at writing on surveillance societies have a look at the online journal Surveillance and Society. This can be accessed at http://www.surveillance-and-society.org/
48. For an overview of surveillance in the United Kingdom, see 'A Report on the Surveillance Society' produced for the UK's Information Commissioner. This can be downloaded from http://www.news.bbc.co.uk/1/shared/bsp/hi/pdfs/02_11_06_surveillance.pdf
49. It is instructive to have at the Claritas homepage at www.claritas.com and the 'My Best Segments' tab to appreciate the depth and range of profiling.
50. Originally designed in 1837 this formed the first computer on paper although never built.
51. This was the first machine to use punch cards to control a sequence of operations.
52. In the United Kingdom, we can access electronic information held about by virtue of the Data Protection Act 1998 (chapter 29). See http://www.opsi.gov.uk/Acts/Acts1998/ukpga_19980029_en_1
53. http://www.zakon.org/robert/internet/timeline/
54. http://www.nethistory.dumbentia.com/
55. Netizen is a portmanteau of internet and citizen referring to someone who belongs to online communities.
56. William Gibson (1984) is the author of Neuromancer, a book regularly quoted as stating that cyberspace is a "consensual hallucination" (p.67).
57. See http://www.eff.org/

58. It can be found at http://www.youtube.com/watch?v=SwDEF-w4rJk

59. Although often conflated to viruses, Trojan horses and worms attack computers in different ways. A virus has to be manually opened and cannot be transmitted without human intervention. Trojan horses appear in the guise of useful software or files but once opened cause varying degree of damage, and it can also open "backdoors" allowing personal data to be compromised. Worms are similar to viruses but can move from computer to computer without human intervention.

60. Malware appears to perform a desirable function but in fact performs undisclosed malicious functions.

61. These can be downloaded from http://www.ftc.gov/os/2007/12/P859900stmt.pdf

62. David Rostan (2008), co-founder and president of ListensToYou, describes that this is an "everybody loses" situation: web users cannot control what personal information (their habits, interests, behaviours, etc.) they trade for the online activities they value (product and service offers, socializing, local event notification, etc.) and, therefore, do not get things they value or trust the ads they do get.

63. See readability tool at http://www.online-utility.org/english/readability_test_and_improve.jsp

64. For a more detailed account of UK information policy for both individuals and organizations, have a look at the Information Commissioner's Office at http://www.ico.gov.uk/

65. The Open Rights Group keep a running catalogue of data debacles at http://www.openrightsgroup.org/orgwiki/index.php/UK_Privacy_Debacles.

66. See International Working Group on Data Protection in Telecommunications. "Data Protection on the Internet: Report and Guidance." Adopted at the 20 meeting, Berlin, 19 November 1997.

67. These can be accessed at http://www.iabuk.net/en/1/behaviouraladvertisinggoodpractice.html

68. This can be accessed at http://www.usdoj.gov/oip/privstat.htm

69. This can be viewed at http://www.publicaccess.org/cableact.html

70. Case details can be viewed at http://cyber.law.harvard.edu/is02/readings/doubleclick.html

71. A full list of companies who have self-certified can be found at http://web.ita.doc.gov/safeharbor/shlist.nsf/webPages/safe+harbor+list

72. This can be found on FTC page at http://www.ftc.gov/opa/2000/05/privacy2k.shtm

73. The Act can be viewed at http://info.sen.ca.gov/pub/01–02/bill/sen/sb_1351–1400/sb_1386_bill_20020926_chaptered.html

74. The FTC proposed principles can be viewed at http://www.ftc.gov/os/2007/12/P859900stmt.pdf

75. The full set of responses can be viewed on the FTC website at http://www.ftc.gov/os/comments/behavioraladprinciples/index.shtm

76. A niche strategy of businesses, such as Amazon.com or Netflix, that sells a large number of unique items in relatively small quantities.

77. See BT Webwise page for more detail at http://www2.bt.com/static/i/btretail/webwise/index.html

78. An illuminating interview with the previous NebuAd CEO, Bob Dykes, can be found at http://www.clickz.com/showPage.html?page=3628009

79. It also raises interesting Minority Report styled questions. For example, user 17556639's searches included how to kill your wife; wife killer; how to kill a wife; poop; dead people; pictures of dead people; killed people; dead pictures; murder photo; steak and cheese; photo of death; death; dead people photos; photo of dead people; www.murderdpeople.com; decapitated photos; car crashes3; car crashes3; car crash photo (The Paradigm Shift, 2008).

80. See 23andme at http://www.23andme.com/

81. Botnets are made up of large numbers of computers that malicious hackers have brought under their control after infecting them with so-called Trojan virus programs.

82. These Regulations implement Articles 2, 4, 5(3), 6 to 13, 15 and 16 of Directive 2002/58/EC of the European Parliament described below.

83. The Information Commissioner's Office is the UK's independent authority set up to promote access to official information and to protect personal information. It reports directly to Parliament and is sponsored by the UK's Ministry of Justice.

84. Available at http://www.ftc.gov/reports/canspam05/051220canspamrpt.pdf

85. Study available at http://www.ftc.gov/reports/optout05/050801optoutetailersrpt.pdf.

86. Available at http://www.consumersinternational.org/shared_asp_files/GFSR.asp?NodeID=97737

87. For the non-broadcast codes see http://www.cap.org.uk/cap/codes/. The codes cover content of advertisements in print, on posters, in new media and the cinema. They also cover all sales promotions, the use of personal data for direct marketing and the delivery of mail order goods or refunds.

88. It does however tell that children under 16 ask their parents for access.

89. Viewable at http://www.youtube.com/watch?v=eGlUN-HW8TA

90. Viewable at http://www.youtube.com/watch?v=V2nL5sSSvd0

91. Report available at http://www.publications.parliament.uk/pa/cm200708/cmselect/cmcumeds/353/353.pdf

92. Report available at http://www.dcsf.gov.uk/byronreview/pdfs/Final%20Report%20Bookmarked.pdf

93. Although see Sasser et al. (2007) for a discussion of how strategy may impede creativity in multiple media integrated marketing communications (IMC) campaigns.

94. Weisberg (1993) established this through the number of recordings available of composers. This measure was used because it represents the combined judgements of musicians, recording companies and the record buying public.

95. Viewable at http://www.uniqlo.jp/uniqlock/

96. Viewable in full at http://www.yellowmachine.us/controlz/#

97. See http:// www.journeys.louisvuitton.com/

98. Viewable at http://www.subservientchicken.com.

99. See http:// www.awards.spotthebull.com/play/game

100. See http://www.pokelondon.com/portfolio/orange/balloonacy/

101. For an extensive list of definitions of interactivity see McMillan and Hwang (2005, 127–130).

102. Viewable at nikeid.nike.com/

103. The tennis court can be downloaded from http://www.fanta.eu/Virtual_Fanta_Tennis.pdf and the mobile software from http:// www.m.fanta.eu. Also see http:// www.uk.youtube.com/watch?v=r-Ya293u34c for Fanta Virtual Tennis in use.

104. For more detail see The Inspiration Room: http:// www.theinspirationroom.com/daily/2007/augmented-reality-at-wellington-zoo/

105. See http://www.dandad.org/annual08/#/categories/ONLN/21142

106. See http://www.dandad.org/annual08/#/categories/WEBS/16236

107. For more on this from a strategic political communication perspective, see Bakir (2010, forthcoming).

108. See video at http://www.youtube.com/watch?v=FZ1st1Vw2kY

109. Also have a look at Henry Jenkins' blog post on transmedia story-telling at http://www.henryjenkins.org/2007/03/transmedia_storytelling_101.html

110. There are blogs on potential for transmedia advertising with many linked to from http:// www.farisyakob.typepad.com/blog/2006/10/transmedia_plan.html

111. Coke Happiness Factory 1 at http:// www.uk.youtube.com/watch?v=NwCn-D5xFdc

112. Coke Happiness Factory 2 at http:// www.uk.youtube.com/watch?v=Uzr4Gq1KI5w

113. Happiness Factory global website at http://www.coca-cola.com/HF/index.jsp

114. See http://www.dandad.org/annual08/#/categories/MMKT/28447

115. The 2008 award winning work can be found at http://www.web-byawards.com/webbys/current.php?media_id=127&season=12

116. After a conference I attended in Vancouver, Canada, in October 2007, I had chance to meet and interview Kalle Lasn.

117. For example, see http://www.adbusters.org/gallery/spoofads

118. It is also interesting to note the rise in shopping as an addictive activity where consumers buy for motives that are not directly related to the actual possession of the goods. See Eccles (2002) for more on this.

119. At the time of writing Wikipedia has a useful introductory account of Resource Description Framework (RDF) languages. See W3C for a range of more technical overviews and introductions http://www.w3.org/RDF/#overview

120. For more on this see W3C Semantic Web Frequently Asked Questions at http://www.w3.org/RDF/FAQ

References

Adbrands.net (2008) The UK's Top 50 Advertisers in 2007, http://www.mind-advertising.com/uk/, date accessed 09 February 2009.

Adland (2008) Happy 30th birthday, spam, from Adland with cake, http:// www.commercial-archive.com/node/143627, date accessed 09 February 2009.

Advertising Age (2008) Agency Report 2008 Index, http:// www.adage.com/datacenter/article?article_id=126698, date accessed 09 February 2009.

Alberti, L. (1972 [1435]) 'On Painting and Sculpture: The Latin texts of De Pictura and De Statua', in J. Bolter and R. Grusin (eds) (1999) *Remediation*, MIT.

Albrechtslund, A. (2008) 'Online Social Networking as Participatory Surveillance', *First Monday*, 13 (3), http:// www.firstmonday.org/htbin/cgiwrap/bin/ojs/index.php/fm/article/view/2142/1949, date accessed 09 February 2009.

Allen, M. (2007) *The History of Web 2.0: Liberty, Economics and the Law of the Father*, Conference paper delivered at Let's Play, Association of Internet Researchers (AOIR), Vancouver 2007.

Allen, K. (2007a) Spending on internet advertising 'to double', *The Guardian*, http://technology.guardian.co.uk/news/story/0,,2125651,00.html?gusrc=rss&feed=20, date accessed 09 February 2009.

Allsop, D.T., Bryce, B.R. and Hoskins, J.A. (2007) 'Word-of-Mouth Research: Principles and Applications', *Journal of Advertising Research*, 47 (4), 398–411.

Alstiel, T. and Grow, G.M. (2006) *Advertising Strategy: Creative Tactics from the Outside/In* (Thousand Oaks, CA: Sage).

Amabile, T. (1996) *Creativity in Context* (Boulder, CO: Westview Press).

Anderson, B. (2006) *Imagined Communities* (London: Verso).

Anderson, C. (2006b) *The Long Tail: Why the Future of Business Is Selling Less of More* (New York: Hyperion).

Anderson, S.D. (2006) 'Technological Chronicles', in P.B. Orlik, S.D. Anderson, L.A. Day and W.L. Patrick (eds) *Exploring Electronic Media: Chronicles and Challenges* (Oxford: Blackwell).

Ang, I. (2000) 'New Technologies, Audience Measurement, and the Tactics of Television Consumption', in J. Caldwell (ed.) *Electronic Media and Technoculture* (New York: Routledge).

AOL (2008) Public comments: # 228, Project No. P859900: Online Behavioral Advertising: Moving the Discussion Forward to Possible

Self-Regulatory Principles, *FTC*, http://www.ftc.gov/os/comments/behavioraladprinciples/080411aol.pdf, date accessed 09 February 2009.

Arthur, C. (2008) Phorm fires privacy row for ISPs. [online]. *The Guardian*, http://www.guardian.co.uk/technology/2008/mar/06/internet.privacy?gusrc=rss&feed=networkfront, date accessed 09 February 2009.

Arvidsson, A. (2004) 'On the "Pre-History of the Panoptic Sort": Mobility in Market Research', *Surveillance and Society*, 1 (4), 456–474.

Arvidsson, A. (2006) *Brands: Meaning and Value in Media Culture* (Oxon: Routledge).

ASA (2005) *Annual Report 2005*, http://www.asa.org.uk/NR/rdonlyres/A14EC76B-5558–4D33-B69B-4A4A538A2363/0/ASA_Annual_Report_2005.pdf, date accessed 09 February 2009.

ASA (2006) *CAP confirms that its Code covers viral advertisements*, http://www.asa.org.uk/cap/news_events/news/2006/CAP+confirms+that+its+Code+covers+viral+advertisements.htm, date accessed 09 February 2009.

ASA (2008) *ASA survey reveals self-regulation is effective in digital media*, http://www.asa.org.uk/asa/news/news/2008/ASA+survey+reveals+self-regulation+is+effective+in+digital+media.htm, date accessed 07 January 2000.

Assael, H. (2005) 'A Demographic and Psychographic Profile of Heavy Internet Users and Users by Type of Internet Usage', *Journal of Advertising Research*, 45 (1), 93–123.

Aun, F. (2007) Forrester Sees Steady Growth for European Online Marketing, *ClickZ*, http:// www.clickz.com/showPage.html?page=3626421, date accessed 09 February 2009.

Aun, F. (2008) One in Five Users Gives Mobile Search and Audio Ads Thumbs Up, *ClickZ*, http://www.clickz.com/showPage.html?page=3626264, date accessed 09 February 2009.

Baker, S. (2008) *The Numerati* (London: Jonathan Cape).

Bakir, V. and Barlow, D. (2007) *Communication in the Age of Suspicion: Trust and the Media* (London: Palgrave-Macmillan).

Ball, K., Lyon, D., Wood, D.M., Norris, C. and Raab, C. (2006) A Report on the Surveillance Society, *The Surveillance Studies Network*, http://www.ico.gov.uk/upload/documents/library/data_protection/practical_application/surveillance_society_full_report_2006.pdf, date accessed 09 February 2009.

Bardini, T. (2006) Hypervirus: A Clinical Report, *Ctheory*, http://www.ctheory.net/articles.aspx?id=504 date accessed 09 February 2009.

Barry, P. (2008) *The Advertising Concept Book* (London: Thames and Hudson).

Bartz, D. (2008) Google says it would support U.S. privacy law, *Reuters*, http:// www.uk.reuters.com/article/internetNews/idUKN103823132 0080612, date accessed 09 February 2009.

Bassett, C. (2008) New Maps for Old? The Cultural Stakes of '2.0', *Fibreculture*. 13, http:// www.journal.fibreculture.org/issue13/issue 13_bassett.html, date accessed 09 February 2009.

Bastholm, L. (2008) Social Storytelling, *Creativity*, http:// www. creativity-online.com/?action=news:article&newsId=131936&sectio nName=pov, date accessed 09 February 2009.

Battelle, J. (2005) *The Search: How Google and Its Rivals Rewrote the Rules of Business and Transformed Our Culture* (New York: Portfolio).

Baudrillard, J. (1994 [1981]) *Simulacra and Simulation* (University of Michigan Press).

Baudrillard, J. (2002) *Screened Out* (London: Verso).

Bauer, R.A. and Greyser, A.A. (1968) *Advertising in America: The Consumer View* (Cambridge, MA: Harvard Business School).

Bauman, Z. (2000) *Liquid Modernity* (Cambridge: Polity Press).

Bauman, Z. (2005) *Liquid Life* (Cambridge: Polity Press).

BBC (2008) *Firm 'broke rules' over data loss*, http:// www.news.bbc. co.uk/1/hi/uk_politics/7575989.stm, date accessed 09 February 2009.

BBC (2008a) *Bank customer data sold on eBay*, http:// www.news.bbc. co.uk/1/hi/uk/7581540.stm, date accessed 09 February 2009.

BBC (2008b) *MoD computer hard drive missing*, http:// www.news.bbc. co.uk/1/hi/uk/7662604.stm, date accessed 09 February 2009.

BBC (2008c) *Mobile internet usage on the rise*, http:// www.news.bbc. co.uk/1/hi/technology/7748372.stm, date accessed 09 February 2009.

Bell, J.A. (1992) 'Creativity, TV Commercial Popularity, and Advertising Expenditures', *International Journal of Advertising*, 11 (2), 168–183.

Beltramini, R.F. (2003) Advertising Ethics: The Ultimate Oxymoron? *Journal of Business Ethics*, 48 (3), 215–216.

Bennett, C.J. (1992) *Regulating Privacy: Data Protection and Public Privacy in Europe and the United States* (Ithaca, NY: Cornell University Press).

Bentham, J. (1843) *The Works of Jeremy Bentham* (Edinburgh: William Tait), available from Google Books, http:// www.books.google.co.uk/ books/pdf/The_Works_of_Jeremy_Bentham.pdf?id=mG1YAAAAM AAJ&output=pdf&sig=ACfU3U0khpJ9ZKUrUnkHRonS2RwDUaCfW A, date accessed 09 February 2009.

Berger, W. (2004) *Advertising Today* (London: Phaidon).

Bergkamp, L. (2003) *European Community Law for the New Economy* (New York: Intersentia).

Berners-Lee, T., Hendler, J. and Lassila, O. (2001) The Semantic Web, *Scientific American*, http://www-personal.si.umich.edu/~rfrost/courses/SI110/readings/In_Out_and_Beyond/Semantic_Web.pdf, date accessed 09 February 2009.

Bhat, S., Bevans, M. and Sengupta, S. (2002) 'Measuring Users' Web Activity to Evaluate and Enhance Advertising Effectiveness', *Journal of Advertising*, 31 (3), 97–106.

Bigo, D. and Guild, E. (2005) *Controlling Frontiers: Free Movement into and within Europe* (London: Ashgate).

Bilton, C. (2007) *Management and Creativity: From Creative Industries to Creative Management* (Oxford: Blackwell).

Black, E (2002) *IBM and the Holocaust* (London: Time Warner).

Blumler, J.G. and McQuail, D. (1969) *Television in Politics* (Chicago: University of Chicago Press).

Bodden, K. (2005) 'Pop Goes The Trademark? Competitive Advertising on the Internet', *Shidler Journal for Law, Commerce and Technology*, 12, http://www.lctjournal.washington.edu/vol1/a012Bodden.html, date accessed 17 April 2006.

Bogart, L. (1958) *The Age of Television* (New York: Frederick Ungar).

Bolter, J. and Grusin, R. (1999) *Remediation* (Massachusetts: MIT).

Boudourides, M.A and Drakou, E. (2000) *Gender@Cyberspace*, http://www.math.upatras.gr/~mboudour/articles/gender@cyberspace.html, date accessed 09 February 2009.

Bourdieu, P. (1984) *Distinction: A Social Critique of the Judgment of Taste* (Cambridge: Harvard University Press).

Bovee, C.L. and Arens, W.F. (1992) *Contemporary Advertising* (Boston: Richard D. Irwin, Inc).

boyd, d.m. and Ellison, N.B. (2007) 'Social Network Sites: Definition, History, and Scholarship', *Journal of Computer-Mediated Communication*, 13 (1), article 11, http:// www.jcmc.indiana.edu/vol13/issue1/boyd.ellison.html, date accessed 09 February 2009.

boyd, d.m. (2006) 'Friends, Friendsters, and Top 8: Writing community into being on social network sites', *First Monday*, 11 (12), http://www.firstmonday.org/htbin/cgiwrap/bin/ojs/index.php/fm/article/view/1418/1336, date accessed 09 February 2009.

Boyd, H.C. (2006) 'Persuasive Talk: Is It What You Say or How You Say It?' *Journal of Advertising Research*, 46 (1), 84–92.

Brackett, L.A. and Carr, B.N. (2001) 'Cyberspace Advertising vs. Other Media: Consumer vs. Mature Student Attitudes', *Journal of Advertising Research*, 41 (5), 23–32.

Brandrepublic (2007) *Dare Scoops Digital Agency of the Year*, http://www.brandrepublic.com/InDepth/Features/773098/Dare-scoops-Digital-Agency-Year/, date accessed 09 February 2009.

Brandrepublic (2008) *Top 100 online advertisers*, http://www.bran-drepublic.com/Research/LeagueTables/795356/Top-100-online-advertisers/, date accessed 09 February 2009.

Brin, D. (1996) The Transparent Society, *Wired*, http://www.wired.com/wired/archive/4.12/fftransparent.html, date accessed 09 February 2009.

Brin, D. (2008) David Brin Rebuts Schneier in Defense of a Transparent Society, *Wired*, http://www.wired.com/politics/security/news/2008/03/brin_rebuttal, date accessed 09 February 2009.

Brin, S. and Page, L. (1998) 'The Anatomy of a Large-Scale Hypertextual Web Search Engine', *Computer Networks and ISDN Systems*, 30 (1–7), 107–117.

Briskman, S. and Smith, M. (2004) Spyware and the Law, *Olswang*, http://insight.zdnet.co.uk/business/legal/0,39020487,39172719–2,00.htm, date accessed 12 April 2006.

Brook, S. (2005a) VW to Sue Polo Ad Duo, *Media Guardian*, http://www.media.guardian.co.uk/site/story/0,14173,1398826,00.html, date accessed 09 February 2009.

Brown, C., Hanc, B-L. and Pangsapa, N. (1999) 'Cognitive Dissonance and Selective Perception', in J.P Jones (ed.) *The Advertising Business* (Thousand Oaks, CA: Sage).

Brown, M. and Muchira, R. 2004) 'Investigation of the Relationship between Internet Privacy Concerns and Online Purchase Behaviour', *Journal of Electronic Commerce Research*, 5 (1), 62–70.

Bruner, J. (1991) 'The Narrative Construction of Reality', *Critical Inquiry*, 18, 1–21.

Bruns, A. (2006) 'Towards Produsage: Futures for User-Led Content Production', in F. Sudweeks, H. Hrachovec, and C. Ess (eds) Proceedings: *Cultural Attitudes towards Communication and Technology 2006*, Perth: Murdoch University, http:// www.produsage.org/files/12132812018_towards_produsage_0.pdf, date accessed 09 February 2009.

Bullmore, J. (1999) 'The Advertising Creative Process', in J.P Jones (ed.) *The Advertising Business* (Thousand Oaks, CA: Sage).

Burgess, J. (2008) ' "All Your Chocolate Rain are Belong to Us?" Viral Video, YouTube and the Dynamics of Participatory Culture' in G. Lovink and S. Niederer (eds) *Video Vortex Reader* (Amsterdam: Institute of Network Cultures).

Burns, E. (2007) China's Online Population Adapts Internet with Speed, *ClickZ*, http://www.clickz.com/showPage.html?page=3627587, date accessed 09 February 2009.

Burns, E. (2007a) Report: Ad Networks Used to Infect Computers, *ClickZ*, http://www.clickz.com/showPage.html?page=3626228, date accessed 09 February 2009.

Burns, E. (2008a) Brands Could Learn From Users in Second Life, *ClickZ*, http://www.clickz.com/showPage.html?page=3630140, date accessed 09 February 2009.

Burns, E. (2008b) Report: In-Game Ads Already Plentiful, Accepted, *ClickZ*, http://www.clickz.com/showPage.html?page=3626497, date accessed 09 February 2009.

Burns, E. (2008c) U.K.'s Online Ad Spend Continues Steady Climb, *ClickZ*, http://www.clickz.com/showPage.html?page=3629054, d date accessed 09 February 2009.

Busch, A. (2006) 'From Safe Harbour to the Rough Sea? Privacy Disputes across the Atlantic', *SCRIPTed*, 3 (4), 304–321, http://www.law.ed.ac.uk/ahrc/script-ed/vol3–4/busch.asp, date accessed 09 February 2009.

BusinessWeek (2006) It's Not All Fun And Games, http://www.businessweek.com/magazine/content/06_18/b3982007.htm, date accessed 09 February 2009.

Button, S. (2008) Consumer protection against unfair trading regulations: can it work? *iMediaConnection*, http://www.imediaconnection.com/content/19583.asp, date accessed 09 February 2009.

Calcutt, A. (1999) *White Noise: An A-Z of the Contradictions in Cyberculture* (London: MacMillan).

Campaign (2007) *Digital shops profits soar by 56 per cent*, 2/29/2008, p. 2

CAP (2003) *The CAP Code*, http://www.cap.org.uk/cap/codes/cap_code/CodeIndex.htm?code_id=19#expanded, date accessed 09 February 2009.

CAP (2006) *Help Note on Advertising Virals*, www.cap.org.uk/cap/advice_online/help_notes, date accessed 09 February 2009.

Cappo, J. (2003) *The Future of Advertising* (New York: McGraw Hill).

Carphone Warehouse/London School of Economics (2008) *Mobile Life: The Connected World*, http://www.mobilelife2007.co.uk/, date accessed 09 February 2009.

Carr, N. (2007) AdBlock Plus can quietly kill ads – and perhaps the internet economy, The *Guardian*, http://www.guardian.co.uk/technology/2007/sep/20/guardianweeklytechnologysection.internet?gusrc=rss&feed=technology, date accessed 09 February 2009.

Carroll, L. (2000) *Alice's Adventures in Wonderland and Through the Looking Glass* (New York: Signet Classics).

Carvajal, D. (2008) Concern in Europe on Cellphone Ads for Children, *The New York Times*, http://www.nytimes.com/2008/03/08/technology/08mobile.html?_r=2&ei=5088&en=5950f0d550bf8b3b&ex=1362888000&adxnnl=1&oref=slogin&partner=rssnyt&emc=rss&adxnnlx=1207314013-mYG0T5F0cg4YBG38YLscyg&oref=slogin, date accessed 09 February 2009.

Castells, M. (2001 [1996]) *The Rise of the Network Society* (Oxford: Blackwell).

Caudill, E.M. and Murphy, P.E. (2000) Consumer Online Privacy: Legal and Ethical Issues, *Journal of Public Policy and Marketing*, 19 (1), 7–19.

CE (2003) *Convention for the Protection of Human Rights and Fundamental Freedoms as amended by Protocol No. 11*, http://www.echr.coe.int/nr/rdonlyres/d5cc24a7-dc13–4318-b457–5c9014916d7a/0/englishanglais.pdf, date accessed 09 February 2009.

Chaudhuri, H.R. and Majumdar, S. (2006) 'Of Diamonds and Desires: Understanding Conspicuous Consumption from a Contemporary Marketing Perspective', *Academy of Marketing Science Review*, 10 (8), 1–18, http://www.amsreview.org/articles/chaudhuri09–2006.pdf, date accessed 09 February 2009.

Chen, K-T., Huang, P. and Lei C-H. (2005) 'Game traffic analysis: An MMORPG perspectives', *Computer Networks*, 50 (16), 3002–3023.

Cheong, H.J. and Morrison, M.A. (2008) 'Consumers' Reliance on Product Information and Recommendations Found in UGC', *Journal of Interactive Advertising*, 8 (2), http://www.jiad.org/article103, date accessed 09 February 2009.

Cheung, J. (2007) Report: 95 percent of all e-mail has that spammy smell, *ars technical*, http:// www.arstechnica.com/news.ars/post/20071212-report-95-percent-of-all-e-mail-has-that-spammy-smell.html, date accessed 09 February 2009.

Cho, C. and Leckenby, J. (1997) 'Interactivity as a Measurement of Advertising Effectiveness: Antecedents and Consequences of Interactivity in Web Advertising', *Proceedings of the 1999 Conference of the American Academy of Advertising*.

Clark, A. (2007) Microsoft buys online advertiser for record £3bn, *The Guardian*, http://www.guardian.co.uk/business/2007/may/19/microsoft.technology, date accessed 09 February 2009.

Clark, C. (1987) 'Science, Superstition, and Consumer Research', *Journal of Advertising Research*, 27 (1), RC-9 – RC-11.

Clarke, A.C. (1973) *Profiles of the Future: An Inquiry into the Limits of the Possible* (London: Pan).

Clarke, R. (2003) *Dataveillance: Fifteen Years on,* http://www.anu.edu.au/people/Roger.Clarke/DV/DVNZ03.html, date accessed 09 February 2009.

ClickZ (2008) Top 50 Advertisers by Media Value in September 2008, http://www.clickz.com/3631918, date accessed 09 February 2009.

comScore (2006) *More than Half of MySpace Visitors are Now Age 35 or Older, as the Site's Demographic Composition Continues to Shift,* http://www.comscore.com/press/release.asp?press=1019, date accessed 09 February 2009.

comScore (2007) *U.K. Social Networking Site Usage Highest in Europe*, http://www.comscore.com/press/release.asp?press=1801, date accessed 09 February 2009.

comScore (2009) *comScore Releases June 2009 U.S. Search Engine Rankings*, http://www.comscore.com/Press_Events/Press_Releases/2009/7/comScore_Releases_June_2009_U.S._Search_Engine_Rankings/(language)/eng-US, date accessed 02 July 2009.

comScore (2009a) *Global Internet Audience Surpasses 1 Billion Visitors*, http://www.comscore.com/Press_Events/Press_Releases/2009/1/Global_Internet_Audience_1_Billion, date accessed 12 February 2009.

Condon, C. (n.d.) Why I'm Called Fuzzyman. [online]. *Nethistory*, http:// www.nethistory.dumbentia.com/fuzzy.html, date accessed 09 February 2009.

Cornell University Law School (2008) *§ 551. Protection of subscriber privacy.* http://www.law.cornell.edu/uscode/47/usc_sec_47_00000551----000-.html, date accessed 09 February 2009.

Cortese, A.J.P. (2004) *Provocateur: Images of Women and Minorities in Advertising* (New York: Rowman and Littlefield).

Coyne, R. (1999) *Technoromanticicism: Digital Narrative, Holism, and the Romance of the Real* (Massachusetts: MIT).

Crawford, S.P. (2005) 'First Do No Harm: The Problem of Spyware', *Berkeley Technology Law Journal*, 20, 1–50.

Crowston, K. and Williams, M. (2000) 'Reproduced and Emergent Genres of Communication on the World Wide Web', *The Information Society*, 16 (3), 201–215.

Culnan, M.J. (2000) 'Protecting Privacy Online: Is Self-Regulation Working?', *Journal of Public Policy and Marketing*, 19 (1), 20–26.

Cuneo, A.Z. (2008) Study: This business is getting personal. *Advertising Age*, 49 (17), http:// www.adage.com/results?endeca=1&return=endeca&search_offset=0&search_order_by=score&x=0&y=0&search_phrase=Study%3A+This+business+is+getting+personal, date accessed 09 February 2009.

Cunningham, T., Hall, A. S. and Young, C. (2006) 'The Advertising Magnifier Effect: An MTV Study', *Journal of Advertising Research*, 46 (4), 369–380.

Dahlen, M. (2001) 'Banner Advertisements through a New Lens', *Journal of Advertising Research*, 41 (4), 23–30.

Dahlen, M., Rasch, A. and Rosengren, S. (2003) 'Love at First Site? A Study of Website Advertising Effectiveness', *Journal of Advertising Research*, 43 (1), 25–33.

Dahlen, M., Rosengren , S. and Törn, F. (2008) 'Advertising Creativity Matters', *Journal of Advertising Research*, 48 (3), 392–403.

Daugherty, T., Eastin, M.S. and Bright, L. (2008) 'Exploring Consumer Motivations for Creating User-Generated Content', *Journal of*

Interactive Advertising, http:// www.jiad.org/article101, date accessed 09 February 2009.

Davison, N. (1991) 'Literary and Electronic Hypertext: Borges, Criticism, Literary Research, and the Computer', *Hispania*, 74 (4), 1159–1161.

De Certeau, M. (1988) *The Practice of Everyday Life* (CA: University of California).

Deleuze, G. (1992) 'Postscript on the Societies of Control', *October*, 59 (4) (Cambridge: MIT).

Department of Commerce (2005) *Safe Harbor Workbook*, http://www.export.gov/safeharbor/sh_workbook.html, date accessed 09 February 2009.

DePaulo, P.J. (1990) 'View from the Front: An Interview with Ernest Dichter, Ph.D.', *The Communicator. The Newsletter for the Society of Consumer Psychology*, 25 (3), 4–5.

Dery, M. (1995) *Flame Wars: The Discourse of Cyberspace* (Durham, NC: Duke University).

Desmond, J., McDonagh, P. and O'Donohoe, S. (2000) 'Counter-Culture and Consumer Society', *Markets and Culture*, 4 (3), 241–279.

developerWorks (2006) developerWorks Interviews: Tim Berners-Lee, *IBM*, http://www.ibm.com/developerworks/podcast/dwi/cm-int082206txt.html, date accessed 09 February 2009.

Dick, P. (1969) *Ubik* (New York: Vintage Books).

DoubleClick (2005) *The Decade in Online Advertising*, www.doubleclick.com/us/knowledge_central, date accessed 09 February 2009.

Drèze, X. and Zufryden, F (1998) *Is Internet Advertising Ready for the Prime Time*, http://www.xdreze.org/Publications/webgrp.pdf, date accessed 20 July 2007. Driessen, H. (2004) 'Jokes and Joking', in N.J.B. Smeler and P.B. Baltes (eds) *International Encyclopedia of the Social and Behavioral Sciences* (Amsterdam and New York: Elsevier Science Ltd).

Ducoffe, R.H. (1996) 'Advertising Value and Advertising on the Web', *Journal of Advertising Research*, 36 (5), 21–35.

Durman, P. (2007) Ad agencies fight for online market, *The Times*, http://www.business.timesonline.co.uk/tol/business/industry_sectors/technology/article1781455.ece, date accessed 09 February 2009.

Eccles, S. (2002) 'The Lived Experiences of Women as Addictive Consumers', *Journal of Research for Consumers*, 4, http://www.jrconsumers.com/academic_articles/issue_4/Eccles.pdf, date accessed 09 February 2009.

The Economist (2006) *The Ultimate Marketing Machine*, July, 69.

The Economist (2007) *Learning to Live with Big Brother*, http://www.economist.com/world/international/displaystory.cfm?story_id=9867324, date accessed 09 February 2009.

Edelman, B. (2006) *Spyware: Research, Testing, Legislation, and Suits*, http://www.benedelman.org/spyware/#legislation, date accessed 20 April 2006.

Edge (2006) *The Making of Adventureland*, 162, 104–107.

Edge (2008) *Welcome to the Edge forum*, http://www.computerandvideogames.com/edge/forum/, date accessed 09 February 2009.

Elliot, S. (2008) Traditional Media Not Dead Yet for Marketing, Study Says, *The New York Times*, http:// www.tvdecoder.blogs.nytimes.com/2008/06/18/traditional-media-not-dead-yet-for-marketing-study-says/?partner=rssnyt&emc=rss, date accessed 09 February 2009.

Elmer, G. (2003) 'A Diagram of Panoptic Surveillance', *New Media and Society*, 5 (2), 231–247.

El-murad, J. and West, D. (2004) 'The Definition and Measurement of Creativity: What Do We Know?' *Journal of Advertising Research*, 44 (2), 188–201.

eMarketer (2007) *Let the Games Begin Advertising!* http://www.emarketer.com/Article.aspx?id=1004739, date accessed 09 February 2009.

eMarketer (2009) *Internet Users Spending Even More Time on Web*, http://www.emarketer.com/Article.aspx?id=1006869, date accessed 09 February 2009.

European Commission (n.d.) European Convention for the Protection of Human Rights and Fundamental Freedoms, Article 8, *Europa*, http://www.ec.europa.eu/justice_home/fsj/privacy/law/treaty_en.htm, date accessed 09 February 2009.

European Union (2002) Directive 2002/58/EC of the European Parliament and of the Council of 12 July 2002 concerning the processing of personal data and the protection of privacy in the electronic communications sector (Directive on privacy and electronic communications), *Eurlex*, http://www.europa.eu.int/smartapi/cgi/sga_doc?smartapi!celexapi!prod!CELEXnumdoc&lg=en&numdoc=32002L0058&model=guichett, date accessed 09 February 2009.

Ewing, A.B. (ed) (2005) *The Patriot Act Reader* (New York: Nova Science).

Export.Gov (n.d.) *Safe Harbor Overview*, http://www.export.gov/safeharbor/SH_Overview.asp, date accessed 09 February 2009.

Faber, R.J. and Stafford, M.R. (2005) 'The Future of Consumer Decision Making in the Age of New Media Promotions and Advertising', in M.R. Stafford and R.J. Faber (eds) *Advertising, Promotion and New Media* (New York: M.E. Sharpe).

Facebook (2007) *Facebook Unveils Facebook Ads*, http://www.facebook.com/press/releases.php?p=9176, date accessed 09 February 2009.

Facebook (2008) Public comments: # 228, Project No. P859900: Online Behavioral Advertising: Moving the Discussion Forward to Possible

Self-Regulatory Principles, *FTC*, http://www.ftc.gov/os/comments/be havioraladprinciples/080411facebook.pdf, date accessed 09 February 2009.

Federal Trade Commission (2007) # 228, Project No. P859900: Online Behavioral Advertising: Moving the Discussion Forward to Possible Self-Regulatory Principles, *Ultraseek*, http://www.search.ftc.gov/query. html?qt=advertising&col=hsr&col=news&col=full, date accessed 09 February 2009.

Federal Trade Commission (2009) *FTC Staff Revises Online Behavioral Advertising Principles*, http://www.ftc.gov/os/2009/02/ P085400behavadreport.pdf, date accessed 14 February 2009.

Federal Trade Commission (2009a) *FTC to Host Ad It Up! Kids in a Commercial World*, http://www.ftc.gov/opa/2009/02/aditup.shtm, date accessed 25 February 2009.

Foucault, M. (1977) *Discipline and Punish* (London: Penguin).

Fowles, J. (1996) *Advertising and Popular Culture* (Thousand Oaks, CA: Sage).

Frauenfelder, M. (2005) *The Computer* (London: Sevenoaks).

FTC (2000) *FTC Recommends Congressional Action to Protect Consumer Privacy Online*, http://www.ftc.gov/opa/2000/05/privacy2k.shtm, date accessed 09 February 2009.

Fuchs, C. (2009) *Social Networking Sites and the Surveillance Society: A Critical Case Study of the Usage of studiVZ, Facebook, and MySpace by Students in Salzburg in the Context of Electronic Surveillance.* Forschungsgruppe Unified Theory of Information (Research Group Unified Theory of Information).

Fujimoto, K. (2005) 'The Third Stage Paradigm: Territory Machines from the Girls' Pager Revolution to Mobile Aesthetics', in M. Ito, D. Okabe, and M. Matsuda (eds) *Personal, Portable, Pedestrian: Mobile Phones in Japanese Life* (Cambridge: MIT).

Fuller, M. (2003) *Essays on the Software Culture: Behind the Blip* (New York: Autonomedia).

Furedi, F. (2002) *The Culture of Fear* (London: Continuum).

Furnham, A. (2002) *Growing up with Advertising* (London: The Social Affairs Unit).

Gallagher, K., Foster, K.D. and Parsons, J. (2001) 'The Medium Is Not the Message: Advertising Effectiveness and Content Evaluation in Print and on the Web', *Journal of Advertising Research*, 41 (4), 57–70.

Gallup, G. (1974) 'How Advertising Works', *Journal of Advertising Research*, 14 (3), 7–11.

Gangadharbatla, H. (2008) 'Facebook Me: Collective Self-Esteem, Need to Belong and Internet Self-Efficacy as Predictors of the iGeneration's Attitudes toward Social Networking Sites', *Journal of*

Interactive Advertising, http:// www.jiad.org/article100, date accessed 09 February 2009.

Garfield, B. (2008) Widgets Are Made for Marketing, So Why Aren't More Advertisers Using Them? *Advertising Age*, http:// www.adage.com/article?article_id=132778, date accessed 09 February 2009.

Garfield, B. (2008a) Your Data With Destiny, *Advertising Age*, http://www.adage.com/digital/article?article_id=130969, date accessed 09 February 2009.

Gere, C. (2002) *Digital Culture* (London: Reaktion).

Gerth, H. and Wright Mills, C. (1946) *From Max Weber: Essays in Sociology* (New York: Oxford University).

Giddens, A. (1990) *The Consequences of Modernity* (Cambridge: Polity).

Golan, G.J. and Zaidner, L. (2008) 'Creative Strategies in Viral Advertising: An Application of Taylor's Six-Segment Message Strategy Wheel', *Journal of Computer-Mediated Communication*, 13 (4), 959–972.

Goodwin, C. (1991) Privacy: Recognition of a Consumer Right, *Journal of Public Policy and Marketing*, 10 (1): 149–166.

Google (2008) *Corporate Information: Technology Overview*, http://www.google.com/corporate/tech.html, date accessed 09 February 2009.

Google (2008a) Public comments: # 228, Project No. P859900: Online Behavioral Advertising: Moving the Discussion Forward to Possible Self-Regulatory Principles, *FTC*, http://www.ftc.gov/os/comments/behavioraladprinciples/080404google.pdf, date accessed 09 February 2009.

Gordon, S. (2003) *Privacy: A Study of Attitudes and Behaviors in US, UK and EU Information Security Professionals*. White Paper, Symantec Security Response, http://sarc.com/avcenter/reference/privacy.attitudes.behaviors.pdf, date accessed 06 April 2006.

Gordon, S. (2005) *Evaluating Additional Security Risks: Spyware and Adware*. White paper: Enterprise Security, http://www.topsectechnology.ie/symantec/pdf/spyware_wp.pdf, date accessed 09 February 2009.

Grabner-Kraeuter, S. (2000) 'The Role of Consumers' Trust in Online-Shopping', *Journal of Business Ethics*, 39 (1–2), 43–50.

Grannick, J. (2007) Online Advertising: So Good, Yet So Bad for Us, *Wired*, http://www.wired.com/politics/law/commentary/circuitcourt/2007/05/circuitcourt_0509, date accessed 09 February 2009.

Green, C. (2002) *Communication, Technology and Society* (London: Sage).

Green, P.E. (1970) 'Measurement and Data Analysis', *Journal of Marketing*, 34 (1), 15–17.

Greene, K. (2007) The Future of Search: The head of Google Research talks about his group's projects, *Technology Review* (MIT), http://www.technologyreview.com/Biztech/19050/?a=f, date accessed 09 February 2009.

Greene, K. (2008) TR10: Reality Mining, *Technology Review* (MIT), http://www.technologyreview.com/read_article.aspx?ch=specialsections&sc=emerging08&id=20247&a=, date accessed 09 February 2009.

Grossberg, L. (1995) 'Cultural Studies vs. Political Economy: Is anyone else Bored with this Debate?' *Critical Studies in Mass Communication*, 12, 72–81.

Grossman, L. (2006) Time's Person of the Year: You, *Time*, http://www.time.com/time/magazine/article/0,9171,1569514,00.html, date accessed February 12 09.

Guadamuz, A. (2007) 'Back to the Future: Regulation of Virtual Worlds', *SCRIPTed*, 4 (3), 242–245, http://www.law.ed.ac.uk/ahrc/script-ed/vol4–3/editorial.asp, date accessed 09 February 2009.

Gunter, B., Oates, C. and Blades, M. (2005) *Advertising to Children on TV* (New Jersey: Erlbaum).

Hafner, K. (1997) The Epic Saga of The Well, *Wired*, http://www.wired.com/wired/archive/5.05/ff_well.html, date accessed 09 January 2008.

Habuchi, I. (2005) 'Accelerating Reflexivity', in M. Ito, D. Okabe and M. Matsuda (eds) *Personal, Portable, Pedestrian: Mobile Phones in Japanese Life* (Cambridge: MIT).

Hackley, C.E. (1999) 'An Epistemological Odyssey: Towards Social Construction of the Advertising Process', *Journal of Marketing Communications*, 5 (3), 157–168.

Haggerty, J. and Ericson, R. (2000) 'The Surveillant Assemblage', *British Journal of Sociology*, 51 (4), 605–622.

Han, J. and Kamber, M. (2001) *Data Mining: Concepts and Techniques* (San Francisco, CA: Morgan Kaufmann).

Hand, D.J. (2002) 'Statistics', in W. Klösgen and J. Zytkow (eds) *Handbook of Knowledge Discovery and Data Mining* (Oxford: Oxford University).

Hardy, I. (2006) Marketers leap into gaming, *BBC*, http://www.news.bbc.co.uk/1/hi/programmes/click_online/5180042.stm, date accessed 09 February 2009.

Hartley, J. (ed.) (2007) *Creative Industries* (Oxford: Blackwell).

Havlena, W.J. and Graham, J. (2004) 'Decay Effects in Online Advertising: Quantifying the Impact of Time Since Last Exposure on Branding Effectiveness', *Journal of Advertising Research*, 44, 327–332.

Haycock, G. (2007) Young ad stars show old pros new tricks, *Reuters*, http://www.reuters.com/article/technologyNews/idUSN2927054520070701?feedType=RSS, date accessed 09 February 2009.

Haythornthwaite, C. and Wellman, B. (2001) 'The Internet in Everyday Life', in B. Wellman and C. Haythornthwaite (eds) *The Internet in Everyday Life* (Malden, MA: Blackwell).

Helm, S. (2000) 'Viral Marketing – Establishing Customer Relationships by "Word-of-Mouse"', *Electronic Markets*, 10, 158–161.

Hendrickx, F. and Castro, H. (2002) *Employment Privacy Law in the European Union: Surveillance and Monitoring* (Groningen: Intersentia).

Herman, A., Coombe, R.J. and Kaye, L. (2006) 'Your Second Life: Goodwill and the Performativity of Intellectual Property in Online Digital Gaming', *Cultural Studies*, 20 (2–3), 184–210.

Hernandez, M.D., Minor, M.S., Suh, J., Chapa, S. and Salas, J.A. (2005) 'Brand Recall in the Advergaming Environment', in M.R Stafford and R.J Faber (eds) *Advertising, Promotion and New Media* (New York: M.E. Sharpe).

Hernandez, S.J. (2007) W3C Spam Policy, *World Wide Web Consortium* (W3C), http://www.w3.org/Mail/Spam, date accessed 09 February 2009.

Hesmondhalgh, D. (2006) *The Cultural Industries* (London: Sage).

Hier, S. (2003) 'Probing the Surveillant Assemblage: On the Dialectics of Surveillance Practices as Processes of Social Control', *Surveillance and Society*, 1 (3), 399–411.

Highmore, B. (2002) *Everyday Life and Cultural Theory* (London: Routledge).

Hill, R. and Johnson, L.W. (2004) 'Understanding Creative Service: A Qualitative Study of the Advertising Problem Delineation, Communication and Response (APDCR) Process', *International Journal of Advertising*, 23 (3), 285–307.

Himpe, T. (2006) *Advertising is Dead, Long Live Advertising* (London: Thames and Hudson).

Hines, M. (2005) Future of search rides on relevance, *CNet News*, http://www.news.cnet.com/2100–1032_3–5555954.html, date accessed 09 February 2009.

Hjorth, L. (2003) 'Cute@keitai.com', in N. Gottlieb and M. McLelland (eds) *Japanese Cybercultures* (London: Routledge).

Hollis, N. (2005) 'Ten Years of Learning on How Online Advertising Builds Brands', *Journal of Advertising Research*, 45 (2), 255–268.

Hood, K. and Schumann, D.W. (2007) 'The Process and Consequences of Cognitive Filtering of Internet Content: Handling the Glut of Internet Advertising', in D.W Schumann and E. Thorson (eds) *Internet Advertising: Theory and Research* (New Jersey: Lawrence Erlbaum).

Hopkins, C. (1998) *My Life in Advertising and Scientific Advertising* (Chicago: NTC Business Books).

House of Commons, Culture, Media and Sport Committee (2007) New Media and the Creative Industries: Fifth Report of Session 2006–07, *House of Commons*, http://www.publications.parliament.uk/pa/cm200607/cmselect/cmcumeds/509/50902.htm, date accessed 09 February 2009.

Howcroft, D. (1999) The Hyperbolic Age of Information: An Empirical Study of Internet Usage, *Information, Communication and Society*, 2 (3), 277–299.

Howe, J. (2008) *Crowdsourcing: Why the Power of the Crowd Is Driving the Future of Business* (NY: Crown Business).

Huhtamo, E. (2004) Hidden histories of mobile media, *Vodafone Receiver*, http://www.vodafone.com/flash/receiver/11/articles/index01.html, date accessed 09 February 2009.

IGA Worldwide (2008) *Landmark IGA-Nielsen Study: 82% of Consumers React Positively to Receiving Contextual In-Game Ads During Game Play*, http://www.igaworldwide.com/aboutus/pr/pressreleases/landmark-iga-nielsen-study.cfm, date accessed 09 February 2009.

Information Commissioner's Office (2008) *The Data Protection Act*, http://www.ico.gov.uk/what_we_cover/data_protection/the_basics.aspx, date accessed 09 February 2009.

Information Commissioner's Office (2008a) *Phorm – Webwise and Open Internet Exchange*, http://www.ico.gov.uk/about_us/news_and_views/current_topics/phorm_webwise_and_oie.aspx, date accessed 09 February 2009.

Information Commissioner's Office (2008b) *Preventing unsolicited marketing*, http://www.ico.gov.uk/upload/documents/library/data_protection/practical_application/stopping_unwanted_marketing_materials.pdf, date accessed 09 February 2009.

Information Commissioner's Office (2008c) *The Privacy and Electronic Communications Regulations 2003*, http://www.ico.gov.uk/what_we_cover/privacy_and_electronic_communications/the_basics.aspx, date accessed 09 February 2009.

Innis, H.A. (1951) *The Bias of Communication* (Toronto: University of Toronto).

Institute of Practitioners in Advertising (2009) *The future of advertising – ad industry should prepare for a consumer-led world or face decline*, http://www.ipa.co.uk/Content/The-future-of-advertising-%E2%80%93-ad-industry-should-prepare-for-a-consumer-led-world-or-face-decline, date accessed 09 February 2009.

Internet Advertising Bureau (2007) *B2B Email Marketing*, http://www.iabuk.net/media/images/UK_Best_Practice_2007_e_FINAL_2623.pdf, date accessed 09 February 2009.

Internet Advertising Bureau (2008) *Government to review increased level of online marketing to children*, http:// www.iabuk.net/en/1/marketingtochildrenonline140408.mxs, date accessed 09 February 2009.

Internet Advertising Bureau (2008a) *IAB Platform Status Report: A Digital Video Advertising Overview*, www.iab.net/media/file/dv-report-v3.pdf, date accessed 09 February 2009.

Internet Advertising Bureau (2008b) *Introduction to in-game advertising*, http://www.iabuk.net/en/1/introductiontoingameadvertising.html, date accessed 09 February 2009.

Internet Advertising Bureau (2008c) *Introduction to mobile advertising*, http://www.iabuk.net/en/1/introductiontomobileadvertising.html, date accessed 09 February 2009.

Internet Advertising Bureau (2008d) *Introduction to social media*, http://www.iabuk.net/en/1/introductiontosocialmedia.html, date accessed 09 February 2009.

Internet Advertising Bureau (2008e) *Mobile advertising: the emerging UK market*, http://www.iabuk.net/media/images/IABMobile AdvertisingReport_2622.pdf, date accessed 09 February 2009.

Internet Advertising Bureau (2008f) *Rich Media Creative Guidelines*, http://www.iab.net/Rich_Media, date accessed 09 February 2009.

Internet Advertising Bureau (2008g) *Targeted Online Advertising*, http://www.iabuk.net/en/1/targetedonlineadvertising010708.mxs, date accessed 09 February 2009.

Internet Advertising Bureau (2009) *Good Practice Principles*, http://www.iabuk.net/en/1/behaviouraladvertisinggoodpractice.html, date accessed 04 March 2009.

Internet Advertising Bureau (2009a) *IAB Online Adspend Study – H1 2008*, http://www.iabuk.net/en/1/researchadspendiabadspends-tudyh12008.mxs, date accessed 09 February 2009.

Internet Advertising Bureau (2009b) *The Online Audience – October 2008*, http://www.iabuk.net/en/1/iabknowledgebankaudienceonlin-eaudience.mxs, date accessed 09 February 2009.

IT World (2008) *Survey: IT staff would steal secrets if laid off*, http://www.itworld.com/security/54579/survey-it-staff-would-steal-secrets-if-laid, date accessed 09 February 2009.

Ito, M. (2005) 'Introduction: Personal, Portable, Pedestrian', in M. Ito, D. Okabe and M. Matsuda (eds) *Personal, Portable, and Pedestrian: Mobile Phones in Japanese Life* (Massachusetts: MIT).

Jackson, D. (2006) Making the Web Mobile, *WC3*, www.w3.org/2006/Talks/mobileweb-3gworld06.pdf, date accessed 09 February 2009.

Jameson, F. (1991) *Postmodernism or The Cultural Logic of Late Capitalism* (London: Verso).

Janger, E.J. and Schwartz, P.M. (2002) The Gramm-Leach-Bliley Act, Information Privacy, and the Limits of Default Rules, *Minnesota Law Review*. 86, http:// www.papers.ssrn.com/sol3/papers.cfm?abstract_id=319144, date accessed 09 February 2009.

Jarvenpaa, S.L., Tractinsky, N. and Saarinen, L. (1999) Consumer Trust in an Internet Store: A Cross-Cultural Validation, *Journal of Computer-Mediated Communication*. 5 (2), http://www3.interscience.

wiley.com/journal/120837783/abstract?CRETRY=1&SRETRY=0, date accessed 09 February 2009.

Jarvis, J. (2007) Chaos theory: advertising cash will soon decrease, *The Guardian*, http://www.guardian.co.uk/media/2007/nov/05/monday-mediasection.comment?gusrc=rss&feed=technology, date accessed 09 February 2009.

Jee, J. and Lee, W-N. (2002) 'The Impact of Personal Factors on Perceived Interactivity, Attitude toward the Web site and Brand Choice', in A.M. Abernethy (ed.) *Proceedings of the 2002 Conference of the American Academy of Advertising* (Auburn, AL: Auburn University).

Jena, R. (2006) Is That a Video Game -- or an Ad? *Businessweek*, http://www.businessweek.com/innovate/content/jan2006/id20060124_792815.htm, date accessed 09 February 2009.

Jenkins, H. (2003) 'Interactive Audiences' in V. Nightingale and K. Ross (eds) *Critical Readings: Media and Audiences* (London: Open University Press).

Jenkins, H. (2006) *Convergence Culture* (New York: New York University).

Jenkins, H. (2006a) *Fans, Bloggers, and Gamers: Exploring Participatory Culture* (New York: New York University).

Johar, G.V., Holbrook, M.B. and Stern, B.B. (2001) 'The Role of Myth in Creative Advertising Design: Theory, Process and Outcome', *Journal of Advertising*, 30 (2), 1–25.

Johnson, B. (2008) As marketers shift to digital, Big 4 keep pace, *Advertising Age*, http:// www.adage.com/digital//article?article_id=125744, date accessed 09 February 2009.

Johnson, F.L. (2008a) *Imaging in Advertising: Verbal and Visual Codes of Commerce* (New York: Routledge).

Johnson, G.C., Bruner, G.C. II and Kumar, A. (2006) 'Interactivity and its facets revisited', *Journal of Advertising*, 35 (4), 35–52.

Jones, J.P. (1999) 'Strategy in Advertising', in J.P Jones (ed.) *The Advertising Business* (Thousand Oaks, CA: Sage).

Jones, J.P. (2004) *Fables, Fashions, and Facts About Advertising* (Thousand Oaks, CA: Sage).

Kalay, Y.E. and Mark, J. (2006) 'Architecture and the Internet: Designing Places in Cyberspace', *First Monday*, Special Issue #5: Virtual Architecture at State of Play III, 6–8, http:// www.firstmonday.org/htbin/cgiwrap/bin/ojs/index.php/fm/article/view/1563/1478, date accessed 09 February 2009.

Kanich, C.L., Kreibich, C., Levchenko, K., Enright, B., Voelker, G.M., Paxson, V. and Savage, S. (2008) 'Spamalytics: An Empirical Analysis of Spam Marketing Conversion', *Proceedings of the 15th ACM Conference on Computer and Communications Security*, http:// www.portal.acm.org/ft_gateway.cfm?id=1455774&type=pdf&coll=ACM&

dl=ACM&CFID=9872424&CFTOKEN=68487029, date accessed 09 February 2009.

Kaplan, D. (2007) Regulation Is Threat to Online Ads, IAB Warns, *The New York Times*, http://www.nytimes.com/paidcontent/PCORG_ 316655.html?ex=1352264400&en=3dcb341cefdc02cd&ei=5088&pa rtner=rssnyt&emc=rss, date accessed 09 February 2009.

Kaplan, D. (2008) Streaming Ads Driving Users Away From Content, *The New York Times*, http://www.nytimes.com/paidcontent/PCORG_ 318930.html?ex=1358830800&en=aa039ef9dddaaa7f&ei=5088&pa rtner=rssnyt&emc=rss, date accessed 09 February 2009.

Kaplan, E.K. (1978) 'The Courage of Baudelaire and Rimbaud: The Anxiety of Faith', *The French Review*, LII (2), 294–306.

Katz, E. and Lazarsfeld, P.F. (1955) *Personal Influence: The Part Played by People in the Flow of Mass Communications* (New York: Free Press).

Katz, E., Blumler, J.G. and Gurevitch, M. (2003 [1974]) 'Utilization of Mass Communication by the Individual', in V. Nightingale and K. Ross (eds) *Critical Readings: Media and Audiences* (Maidenhead: Open University Press).

Kaye, K. (2008) Obama's Online Ad Spend Approached $8 Million, *ClickZ*, http://www.clickz.com/showPage.html?page=3631586, date accessed 09 February 2009.

Keller, E. (2007) 'Unleashing the Power of Word of Mouth: Creating Brand Advocacy to Drive Growth', *Journal of Advertising Research*, 47 (4), 448–452.

Kelley, L.D. and Jugenheimer, D.W. (2004) *Advertising Media Planning: A Brand Management Approach* (New York: M.E. Sharpe).

Kelly, S. (2008) Warnings of internet overload, *BBC*, http:// www. news.bbc.co.uk/1/hi/programmes/click_online/6756899.stm, date accessed 09 February 2009.

Kim, S. (2008) 'A Framework for Advertising in the Digital Age', *Journal of Advertising Research*, 48 (3), 310–312.

King, L. (2008) UK gov't loses personal data on 4M people in one year, *Computerworld*, http://www.computerworld.com.au/index.php/id; 50110485, date accessed 09 February 2009.

Kiousis, S. (2002) 'Interactivity: A Concept Explication', *New Media and Society*, 4 (3), 355–383.

Kirby, J. and Marsden, P. (2005) *Connected Marketing* (London: Butterworth-Heinemann).

Kiss, J. (2007) Most teens are MySpacers, *The Guardian*, http://www. guardian.co.uk/media/2007/may/17/digitalmedia.socialnetworking, date accessed 09 February 2009.

Klaassen, A. (2008) Publicis Acquires Search Agency Performics From Google, *Advertising Age*, http:// www.adage.com/digital/ article?article_id=130168, date accessed 09 February 2009.

Klaassen, A. (2008a) Some Respite for Consumers as Ad Clutter Clears on Web, *Advertising Age*, http:// www.adage.com/digital/article?article_id=132029, date accessed 09 February 2009.

Klein, K. (2008) Demystifying Web 2.0, *Business Week Online*, http:// www.businessweek.com/smallbiz/content/jun2008/sb20080616_188170.htm, date accessed 09 February 2009.

Klein, N. (2000) *No Logo* (London: Flamingo).

Klingmann, A. (2007) *Brandscapes: Architecture in the Experience Economy* (Massachusetts: MIT).

Kneller, G.F. (1965) *The Art and Science of Creativity* (New York: Holt, Rinehart and Winston).

Koskela, H. (2003) ' "Cam Era" – the Contemporary Urban Panopticon', *Surveillance and Society*, 1 (3), 292–313.

Koslow, S., Sasser, S.L. and Riordan, E.A. (2003) 'What Is Creative to Whom and Why? Perceptions in Advertising Agencies', *Journal of Advertising Research*, 42 (1), 96–110.

Koslow, S., Sasser, S.L. and Riordan, E.A. (2006) 'Do Marketers Get the Advertising They Need or the Advertising They Deserve? Agency Views of How Clients Influence Creativity', *Journal of Advertising*, 35 (3), 81–101.

Kover, A.J., Goldberg, S.M. and James, W.L. (1995) 'Creativity vs. Effectiveness? An Integrating Classification for Advertising', *Journal of Advertising Research*, 35 (6), 29–38.

Kover, A.J., James, W.L. and Sonner, B.S. (1997) 'To Whom Do Advertising Creatives Write? An Inferential Answer', *Journal of Advertising Research*, 37 (1), 41–53.

Kraidy, M. and Goeddertz, T. (2003) 'Transnational Advertising and International Relations: US Press Discourses on the Benetton "We on Death Row" Campaign', *Media, Culture and Society*, 25 (2), 147–165.

Kravets, D. (2007) VW 'Nazi' Subpoena Points Up YouTube Privacy Risks, *Wired*, http://www.wired.com/entertainment/hollywood/news/2007/09/vw_parody_ad, date accessed 09 February 2009.

Krishnamurthy, S. and Dou, W. (2008) 'Advertising with User-Generated Content: A Framework and Research Agenda', *Journal of Interactive Advertising*, 8 (2), http://www.jiad.org/article99, date accessed 09 February 2009.

Kroker, A. and Weinstein, M.A. (1994) *Data Trash: the Theory of the Virtual Class* (New York: St Martin's Press).

Krugman, H.E. (1999) 'Television Advertising: Learning Without Involvement', in J.P. Jones (ed.) *The Advertising Business* (Thousand Oaks, CA: Sage).

Kuner, C. (2003) *European Data Privacy Law and Online Business* (Oxford: Oxford University Press).

Kushner, D. (2008) Webkinz Effect: Plush-Toy Fad Begets Imitators, *Wired*, http://www.wired.com/entertainment/theweb/magazine/16–11/st_webkinz, date accessed 09 February 2009.

Langville, A.H. and Mayer, C.D. (2006) *Google's PageRank and Beyond: The Science of Search Engine Rankings* (New Jersey: Princeton University).

Lanier, C.D. Jr. and Saini, A. (2008) 'Understanding Consumer Privacy: A Review and Future Directions', *Academy of Marketing Science Review*, 12 (2), 1–45, http://www.amsreview.org/articles/lanier02–2008.pdf, date accessed 09 February 2009.

Lash, S. (1990) *Sociology of Postmodernism* (London: Routledge).

Lasn, K. (1999) *Culture Jam: The Uncooling of America* (New York: Eagle Brook).

Latour, B. (1991) 'Technology is Society Made Durable', in J. Law (ed.) *A Sociology of Monsters: Essays on Power, Technology and Domination* (London: Routledge).

Lazzarato, M. (1996) 'Immaterial Labour', in P. Virno and M. Hardt (eds) *Radical Thought in Italy* (Minneapolis: University of Minnesota).

Lazzarato, M. (2004) From Capital-Labour to Capital-Life, *Ephemera*, 4 (3), 187–208.

Lea, M., O'Shea, T., Fung, P. and Spears, R. (1992) ' "Flaming" in Computer-mediated Communication: Observations, Explanations, and Implications', in M. Lea (ed.) *Contexts of Computer-mediated Communication* (New York: Harvester-Wheatsheaf).

Learmonth, M. (2009) Twitter: We Can Do What Google Can't, *Advertising Age*, http://www.adage.com/digital/article?article_id=135016, date accessed 04 March 2009.

Leberecht, T. (2008) Chinese social network QQ outperforms Facebook and Co., *CNet*, http://www.news.cnet.com/8301–13641_3–9912252-44.html?hhTest=1, date accessed 09 February 2009.

Leckenby, J.D. (2005) 'The Interaction of Traditional and New Media', in. M.R. Stafford and R.J. Faber (eds) *Advertising, Promotion and New Media* (New York: M.E. Sharpe).

Lee, E-J. (2007) 'Computer Agents as Sources of Trust in Internet Advertising', in D.W. Schumann and E. Thorson (eds) *Internet Advertising: Theory and Research* (New Jersey: Lawrence Erlbaum).

Lefebvre, H. (1971) *Everyday Life in the Modern World* (New York: Harper Torchbook).

Leiss, W., Kline, S., Jhally, S. and Botterill, J. (2005) *Social Communication in Advertising: Consumption in the Mediated Marketplace* (New York: Routledge).

Lessig, L. (1999) *Code and other Laws of Cyberspace* (New York: Basic Books).

Lessig, L. (2001) *The Future of Ideas* (New York: Random House).

Lessig, L. (2006) *Code version 2.0* (New York: Basic Books).

Leyden, J. (2008) Call for reform as UK data protection rules turn 10, *The Register*, http://www.theregister.co.uk/2008/07/16/dpa_10/, date accessed 09 February 2009.

Li, H., Daugherty, T. and Biocca, F. (2005) 'Impact of 3-D Advertising on Product Knowledge, Brand Attitude, and Purchase Intention', in M.R. Stafford and R.J. Faber (eds) *Advertising, Promotion and New Media* (New York: M.E. Sharpe).

Lindstrom, M. (2001) *Clicks, Bricks and Brands* (London: Kogan Page).

Lister, M., Dovey, J., Giddings, S., Grant, I. and Kelly, K. (2003) *New Media: A Critical Introduction* (London: Routledge).

Liu, Y. (2003) 'Developing a Scale to Measure the Interactivity of Websites', *Journal of Advertising Research*, 43 (2), 207–216.

Liu, Y. and Shrum, L.J. (2005) 'Rethinking Interactivity: What It Means and Why It May Not Always Be Beneficial', in M.R. Stafford and R.J. Faber (eds) *Advertising, Promotion and New Media* (New York: M.E. Sharpe).

Lohtia, R., Donthu, N. and Herschberger, E.K. (2003) 'The Impact of Content and Design Elements on Banner Advertising Click-Through-Rates', *Journal of Advertising* Research, 43 (4), 410–418.

Lombard, M. (2001) 'Interactive Advertising and Presence: A Framework', *Department of Advertising. The University of Texas*, http://www.jiad.org/vol1.no2/lombard, date accessed 09 February 2009.

Lovink. G. (2002) *After the Dotcom Crash: Recent Literature on Internet, Business and Society*, http://www.australianhumanitiesreview.org/archive/Issue-September-2002/lovink.html, date accessed 12 January 09.

Luhmann, N. (1979) *Trust and Power* (Chichester: Wiley).

Lupton, D. (1999) *Risk* (New York: Routledge).

Lynn, R. (2007) Second Life Without Sex Would Be a Sad Life, Indeed, *Wired*, http://www.wired.com/culture/lifestyle/commentary/sexdrive/2007/06/sexdrive_0622, date accessed 09 February 2009.

Lynn, R. (2008) Second Life Without Sex Would Be a Sad Life, Indeed, *Wired*, http://www.wired.com/culture/lifestyle/commentary/sexdrive/2007/06/sexdrive_0622, date accessed 09 February 2009.

Lyon, D. (1994) *The Electronic Eye: The Rise of Surveillance Society* (Minneapolis: University of Minnesota Press)

Lyon, D. (2001) *Surveillance Society: Monitoring Everyday Life* (Buckingham: Open University Press).

Lyon, D. (2003) 'Surveillance as Social Sorting: Computer Codes and Mobile Bodies', in D. Lyon (ed.) *Surveillance as Social Sorting: Privacy, Risk and Digital Discrimination* (New York: Routledge).

Machillis, S. (2007) '80 Mbytes of storage for under $12k!' and other ad favorites through the years, *Computerworld*, http://www.

computerworld.com/action/article.do?command=viewArticleBasic&articleId=9023960&pageNumber=1, date accessed 09 February 2009.

Mann, S. (2004) ' "Sousveillance": inverse surveillance in multimedia imaging, *Proceedings of the 12th annual ACM international conference on Multimedia*, New York: USA.

Mann, S., Nolan, J. and Wellman, B. (1998) 'Sousveillance: Inventing and Using Wearable Computing Devices for Data Collection in Surveillance Environments', *Surveillance and Society*, 1(3), 331–355.

Manovich, L. (2003) *The Language of New Media* (Cambridge: MIT).

Manovich, L. (2006) 'The Poetics of Urban Media Surfaces', *First Monday*, Special Issue #4: Urban Screens: Discovering the potential of outdoor screens for urban society, http://www.firstmonday.org/htbin/cgiwrap/bin/ojs/index.php/fm/article/view/1545/1460, date accessed 09 February 2009.

Market Resource Guide (2008) *Top Internet Advertisers*. Vol. 92 (Detroit: Crain Communications).

Markoff, J. (2006) Entrepreneurs See a Web Guided by Common Sense, *The New York Times*, http://www.nytimes.com/2006/11/12/business/12web.html?ex=1320987600&en=254d697964cedc62&ei=5088, date accessed 09 February 2009.

Marshall, J. (2007) Small U.K. Businesses Reluctant to Embrace Search Marketing, *ClickZ*, http://www.clickz.com/showPage.html?page=3627573, date accessed 09 February 2009.

Martin, B.A.S., Durme, J.V., Raulas, M. and Merisaco, M. (2003) 'Email Advertising: Exploratory Insights from Finland', *Journal of Advertising Research*, 43 (3), 293–300.

Marvin, C. (1988) *When Old Technologies Were New: Thinking About Electronic Communication in the Late Nineteenth Century* (New York: Oxford University).

Massumi, B. (1993) *The Politics of Everyday Fear* (Minnesota: University of Minnesota).

Mathieson, R. (2005). *Branding Unbound: The Future of Advertising, Sales, and the Brand Experience in the Wireless Age* (New York: AMACOM)

Matwyshyn, A.M. (2006) 'Penetrating the Zombie Collective: Spam as an International Security Issue', *SCRIPTed*, 4 (3), 370–388, http://www.law.ed.ac.uk/ahrc/script-ed/vol3–4/matwyshyn.asp, date accessed 09 February 2009.

Maury, M.D. and Kleiner, D.S. (2002) 'E-Commerce, ethical Commerce?', *Journal of Business Ethics*, 36 (1–2), 21–31.

Mäyrä, F. (2008) *Introduction to Game Studies* (London: Sage).

McCormack, D. (2002) *Web 2.0: The Resurgence of the Internet and E-Commerce* (Boston: Aspatore).

McCormick, N. (2008) Barack Obama's 'Yes We Can' video, *The Telegraph*, http://www.telegraph.co.uk/culture/music/3671190/Barack-Obama%27s-%27Yes-We-Can%27-video.html, date accessed 09 February 2009.

McCullogh, M. (2006) 'On Urban Markup: Frames Of Reference In Location Models For Participatory Urbanism', *Leonardo Electronic Almanac*, 14 (3), http:// www.leoalmanac.org/journal/Vol_14/lea_v14_n03–04/mmccullough.asp, date accessed 09 February 2009.

McIlroy, M. (2008) Second Life Voted Last Year's Most Over-hyped Trend, *Advertising Age*, http://www.adage.com/digital/article?article_id=125832, date accessed 09 February 2009.

McIlroy, M. (2008a) Survey: More Buyers Expect to Spend Less in Most Media, *Advertising Age*, http://www.adage.com/mediaworks/article?article_id=128186, date accessed 09 February 2009.

McKenna, P. (2008) US and UK rival China for government surveillance, *New Scientist*, http:// www.technology.newscientist.com/channel/tech/dn13145-us-and-uk-rival-china-for-government-surveillance.html?feedId=online-news_rss20, date accessed 09 February 2009.

McLure, H. (2000) 'The Wild, Wild Web: The Mythic American West and the Electronic Frontier', *Western Historical Quarterly*, 31 (4), 457–476.

McMillan, S.J. (2007) 'Internet Advertising: One Face or Many', in. D.W. Schumann and E. Thorson (eds) *Internet Advertising: Theory and Research* (New Jersey: Lawrence Erlbaum).

McMillan, S.J. and Hwang, J.S. (2005) 'Measures of Perceived Interactivity: An Exploration of the Role of Direction of Communication, User Control, and Time in Shaping Perceptions of Interactivity', in M.R. Stafford and R.J. Faber (eds) *Advertising, Promotion and New Media* (New York: M.E. Sharpe).

McRobb, S. and Rogerson, S. (2004) 'Are They Really Listening? An Investigation into Published Online Privacy Policies at the Beginning of the Third Millennium', *Information Technology and People*, 17 (4), 442–461.

McStay, A. (2006) *A Critical Exploration of Users' Resistances, Co-optation and Perceptions of Creativity within Online Advertising* (PhD thesis).

McStay, A. (2007a) 'Regulating the Suicide Bomber: A Critical Examination of Online Viral Advertising and Simulations of Self-Broadcasting', *Ethical Space: Journal of Communication*, 4 (1/2), 40–48.

McStay, A. (2007b) 'Trust, Data-mining and Instantaneity: The Creation of the Online Accountable Consumer', in V. Bakir and D. Barlow (eds) *Communication in the Age of Suspicion: Trust and the Media* (London: Palgrave-Macmillan).

McStay, A. (forthcoming 2009) 'Understanding audience's perceptions of creativity in online advertising: the benefits of a qualitative approach', *The Qualitative Report*.

McStay, A. and Bakir, V. (2006) 'Privacy, Online Advertising and Marketing Techniques: The Paradoxical Disappearance of the User', *Ethical Space: Journal of Communication*, 3 (1), 24–31.

McVeigh, B.J. (2003) 'Individualization, Individuality, Interiority, and the Internet: Japanese University Students and E-mail', in N. Gottlieb and M. McLelland (eds) *Japanese Cybercultures* (London: Routledge).

Meadows, S.M. (2008) *I, Avatar: The Culture and Consequences of Having a Second Life* (Berkeley, CA: New Riders).

Mehta, A .(2000) 'Advertising Attitudes and Advertising Effectiveness', *Journal of Advertising Research*, 40 (3), 67–72.

Merisavo, M., Kajalo, S., Karjaluoto, H., Virtanen, V., Salmenkivi, S., Raulas, M. and Lappäniemi, M. (2007) 'An Empirical Study of the Drivers of Consumer Acceptance of Mobile Advertising', *Journal of Interactive Advertising*, 7 (2), http://www.jiad.org/article92, date accessed 09 February 2009.

Messaging Anti-Abuse Working Group (MAAWG) (2007) *Email Metrics Program: The Network Operators' Perspective*, http://www.maawg. org/about/MAAWG20072Q_Metrics_Report.pdf, date accessed 09 February 2009.

Mayer, J.P. (1943) *Max Weber and German Politics* (London: Faber and Faber).

Miller, S. (2008) Study: E-Mail is The Most Effective Form of Direct Response, *Brandweek*, http://www.brandweek.com/bw/content_display/news-and-features/direct/e3i36f09c881b6aded42e6f8-b75821fc0b5, date accessed 09 February 2009.

Milne, G.R. (2000) 'Privacy and Ethical Issues in Database/Interactive and Overview of the Special Issue', *Journal of Public Policy and Marketing*, 19 (1), 1–6.

Mindlin, A. (2008) Web Videos Where Ads Are Acceptable, *The New York Times*, http://www.nytimes.com/2008/08/18/technology/18drill.html?_r=2&partner=rssnyt&emc=rss&oref=slogin&oref=slogin, date accessed 09 February 2009.

Miyazaki, A.D. and Fernandez, A. (2000) Internet Privacy and Security: An Examination, *Journal of Public Policy and Marketing*, 19 (1), 54–62.

Morissey, B. (2003) Web Leads for Busy Execs, *ClickZ*, http://www.clickz.com/showPage.html?page=2107991, date accessed 09 February 2009.

Morissey, B. (2006) Pontiac Drives Into Second Life, *Adweek*, http://www.adweek.com/aw/iq_interactive/article_display.jsp?vnu_content_id=1003286949, date accessed 09 February 2009.

Morissey, B. (2008) Can Search's 'Beautiful System' Extend to Display? *Adweek*, http://www.adweek.com/aw/content_display/news/digital/ e3i5c4d8ac24396d86e1a5f0182c9f518fb, date accessed 09 February 2009.

Moskalyuk, A. (2008) MySpace got 76% of US social network traffic in 2007, *ZDNet*, http://www.blogs.zdnet.com/ITFacts/?p=14238, date accessed 09 February 2009.

Moss, J. (1998) *The Later Foucault* (London: Sage).

Murthy, R. (2006) 'Story Space: A Theoretical Grounding for the New Urban Annotation', *First Monday*, Special Issue #4: Urban Screens: Discovering the potential of outdoor screens for urban society, http://www.firstmonday.org/htbin/cgiwrap/bin/ojs/index.php/fm/ article/view/1547/1462, date accessed 09 February 2009.

Nakashima, R. (2008) TV Networks Seek Formula for Online Ads, *Wired*, http:// www.news.wired.com/dynamic/stories/N/NETWORKS_ONL INE?SITE=WIRE&SECTION=HOME&TEMPLATE=DEFAULT&CTIM E=2008-04-12-05-49-50, date accessed 09 February 2009.

Nasco, S.A. and Bruner II, G.C. (2007) 'Perceptions and Recall of Advertising Content Presented on Mobile Handheld Devices', *Journal of Interactive Advertising*, 7 (2), http://www.jiad.org/article93, date accessed 09 February 2009.

Naughton, J. (2007) Blocking ads can be fun - and also downright dangerous, *The Guardian*. http://www.guardian.co.uk/business/2007/ sep/23/digitalmedia.media, date accessed 09 February 2009.

Neate, R. (2008) Facebook to be Britain's most used website, *Telegraph*, http://www.telegraph.co.uk/digitallife/main.jhtml?xml=/ connected/2008/06/10/dlface110.xml, date accessed 09 February 2009.

Negus, K. and Pickering, M. (2004) *Creativity, Communication and Cultural Value* (London: Sage).

Nelson, M.G. (2007) Teens Want Branded Online Social Experiences, Study Says, *ClickZ News*, http://www.clickz.com/showPage.html? page=3626320, date accessed 09 February 2009.

Nelson, M.G. (2007a) Users Request More Targeted Ads, Study Says, *ClickZ*, http://www.clickz.com/showPage.html?page=3627288, date accessed 09 February 2009.

Neuman, W.R. (1991) *The Future of the Mass Audience* (New York: Cambridge University).

NewMediaAge (2008) *Top 100 Interactive Agencies 2008*, http:// www. top100.nma.co.uk/section.php?section_id=1, date accessed 09 February 2009.

Nielsen (2006) *Nielsen To Provide Video Game Rating Service*, http://www. nielsenmedia.com/nc/portal/site/Public/menuitem.55dc65b4a7d5a dff3f65936147a062a0/?vgnextoid=aea42f5dde75e010VgnVCM1000 00ac0a260aRCRD, date accessed 09 February 2009.

Nissenbaum, H. (2001) Can Trust be secured Online? A Theoretical Perspective, *Boston University*, http://www.univ.trieste.it/%7Eetica/ 1999_2/nissenbaum.html, date accessed 09 February 2009.

Nixon, S. (2003) Advertising Cultures (London: Sage).

Norris, S. (2008) Paid search on mobile: looking beyond the hype, *iMedia*, http://www.imediaconnection.com/content/19634.asp, date accessed 09 February 2009.

Norris, V. (2007) 'Advertising History – According to the Textbooks', in R. Hovland, J. Wolberg and E. Haley (eds) *Readings in Advertising, Society, and Consumer Culture* (New York: ME Sharpe).

Novak, T., Hoffman, D. and Yung, Y. (2000) 'Measuring the Customer Experience in Online Environments: A Structural Modeling Approach', *Marketing Science*, 19 (1), 22–44.

Oates, C., Blades, M., Gunter, B. and Don, J. (2003) 'Children's Understanding of Television Advertising: A Qualitative Approach', *Journal of Marketing Communications*, 9 (2), 59–71.

Office of Public Sector Information (n.d.) *Data Protection Act 1998 (c. 29)*, http://www.opsi.gov.uk/acts/acts1998/ukpga_19980029_en_1, date accessed 09 February 2009.

Ogilvy, D. (1985) *Ogilvy on Advertising* (New York: Random House).

O'Hara, K. (2004) *Trust: From Socrates to Spin* (Cambridge: Icon Books).

Oliver and Ohlbaum Associates (2008) The Growth of the Internet and The Implications for UK TV content, *Ofcom*, http://www.ofcom.org. uk/consult/condocs/psb2_phase2/annex13.pdf, date accessed 09 February 2009.

O'Reilly, T. (2005) What is Web 2.0: Design Patterns and Business Models for the Next Generation of Software, *O'Reilly*, http://www. oreillynet.com/pub/a/oreilly/tim/news/2005/09/30/what-is-web-20. html, date accessed 09 February 2009.

Organisation for Economic Co-Operation and Development (OECD) (2007) *Broadband and ICT access and use by households and individuals*, http://www.oecd.org/dataoecd/44/11/39869349.pdf, date accessed 09 February 2009.

Orlik, P.B., Anderson, S.D., Day, L.A. and Patrick, W.L. (2006) *Exploring Electronic Media: Chronicles and Challenges* (Oxford: Blackwell).

Ostrow, J.W. (1984) 'Setting Frequency Levels: An Art or a Science?' *Journal of Advertising Research*, 24 (4), I–9 – I–11.

Pan, B., Hembrooke, H., Joachims, T., Lorigo, L., Gay, G. and Granka, L. (2007) 'In Google We Trust: Users' Decisions on Rank, Position, and Relevance', *Journal of Computer-Mediated Communication*, 12 (3), article 3, http:// www.jcmc.indiana.edu/vol12/issue3/pan.html, date accessed 09 February 2009.

Palmer, D.E. (2005) 'Pop-ups, Cookies, and Spam: Toward a Deeper Analysis of the Ethical Significance of Internet Marketing Practices', *Journal of Business Ethics*, 58, 271–280.

Parekh, R. and Klaassen, A. (2008a) As the Lines Blur, Digital Agencies Are Taking Lead, *Advertising Age*, http://www.adage.com/agencynews/article?article_id=132026, date accessed 09 February 2009.

Parikka, J. (2005) 'Contagion and Repetition: On the Viral Logic of Network Culture. Ephemera', *Fibreculture*, http://www.journal.fibreculture.org/issue4/issue4_parikka.html, date accessed 09 February 2009.

Parikka, J. (2007) 'Contagion and Repetition: On the Viral Logic of Network Culture', Ephemera, *Theory and Politics in Organization*, 7 (2), 287–308.

Park, S.R., Nah, F.F.-H., DeWester, D. and Eschenbrenner, B. (2008) 'Virtual World Affordances: Enhancing Brand Value', *Journal of Virtual Worlds Research*, 1 (2), 1–18, http://www.journals.tdl.org/jvwr/article/view/350/267, date accessed 09 February 2009.

Patelis, K. (2000) 'The Political Economy of the Internet', in J. Curran (ed,) *Media Organisations in Society* (London: Arnold).

Paul, B. and Cassar, K. (2008) Global Shoppers In Line to Shop Online:

Virtual Shopping a Virtual Reality Around the World, Nielsen, http://www.nielsen.com/consumer_insight/issue7/ci_story4.html, date accessed 09 February 2009.

Perlando, V.R. and Barwise, P. (2005) 'Mobile Advertising: A Research Agenda', in M.R. Stafford and R.J. Faber (eds) *Advertising, Promotion and New Media* (New York: M.E. Sharpe)

Petty, R.D. (2000) 'Marketing Without Consent: Consumer Choice', *Journal of Public Policy and Marketing*, 19 (1), 42–54.

Pew Internet and American Life Project (2008) *Reports: Technology and Media Use*, http://www.pewinternet.org/PPF/r/257/report_display.asp, date accessed 09 February 2009.

Pfanner, E. (2008) Ad Leaders See Web's Threat and Promise, *New York Times*, http://www.nytimes.com/2008/06/23/business/media/23cannes.html?_r=1&partner=rssnyt&emc=rss&oref=slogin, date accessed 09 February 2009.

Phelps, J.E., Lewis, R., Mobilio, L., Perry, D. and Raman, N. (2004) 'Viral Marketing or Electronic Word-of-Mouth Advertising: Examining Consumer Responses and Motivations to Pass Along Email', *Journal of Advertising Research*, 44 (4), 333–348.

Phillips, D. and Curry, M. (2003) 'Privacy and the Phentic Urge: Geodemographics and the Changing Spatiality of Local Practice', in D. Lyon (ed.) *Surveillance as Social Sorting: Privacy, Risk and Digital Discrimination* (New York: Routledge).

Phorm (2008) Re: # 228 Project No. P859900: Phorm, Inc.'s Comments to the Statement of the Federal Trade Commission's Bureau of Consumer Protection Proposing Governing Principles For Online Behavioral Advertising, *FTC*, http://www.ftc.gov/os/comments/beha vioraladprinciples/080411phorminc.pdf, date accessed 09 February 2009.

Pidd, H. (2007) Food manufacturers target children on internet after regulator's TV advertising clampdown, *The Guardian*, http://www. guardian.co.uk/media/2007/jul/31/newmedia.advertising1, date accessed 09 February 2009.

Plummer, J.T. (2004) 'Editorial: To Our Readers and Supporters from the New Editor', *Journal of Advertising Research*, 44 (3), 223–224.

Plummer, J.T., Rappaport, S., Hall, T. and Barocci, R. (2007) *The Online Advertising Playbook* (New Jersey: Wiley).

Porter, L. and Golan, G.J. (2006) 'From Subservient Chickens to Brawny Men: A Comparison of Viral Advertising to Television Advertising', *Journal of Interactive Advertising*, 6 (2), 30–38.

Poster, M. (1996) 'Databases as Discourse, or Electronic Interpellations', in P. Heelas, S. Lash, and P. Morris (eds) *Detraditionalization* (Oxford: Blackwell).

Poster, M. (2004) 'Consumption and Digital Commodities in the Everyday', *Cultural Studies*, 18 (2/3), 409–423.

Poster, M. (2005) 'Future Advertising: Dick's Ubik and the Digital Ad', in S. Cohen and R. Rutsky (eds) *Consumption in an Age of Information* (Oxford: Berg).

Powers, T.M. (2003) 'Real Wrongs in Virtual Communities', *Ethics and Information Technologies*, 5, 191–198.

Quenqua, D. (2008) Poll Shows Consumers Misinformed about Data Collection Online, *ClickZ*, http://www.clickz.com/showPage. html?page=3630995, date accessed 09 February 2009.

Radicati Group (2008) *The Radicati Group, Inc. Releases Q2 2008 Market Numbers Update*, http://www.radicati.com/?p=638, date accessed 09 February 2009.

Randazzo, S. (1993) *Mythmaking on Madison Avenue: How Advertisers Apply the Power of Myth and Symbolism to Create Leadership Brands* (Chicago: Probus).

Rapp, S. and Collins, T. (1990) *The Great Marketing Turnaround* (Englewood Cliffs, NJ: Prentice Hall Trade).

Rashid, O., Coulton, P. and Edwards, R. (2006) 'Providing Location Based Information/Advertising for Existing Mobile Phone Users', *Personal and Ubiquitous Computing*, 12 (1), 3–10.

Raymond, C. (1978) 'Editorial: The Enemies of Science', *Journal of Advertising Research*, 18 (1), 59.

Reid, D. (2007) The Evolution of the Web, *BBC*, http:// www.news.bbc. co.uk/1/hi/programmes/click_online/6708491.stm, date accessed 09 February 2009.

Reid, L., King, K. and DeLorme, D. (1998) 'Top-level Creatives Look at Advertising Creativity Then and Now', *Journal of Advertising*, 27 (2), 1–16.

Reidenberg, J.R (2000) Resolving Conflicting International Data Privacy Rules in Cyberspace, *Stanford Law Review*. 52 (2), 1315–1376.

Reisinger, D. (2008) Facebook, MySpace reign supreme in mobile market, *CNet News*, http:// www.news.cnet.com/8301–17939_109–10058697-2.html, date accessed 09 February 2009.

Riegner, C. (2007) 'Word of Mouth on the Web: The Impact of Web 2.0 on Consumer Purchase Decisions', *Journal of Advertising Research*, 47 (4), 436–447.

Rettie, R., Robinson, H. and Jenner, B. (2003) Does Internet Advertising Alienate Users? *Kingston University*, http://www.kingston.ac.uk/~ku03468/docs/Does%20Internet%20Advertising%20Alienate%20Users.pdf, date accessed 09 February 2009.

Reuters (2008) *Mobile ads years away from breakthrough: execs*, http:// www.reuters.com/article/technologyNews/idUSL2160737920080521?feedType=RSS&feedName=technologyNews&pageNumber=2&virtualBrandChannel=0, date accessed 09 February 2009.

Reuters (2008a) *Google CEO bullish on mobile Web advertising*, http:// www.reuters.com/article/technologyNews/idUSL2563364020080125?feedType=RSS&feedName=technologyNews, date accessed 09 February 2009.

Rheingold, H. (1993) *The Virtual Community* (New York: HarperPerennial).

Richard, B. (2008) 'Media Masters and Grassroot Art 2.0 on YouTube', in G. Lovink and S. Niederer (eds) *Video Vortex Reader* (Amsterdam: Institute of Network Cultures).

Riding, C.M. and Gefen, D. (2004) 'Virtual Community Attraction: Why People Hang Out Online', *Journal of Computer Mediated Communication*, 10 (1), article 4, http://www.jcmc.indiana.edu/vol10/issue1/ridings_gefen.html, date accessed 09 February 2009.

Robins, K. (1995 [2000]) 'Cyberspace and the World We Live In', in M. Featherstone, and R. Burrows (eds) *Cyberspace, Cyberbodies, Cyberpink: Cultures of Technological Embodiment* (London: Sage).

Robins, K. and Webster, F. (1999) *Times of the Technoculture* (London: Routledge).

Rodgers, S. and Harris, M.A. (2003) 'Gender and e-Commerce: An Exploratory Study', *Journal of Advertising Research*, 43 (3), 322–329.

Rodgers, S., Cannon, H.M. and Moore, J. (1999) 'Segmenting Internet Markets', in D.W. Schumann and E. Thorson (eds) *Internet Advertising: Theory and Research* (New Jersey: Lawrence Erlbaum).

Rodgers, Z. (2007) Advertisers Home in on Standards, Best Practices in Video, *ClickZ*, http://www.clickz.com/showPage.html?page=3626498, date accessed 09 February 2009.

Rodgers, Z. (2008) Credit Collapse Dampens Prospects for Web Advertising, *ClickZ*, http://www.clickz.com/showPage.html?page=3631127, date accessed 09 February 2009.

Rodowick, D.N. (2001) *Reading the Figural* (Durham: Duke University).

Rogers, T.W. (1994) 'Detournement for fun and (political) profit', *Ctheory*, http:// www.ctheory.net/text_file.asp?pick=242, date accessed 09 February 2009.

Röhle, T. (2008) 'Desperately Seeking the Consumer: Personalized Search Engines and the Commercial Exploitation of User Data', *First Monday*, 12 (9), http:// www.firstmonday.org/htbin/cgiwrap/bin/ojs/index.php/fm/article/view/2008/1883, date accessed 09 February 2009.

Romeo, A., Denham, S. and Neves, J. (2004) *How and Why Online Advertising has been Getting Better over Time*, presented at the ARF/ESOMAR Worldwide Audience Measurement (WAM) Conference in Geneva, Switzerland.

Rosen, E. (2000) *The Anatomy of Buzz* (London: HarperCollins).

Ross, K. and Nightingale, V. (2003) *Media and Audiences* (London: Open University Press).

Rostand, D. (2008) Crisis in Advertising: Privacy vs. Relevancy, *AdLab*, http:// www.adverlab.blogspot.com/2008/10/crisis-in-advertising-privacy-vs.html, date accessed 09 February 2009.

Rubel, S. (2007) With so many start-ups, only you can save Web 2.0, *Advertising Age*, http:// www.adage.com/digital/article?article_id=121718, date accessed 09 February 2009.

Rubel, S. (2008) For the future of digital, get your head in the cloud, *Advertising Age*, http:// www.adage.com/abstract.php?article_id=130488, date accessed 09 February 2009.

Runco, M.A. and Charles, R.E. (1993) 'Judgments of Originality and Appropriateness as Predictors of Creativity', *Personality and Individual Differences*, 15 (5), 537–546.

Rushkoff, D. (1994) *Media Virus* (New York: Random House).

Russell, T. (2008) Study Shows Targeted Ads Make Users Uneasy, *Wired*, http:// www.blog.wired.com/business/2008/04/study-shows-tar.html, date accessed 09 February 2009.

Samuels, P. (2008) In-game advertising: the advertiser's context, *iMedia Connection*, http://www.imediaconnection.com/content/18701.asp, date accessed 09 February 2009.

Sanders, L. (2007) Buying into digital: A look at the holding companies, *Advertising Age*, http:// www.adage.com/digital/article.php?article_id=116611, date accessed 09 February 2009.

Sasser, S.L., Koslow, S. and Riordan, E.A. (2007) 'Creative and Interactive Media Use by Agencies: Engaging an IMC Media Palette for Implementing Advertising Campaigns', *Journal of Advertising Research*, 47 (3), 237–256.

Schutz, W.C. (1966) *The Interpersonal Underworld* (Palo Alto, CA: Science and Behavior Books).

Schari, A. (2008) The geospatial web – blending physical and virtual spaces, *Vodafone Receiver*, http://www.receiver.vodafone.com/the-geospatial-web, date accessed 09 February 2009.

Schari, A. (2007) *The Geospatial Web: How Geobrowsers, Social Software and the Web 2.0 are Shaping the Network Society* (London: Springer).

Schlosser, A.E., Shavitt, S. and Kanfer, A. (2000) 'Survey of Internet "users" Attitudes towards Internet Advertising', *Journal of Interactive Marketing*, 13 (3), 34–54.

Schmitt, G. (2009) Mobile Marketing: Is 'App-vertising' the Answer? *Advertising Age*, http:// www.adage.com/digitalnext/post.php?article_id=136622, date accessed 15 May 2009.

Schneier, B. (2008) The Myth of the 'Transparent Society', *Wired*, http://www.wired.com/politics/security/commentary/securitymatters/2008/03/securitymatters_0306, date accessed 09 February 2009.

Second Life (2008) *Advertising in Second Life*, http:// www.wiki.secondlife.com/wiki/Advertising_in_Second_Life, date accessed 09 February 2009.

Second Life (2008a) *Terms of Service*, http:// www.secondlife.com/corporate/tos.php, date accessed 09 February 2009.

Shade, L.S. (2002) *Gender and Community in the Social Construction of the Internet* (New York: Peter Lang).

Shankland, S. and Needleman, R. (2009) Wolfram Alpha shows data in a way Google can't, *CNET*, http:// www.news.cnet.com/8301– 17939_109–10233763-2.html, date accessed 07 May 2009.

Shannon, E. and Weaver, W. (1949) *A Mathematical Model of Communication* (Urbana: University of Illinois).

Shavitt, S., Vargas, P. and Lowrey, P. (2004) 'Exploring the Role of Memory for Self-selected Ad Experiences: Are some Advertising Media Better Liked than Others?' *Psychology and Marketing*, 21 (12), 1011–1032.

Sheehan, K.B. and Hoy, M.G. (1999) 'Flaming, Complaining, Abstaining: How Online Users Respond to Privacy Concerns', *Journal of Advertising*, 28 (3), 37–51.

Sheehan, K.B. and Hoy, M.G. (2000) 'Dimensions of Privacy Concern among Online Consumers', *Journal of Public Policy and Marketing*, 19 (1), 62–74.

Shen, F. (2002) 'Banner Advertisement Pricing, Measurement, and Pretesting Practices: Perspectives from Interactive Agencies', *Journal of Advertising*, 31 (3), 59–67.

Sherman, R. (2008) Privacy Policies are Great – for PhDs, *BNET*, http://www.industry.bnet.com/technology/1000391/privacy-policies-are-great-for-phds/, date accessed 09 February 2009.

Sherman, T. (2007) Vernacular Video, *Wired*, http:// www.blog.wired.com/sterling/2007/01/vernacular_vide.html, date accessed 09 February 2009.

Sherman, T. (2008) 'Vernacular Video', in G. Lovink and S. Niederer (eds) *Video Vortex Reader* (Amsterdam: Institute of Network Cultures).

Shifman, L. (2007) 'Humor in the Age of Digital Reproduction: Continuity and Change in Internet-Based Comic Texts', *International Journal of Communication*, 1, 187–209.

Silver, D. (2000) 'Looking Backwards, Looking Forwards: Cyberculture Studies 1990–2000', in D. Gauntlett (ed.) *WebStudies: Rewiring Media Studies for the Digital Age* (London: Arnold).

Simmel, G. (2002) 'The Metropolis and Mental Life', in L. Spillman (ed.) *Cultural Sociology* (London: Blackwell).

Simmons, D. (2008) Virtual worlds with real purposes, *BBC*, http://www.news.bbc.co.uk/1/hi/programmes/click_online/7754038.stm, date accessed 09 February 2009.

Singer, E. (2008) The Genetic Early Adopters, *Technology Review*, http://www.technologyreview.com/Biotech/21341/?a=f, date accessed 09 February 2009.

Singer, E. (2008a) Five Thousand Bucks for Your Genome: A new sequencing service could change the face of human genomics, *Technology Review*, http://www.technologyreview.com/biomedicine/21466/, date accessed 09 February 2009.

Slater, D. (2002) 'Social Relationships and Identity, Online and Offline', in L.A. Lievrouw and S. Livingstone (eds) *Handbook of New Media: Social Shaping and Consequences of ICTs* (London: Sage).

Smart, B. (1993) *Postmodernity* (London: Routledge).

Smith, R. and Yang, X. (2004) 'Towards a General Theory of Creativity: Examining the Role of Divergence', *Marketing Theory*, 4 (1/2), 31–58.

Smith, W. (1956) 'Product Differentiation and Market Segmentation as Alternative Marketing Strategies', *Journal of Marketing*, 21 (1), 3–8.

Smithers, R. (2008) Ban junk food advertising on internet, say campaigners, *The Guardian*, http://www.guardian.co.uk/technology/2008/mar/15/advertising.food.date accessed 09 February 2009.

Solove, D. (2004) *The Digital Person: Privacy and Technology in the Digital Age* (New York: New York University).

Sophos (2006) *Sophos reveals 'Dirty Dozen' spam producing countries*, http://www.sophos.com/pressoffice/news/articles/2006/11/dirty-dozq306.html, date accessed 09 February 2009.

Spence, J. (2008) 'Demographics of Virtual Worlds', *Journal of Virtual Worlds Research*, 1 (2), 1–44, http:// www.journals.tdl.org/jvwr/article/view/360/272, date accessed 09 February 2009.

Spurgeon, C. (2008) *Advertising and New Media* (Oxon: Routledge).

Stafford, M.R. and Stafford, T.F. (2000) 'Identifying the uses and gratifications of Web use', in M.A. Shaver (ed.) *Proceedings of the 2000 Conference of the American Academy of Advertising* (East Lansing: Michigan State University).

Stafford, M.R. and Faber, R.J. (2005) 'The Future of Consumer Decision Making in the Age of New Media Promotions and Advertising' in M.R. Stafford and R.J. Faber (eds) *Advertising, Promotion and New Media* (M.E. Sharpe: New York).

Stafford, T.F. (2005) 'Mobile Promotional Communication and Machine Persuasion: A New Paradigm for Source Effects?' in M.R. Stafford and R.J. Faber (eds) *Advertising, Promotion and New Media* (New York: M.E. Sharpe).

Staples, W.G. (2000) *Everyday Surveillance: Vigilance and Visibility in Postmodern Life* (Lanham, MD: Rowman & Littlefield).

Steiger, R. (2008) Merging the Real World and the Internet, *Advertising Age*, http://www.adage.com/digitalnext/post.php?article_id=126464, date accessed 09 February 2009.

Sterling, B (1988) *Globalhead* (New York: Spectra).

Sterling, B. (1992) *The Hacker Crackdown: Law and Disorder on the Electronic Frontier*, http://www.gutenberg.org/files/101/101.txt, date accessed 09 February 2009.

Stern, B. (2004) 'The Importance of Being Ernest: Commemorating Dichter's Contribution to Advertising Research', *Journal of Advertising Research*, 44 (02), 165–169.

Sternberg, R. (1999) *Handbook of Creativity* (New York: Cambridge University).

Steuer, J. (1992) 'Defining Virtual Reality: Dimensions Determining Telepresence', *Journal of Communication*, 42 (4), 73–93.

Stewart, D.W. and Pavlou, P.A. (2002) 'From Consumer Response to Active Consumer: Measuring the Effectiveness of Interactive Media', *Journal of the Academy of Marketing Science*, 30 (4), 376–396.

Stewart, J. (1986) 'The Role and Evolution of the Advertising Planner', *Journal of Advertising Research*, 26 (5), 22–24.

Stone, A.R. (1996) *The War of Desire and Technology at the Close of the Mechanical Age* (Cambridge, MA: MIT).

Stone, B. (2007) MySpace to Discuss Effort to Customize Ads, *The New York Times*, http://www.nytimes.com/2007/09/18/technology/18myspace. html?ex=1347768000&en=28ff3d3a5ba194ff&ei=5088&partner=rss nyt&emc=rss, date accessed 09 February 2009.

Stone, G., Besser, D. and Lewis, L.E. (2000) 'Recall, Liking and Creativity in TV Commercials: A New Approach', *Journal of Advertising Research*, 40 (3), 7–18.

Story, L. (2007) It's an Ad, Ad, Ad, Ad World, *New York Times*, http://www.nytimes.com/2007/08/06/business/media/06digitas.html?ex=1344052800&en=58385a0b46134a2f&ei=5088&partner=rssnyt&emc=rss, date accessed 09 February 2009.

Story, L. (2007a) Online Customised Ads Move a Step Closer, *New York Times*, http://www.nytimes.com/2007/07/02/technology/02yahoo. html?ex=1341028800&en=0279c19e5ab34dda&ei=5088&partner= rssnyt&emc=rss, date accessed 09 February 2009.

Story, L. (2007b) Outcome of an Ad Contest Starts an Uproar on YouTube, *New York Times*, http://www.nytimes.com/2007/06/27/ technology/27malibu.ready.html?ex=1340596800&en=90585f4 c2f76ae0d&ei=5088&partner=rssnyt&emc=rss, date accessed 09 February 2009.

Story, L. (2007c) The High Price of Creating Free Ads, *New York Times*, http://www.nytimes.com/2007/05/26/business/26content.ready.ht ml?ex=1337832000&en=a8f6300e54b452d6&ei=5088&partner=rss nyt&emc=rss, date accessed 09 February 2009.

Story, L. (2008) Where Every Ad Knows Your Name, *New York Times*, http:// www.bits.blogs.nytimes.com/2008/03/10/where-every-ad-knows-your-name/, date accessed 09 February 2009.

Strickland, M. (2008) What the Semantic Web – or Web 3.0 – Can Do for Marketers, *Advertising Age*, http:// www.adage.com/digitalnext/ post.php?article_id=132815, date accessed 09 February 2009.

Sudhaman, A. (2006) The virtual world of Second Life. *Media: Asia's Media & Marketing Newspaper*, 11 March 2006, 13.

Sullivan, L. (2008) *Hey Whipple, Squeeze This* (New Jersey: Wiley).

Sundar, S.S. and Kalyanaraman, S. (2004) 'Arousal, Memory, and Impression-Formation Effects of Animation Speed in Web Advertising', *Journal of Advertising*, 33 (1), 7–17.

Sweney, M. (2007) Publicis to launch 'one-stop' model, *The Guardian*, http://www.guardian.co.uk/media/2007/nov/13/advertising?gusrc= rss&feed=media, date accessed 09 February 2009.

Sweney, M. (2008) UK ad market will not grow again until 2010, says Publicis chairman, *The Guardian*, http://www.guardian.co.uk/media/2008/ oct/29/publicis-downturn, date accessed 09 February 2009.

Taylor, C. (2008) The Future of Advertising: The State of the News Media an Annual Report on American Journalism, *Project for Excellence in*

Journalism, http://www.stateofthenewsmedia.org/2008/narrative_special_advertising.php?media=13, date accessed 09 February 2009.

Teinowitz, I. (2008) Marketers intent on engaging consumers across multiple media, *Advertising Age*, http:// www.findarticles.com/p/articles/mi_hb6398/is_200804/ai_n25583364, date accessed 09 February 2009.

The Economist (2007) *Got Game*, http://www.economist.com/business/displaystory.cfm?story_id=9304254, date accessed 09 February 2009.

The Economist (2008) *Shopped out*, http://www.economist.com/world/britain/displaystory.cfm?story_id=12856490, date accessed 09 February 2009.

The Economist (2009) *China is number one*, http://www.economist.com/daily/chartgallery/displaystory.cfm?story_id=13007996&fsrc=rss, date accessed 09 February 2009.

The Guardian (2007) *In praise of ... Silver surfers*, http://www.guardian.co.uk/commentisfree/2007/aug/24/comment.technology, date accessed 09 February 2009.

The Paradigm Shift (2008) *AOL Search Data Shows Users Planning to commit Murder*, http:// www.plentyoffish.wordpress.com/2006/08/07/aol-search-data-shows-users-planning-to-commit-murder/, date accessed 09 February 2009.

Thompson, C. (2008) Brave New World of Digital Intimacy, *The New York Times*, http://www.nytimes.com/2008/09/07/magazine/07awareness-t.html?_r=3&pagewanted=1&partner=rssnyt&emc=rss&oref=slogin&oref=slogin, date accessed 09 February 2009.

Thorson, K. and Watson, B. (2007) 'The New Online Campaign: Translating Information Into Action', in D.W. Schumann and E. Thorson (eds) *Internet Advertising: Theory and Research* (New Jersey: Lawrence Erlbaum).

Till, B.D. and Baack, D.W. (2005) 'Recall and Persuasion: Does Creative Advertising Matter?' *Journal of Advertising*, 34 (3), 47–57.

Toffler, A. (1980) *The Third Way* (London: Pan).

TRUSTe (2009) Consumers Want Relevant Ads Online, But Still Worry About Their Online Privacy, http:// www.truste.org/about/press_release/03_04_09.php, date accessed 05 March 2009.

Tse, A.C.B. and Chan, C. (2004) 'The Relationship between Interactive Functions and Website Ranking', *Journal of Advertising Research*, 44 (4), 369–374.

Tungate, M. (2007) *Adland: A Global History of Advertising* (London: Kogan Page).

Turkle, S. (1995) *Life on the Screen: Identity in the Age of the Internet* (New York: Touchstone).

Turrow, J. (2006) *Niche Envy: Marketing Discrimination in the Digital Age* (Massachusetts: MIT).

Tynan, D. (2008) The Next 25 Years in Tech, *PCWorld*, http://www.pcworld.com/article/141791–2/the_next_25_years_in_tech.html, date accessed 09 February 2009.

Veblen, T. (1899 [2008]) *The Theory of the Leisure Class* (Charleston, South Carolina: Forgotten Books).

Vedrashko, I. (2006) Advertising in Computer Games, http:// www.gamesbrandsplay.com/files/vedrashko_advertising_in_games.pdf, date accessed 09 February 2009.

Verkaik, R. (2007) Google is watching you, *The Independent*, http://www.independent.co.uk/news/science/google-is-watching-you-450084.html, date accessed 09 February 2009.

Verna, P. (2007) Video Game Advertising: Getting to the Next Level, *eMarketer*, http://www.emarketer.com/Reports/All/Emarketer_2000386.aspx, date accessed 09 February 2009.

Virilio, P. (1986 [1977]) *Speed and Politics: An Essay on Dromology* (New York: Semiotext(e)).

Virilio, P. (1997) *Open Sky* (London: Verso).

Virzi, A.M. (2008) Undecided: What Was Digital's Impact on the Election? *ClickZ*, http://www.clickz.com/showPage.html?page=3631556, date accessed 09 February 2009.

W3C (2008) *W3C Semantic Web Activity*, http://www.w3.org/2001/sw/, date accessed 09 February 2009.

W3C (2008a) *W3C Semantic Web Frequently Asked Questions*, http://www.w3.org/RDF/FAQ, date accessed 09 February 2009.

Weber, M. (1994) *Political Writings* (Cambridge: Cambridge University Press).

Weisberg, R.W. (1993) *Creativity: Beyond the Myth of Genius* (New York: Freeman).

Welch, R. and Krishnamoorthy, S. (2000) E-testing – Measuring the Effectinevess of Internet Advertising on Offline Purchasing [online], *Advertising Research Foundation*. Available from: http://www.arfsite.org/resources/pastresearch.html, date accessed 11/02/09]

Wesch, M. (2007) Web 2.0 ... The Machine is Us/ing Us, *YouTube*, http://www.uk.youtube.com/watch?v=NLlGopyXT_g, date accessed 09 February 2009.

Westin, A.F. (1967) *Privacy and Freedom* (New York: Atheneum).

White, A. and Smith, B.L. (2001) 'Assessing Advertising Creativity Using the Creative Product Semantic Scale', *Journal of Advertising Research*, 41 (6), 27–34.

White, R. (2000) *Advertising* (London: McGraw Hill).

Wiedemann, J. (ed.) (2006) *Advertising Now! Online* (Cologne: Taschen).

Wilmshurst, J. and Mackay, A. (2002) *The Fundamentals of Advertising* (Oxford: Butterworth-Heinemann),

Wind, Y. (1978) 'Issues and Advances in Segmentation Research', *Journal of Marketing Research*, 15 (3), 317–337.

Wood, D (2003) Editorial. Foucault and Panopticism Revisited. *Surveillance and Society*, 1 (3), 234–239.

World Privacy Forum (2008) Public comments: # 228, Project No. P859900: Online Behavioral Advertising: Moving the Discussion Forward to Possible Self-Regulatory Principles, *FTC*, http://www.ftc.gov/os/comments/behavioraladprinciples/080411worldprivacyforum.pdf, date accessed 09 February 2009.

Wray, R. (2007) Blyk's free mobile launch delayed, *The Guardian*, http://www.guardian.co.uk/technology/2007/jul/09/news.mobilephones, date accessed 09 February 2009.

Wu, S. (2007) Virtual Goods: the next big business model, *TechCrunch*, http://www.techcrunch.com/2007/06/20/virtual-goods-the-next-big-business-model/, date accessed 09 February 2009.

Wurster, C. (2002) *Computers* (Cologne: Taschen).

Yahoo (2008) *Squeeze Every Drop of Meaning from Data*, http://www.research.yahoo.com/node/89, date accessed 09 February 2009.

Yar, M. (2003) 'Panoptic Power and the Pathologisation of Vision: Critical Reflections on the Foucault Thesis', *Surveillance and Society*, 1 (3), 254–271.

Yeshin, T. (2005) *Advertising* (London: Thomson Learning).

York, E. B. (2007) The Hottest Thing in Kids Marketing? Imitating Webkinz, *Advertising Age*, http://www.adage.com/abstract.php?article_id=120933, date accessed 09 February 2009.

Youn, S. and Lee, M. (2005) 'Advergame Playing Motivations and Effectiveness: A "Uses and Gratifications" Perspective', in M.R. Stafford and R.J. Faber (eds) *Advertising, Promotion and New Media* (New York: M.E. Sharpe).

Ziff, R. (1971) 'Psychographics for Market Segmentation', *Journal of Advertising Research*, 11 (2), 3–9.

Zinkhan, J.M. (1993) 'Creativity in Advertising', *Journal of Advertising*, 22 (2), 1–3.

Index

Printed and bound by CPI Group (UK) Ltd, Croydon, CR0 4YY